The Dashwoods
—— *of* ——
West Wycombe

The Dashwoods
—— *of* ——
West Wycombe

SIR FRANCIS DASHWOOD

AURUM PRESS

Text copyright © Sir Francis Dashwood 1987
First published 1987 by Aurum Press Limited, 33 Museum Street,
London WC1A 1LD
Reprinted in paperback 1990

Dashwood *Sir*, Francis
The Dashwoods of West Wycombe.
1. Buckinghamshire. West Wycombe. (Family) Dashwood,
history
I. Title
929'.2'0942

ISBN 1 85410 108 0

Phototypeset by Bookworm Typesetting, Manchester
Printed and bound in Great Britain by
Biddles Ltd, Guildford and King's Lynn

CONTENTS

Introduction   1

THE DASHWOODS

1   The Early Dashwoods   11

2   The Exclusive Clubs   18
    *The Dilettanti Society • the Divan Club • the Lincoln
    Club • the Hell-Fire Club*

3   Expedition to Russia   52

4   The Public Life of Sir Francis   57
    *Forty years in Parliament • Postmaster-General • Plan of
    Reconciliation • the revision of the Prayer Book*

5   The Next Fifty Years   71

6   The Progressive Tory   86

7   Down Under   93

8   Pa and Ma   105

9   Getting Started   118
    *Childhood days • Eton, rabbits and jazz • the war •
    home again • America • my first job • a foot in industry •
    . . . and politics*

10 Securing the Future   153
    *The Caves • life at Chipps • Wales • financial crisis •
    dances • my family now*

WEST WYCOMBE

11 The House   189

12 The Gardens   220

    Chronology   233

    Family Tree   234

    Bibliography   236

    Index   238

TO
VICTORIA AND MARCELLA

ACKNOWLEDGEMENTS

Over the years many people have helped me with research and advice and to all of them I would like to express my gratitude, especially to Sir Brinsley Ford and Viscount Boyne in connection with the Dilettanti Society, Mrs Susan Rogers for taking me round her charming home in Medmenham Abbey, and Sir John Pestell and Mr P. J. Langton, also of Medmenham.

Others to whom I would like to express my gratitude are the Hon. Alastair Bruce, Lt-Col. A. Clerke-Brown, Sir Richard Dashwood, Bt, Mr Peter Jackson, Mr James Kent, Mr P. Lefroy, Mr Noel Mander, Mr Donald McCormack, Mrs Tom Meyer, the Hon. Victor Montagu, Mrs Eugenia Rawls and Mr Eric Towers.

I have also received much help from Lord Blake, Mr Howard Colvin, Miss Betty Kemp and Mr F. W. J. Scovil of Oxford University and Mr W. O. Hassall and Mr Steven Tomlinson of the Bodleian Library, Oxford; Sir Jack Plumb of Christ's College and Mr Michael Crawford and Mr R. G. Killick of Cambridge University; Mr John Harris of the Royal Institute of British Architects; Sir Colin Cole of the College of Arms; Mr John Hopkins of the Society of Antiquaries in London; Mr Christopher Wall of the National Trust; Mr Jon Darius of the Science Museum; Mr A. S. Ireson of the Men of Stones; Mr David Fletcher of the Tank Museum; from Buckinghamshire Mr H. A. Hanley, the County Archivist; from Dorset Miss Margaret Holmes of the County Record Office and Mrs Stella Campbell; from Gloucestershire Mrs D. J. H. Smith, the Diocesan Archivist; from Lincolnshire Dr G.A. Knight, the Principal Archivist, and the Rev. Henry Thorold; from the City of London Livery Companies, Mr Robert Strick of the Drapers', Miss Janet Taylor of the Brewers' and Major John Laurie of the Saddlers'; Mr Paul Quarrie of the Eton College Library; and Mr David Wright of the National Horseracing Museum.

The Guildhall Library and Art Gallery, the National Portrait Gallery, the Victoria and Albert Museum and the Historical

Manuscripts Commission Reports were also invaluable sources of information.

From the United States, useful information was supplied by the Library of Congress in Washington, Yale University, the American Philosophical Society, Mr Ben Hibbs of Philadelphia, Mr William B. Willcox of the William L. Clements Library at the University of Michigan, and the Huntingdon Library in California; from Auckland, New Zealand, Miss Angela Finnerty of the Society of Genealogists, Mrs Nell Hartley, Mr Keith Vautier, and Miss Jill Tasker of the New Zealand High Commission in London; and from South Africa Mrs F. P. Kuttel.

I also owe a great debt of gratitude to my secretary Miss Ina Swain for the laborious typing of semi-legible drafts, to Mrs P. L. Reynolds and Mrs Frances Bird for their unstinting assistance, and to Mrs Angela Dyer, whose contribution as editor was paramount.

But without the constructive criticism and enthusiastic encouragement of the Hon. John Grigg the project might well have foundered.

PICTURE CREDITS

Between pages 88 and 89 Plate I (*top*) Courtauld Institute of Art; (*bottom*) *Illustrated London News*. Plate II Courtauld Institute of Art. Plate III (*bottom left*) Edmund Harrington; (*bottom right*) Vandyk. Plate IV Cecil Beaton photograph, courtesy of Sotheby's, London. Plate V (*top*) Courtauld Institute of Art; (*bottom*) MK Photography. Plate VI (*bottom*) Ronald Goodearl. Plate VII Peter Titmuss Photography. Plate VIII (*top left*) Barry Swaebe; (*bottom*) Stefano Massimo.

Between pages 184 and 185 Plate I (*top*) Peter Titmuss Photography; Plates II, III François Halard; Plate IV (*top*) National Trust/John Bethell; (*bottom*) François Halard; Plate V *Country Life*; Plate VI (*top*) British Tourist Authority/Barry Hicks; Plates VI–VII Photograph by Snowdon from *Vogue* 1979 © The Condé Nast Publications Ltd. Plate VIII (*top*) Topham Picture Library; (*centre, bottom*) British Tourist Authority/Barry Hicks.

The picture reproduced on p.32 was kindly lent by Mrs Susan Rogers; pp.193, 195 Courtauld Institute of Art.

Introduction

WEST WYCOMBE has been the seat of the Dashwood family for about three hundred years. The house and the gardens have changed little save from the normal ravages of time, and during the last thirty years I have endeavoured to re-create everything as it was at the height of its splendour two hundred years ago.

The house itself is sometimes described as 'having been run up like a stage set' and with its porticoes and colonnades and the extraordinarily ornate interior, copied from the most famous palaces in Rome and Asia Minor, there is some justification for this description. Overlooking a lake in the shape of a swan with numerous temples and follies inspired by those from ancient Rome and Greece, West Wycombe can justly claim to be amongst the most beautiful and distinctive seats in the world.

It also has a most colourful history, summed up by Lord Esher when, as President of the National Trust, he accepted the gift from my father in 1944: 'It gives me great pleasure to accept this ancient house of vice, or rather I should say, this house of ancient vice.'

My family too has a colourful history. The stories involving sexual frolics, enterprise and courage, and spreading over a large part of the globe from North America to New Zealand, India and Russia, range from the heroic to the hilarious.

Benjamin Franklin, a frequent visitor to West Wycombe in the eighteenth century, described the gardens as 'a paradise'; and so they still are, with the swan-shaped lake, delightful little flint and wooden bridges, waterfalls, temples and statues, and on the hilltop the imposing hexagonal Mausoleum and the church tower capped by a glittering golden ball – all of this set amidst the rolling hills and hanging woods of a typical Chiltern landscape.

Living in a stately home in such surroundings is a great treat, but it is no picnic with all the problems of the staff and the enormous cost of restoration, and of course of living here. The days of the old family retainers, the butler and the chauffeur, are pretty well over, and in many cases such family seats are no longer private and the accent is on making everything pay its own way.

The house and gardens belong to the National Trust and I am their tenant on an annual lease. They are open to visitors in June, July and August and I have always refused to commercialize them – there are no gimmicks, gift shops or tea rooms. We just try to retain the atmosphere of a much-loved family home and to keep the rooms as they are when we use them and filled with flowers, so that visitors can share the feeling of what it is like to live here.

No doubt we could attract hordes more visitors, but, contrary to popular belief, the income from admission charges and souvenirs provides only a modest contribution to the general cost of upkeep, except in very rare cases where everything has been sacrificed to the public's benefit and with such success that the family has had to move out. That seems pointless to me. And it makes little sense to go to all this effort unless our friends, too, can enjoy it.

We no longer concentrate on the traditional weekend house parties as it would be too exhausting to cope with these after working hard in the City and leading a hectic social life in London. Instead, my wife Marcella hit on the answer of having lunch and dinner parties for forty or so a few times a year. The Palmyra Room takes that number and then, after dinner, everyone can wander round the different drawing rooms or listen to a concert by some well-known pianist or singers, such as the sextet from King's College Choir. I suppose this has always happened – my mother had Elisabeth Schwarzkopf amongst others – but perhaps not to quite the same extent. And we do, of course, have regular family weekends.

West Wycombe is also ideal for entertaining on a grand scale and seems to produce its own intoxicating atmosphere. I can think of a dozen or more marvellous parties we have given during the past thirty years, some of which I describe later in the book.

One of the most spectacular was in the summer of 1986 when 14,000 visitors attended three consecutive charity evenings in order to raise money for the National Trust and the National Society for Cancer Relief. All the guests were encouraged to wear eighteenth-century dress and to bring their own picnics. Throughout each evening there was continuous entertainment in the porticoes and Colonnade of the house and in different temples in the gardens – a belly-dancer, a contortionist, a fire-eater, Cossack dancers, a harp duo and an oboe quartet, a Viennese string orchestra. Two actors mimed famous arias from Verdi and Puccini from a gondola on the lake; and this was followed by the sixty-strong Wycombe Orpheus male choir holding flaming torches in their hands on one of the islands and singing popular songs like 'John Brown's Body' and 'The Saints Go Marching In'. The grand finale was a magnificent display of fireworks across the water (by the Rev. Ron Lancaster, who arranged the fireworks for Prince Charles and Princess Diana's wedding), set to excerpts from Handel's *Firework Music* and Tchaikovsky's *1812 Overture*, whilst the lawns twinkled with 1200 candles held by the enraptured audience.

Luckily we had fine weather and no rain on all three evenings, so the event was a great success and raised a large sum for the two charities.

The trouble with all such stately homes is that they need constant maintenance and attention and frequently a great deal of restoration. This has been especially true of West Wycombe, partly because nothing major had been done for almost a hundred years from 1860 to 1950, and partly because the house is profusely decorated so that restoration work tends to be laborious and expensive; moreover the numerous temples and follies surrounding the house were all in need of similar restoration.

The money to pay for all this work has come partly from government grants and partly from the National Trust, with massive contributions from me. The profits from the Caves, first opened up by me in 1951 and now a popular tourist attraction, go to the National Trust to help with general restoration and maintenance.

Another useful source of income is generated by filming. Many shots of the house and gardens appeared in the film *Sahara* with Brooke Shields, in *Rough Cut* with Burt Reynolds and Lesley-Anne Down, and in Paul McCartney's *Broad Street*; and just recently Agatha Christie's thriller *Dead Man's Folly* with Peter Ustinov as Hercule Poirot was filmed here and has been released as a TV cassette. West Wycombe was also one of the seventeen houses with their gardens which were seen by millions of television viewers in the United States in connection with the splendid and successful 'Treasure Houses of Britain' exhibition in Washington in 1986.

The costs of running the house and living in it naturally fall solely on me, and it has only been possible to survive here by selling land and other assets – much to my reluctance. But I have been determined that this whittling down policy should be accompanied by a dynamic and enterprising one to rebuild the family's fortunes, and it was this that drove me to Lloyd's in 1969 to start my own underwriting business, and to Australia, Canada and the United States to develop my agricultural enterprises. Such furniture and pictures as I have sold have been replaced, and I have added greatly to the whole collection by acquiring many magnificent pieces; some of them originally belonged here, and the remainder are well up to the quality and style of the collection as it must have been two hundred years ago.

The fact is that my love of West Wycombe has overruled all financial considerations. Bringing about careful changes and upgrading in such an environment is one of the great joys of living here. It brings a feeling of life and excitement to a house in place of the dreary museum-like atmosphere which prevails in so many stately homes which are no longer in private hands. I would not want to live in my home if the policy of sterile preservation prevailed. Change there has to be, and I hope that all those ancestors looking down from the walls approve of my contribution.

A BARONET

Although I am the Premier Baronet of Great Britain, our title was only acquired in 1707 at the time when England and Scotland were united to form Great Britain. Baronetcies of an earlier date still survive — in fact seventeen of the original seventy-five which were created in 1611. The earliest of these is held by Sir Nicholas Bacon who is Premier Baronet of England and therefore first in order of precedence.

The title 'Sir' derives from 'Cyr', an abbreviation of the Greek word *Kurios* which was much used by the Greek emperors and in France by the monarch. In feudal times it was widely used — as, for instance, 'Sir Knight'.

The award of a title is a simple and effective way of rewarding some valuable contribution to society. 'Sir' or 'Lord' is such a short and easy form of address and much better than tacking on something cumbrous to the name, such as 'Order of Lenin, First Class'. And I like to be reminded of great heroes of the past. A name like 'The Duke of Wellington' conjures up for me that epic battle at Waterloo.

Titles do, however, confuse foreigners, especially Americans, so I always say, 'Do call me Francis or Sir Francis, but please not Sir Dashwood or Sir Bart.'

I am descended not from the Sir Francis of Hell-Fire Club fame, the 2nd Baronet who transformed West Wycombe, but from his half-brother, Sir John Dashwood-King, who was the son of Mary King. Through John's marriage to Sarah Moore in 1761, I can claim to be the closest relation to the poet John Milton, as Sarah was the great granddaughter of Milton's sister Ann.

The difference between a knight and a baronet, both of whom use the title of Sir, is that the former is for life only whilst the latter passes on to the heir and later generations. The addition of the letters 'Bt.' after the surname denotes this hereditary distinction.

Baronet is a very ancient title. Baronets were first recorded in 1313 at the Battle of Strivelin between King Edward II of England and Robert I of Scotland, and again in 1321 at the Battle of

Bannenberg where they occupied a place near the Royal Standard in battle. They also took part in state ceremonies, carrying the canopy, the standard and the coronet of the Prince of Wales. But after 1340 the title seems to have more or less died out.

In 1611, however, King James I decided to revive this class of nobility, largely to pay for the soldiers needed to protect the English and Scottish settlers who had been encouraged to establish themselves in Ulster. The honour cost thirty soldiers for three years or £1095, as well as a fee of £1200 to the Heralds for their patents, which had to be paid into the Exchequer. The King also promised to limit the creation to two hundred, each of whom was to have an income from landed estates of £1000 a year. At that date this meant very extensive holdings of land and there was a rush to acquire the new titles; these new Baronets represented the great landed families and with their large estates, fine country houses and influential standing in the counties, they considered themselves superior in many instances to those who had previously been raised to the peerage.

Baronets were entitled to 'display the Bloody Hand of Ulster' on their coats of arms. The story goes that Heremon O'Neill, the first King of Ireland 1028–1015 BC, sailed there from Spain with a fleet, having sworn that he would be the first ashore. On discovering that he had been beaten to it,

> He seized his sword, cut off his hand
> and held it dripping red
> then flung it on the beach
> that curved so close ahead.

Baronets were also 'to have place in the Armies of Us, Our Heirs and successors in the Troop nigh to the Banner of Us ... in defence of the same.'

The success of James I's scheme led to further orders of Baronets for Ireland (1619) for the same purpose, for Scotland and Nova Scotia (1625) to encourage the colonization of Nova Scotia, New Brunswick and Anticosti Island in the Gulf of St Lawrence, for Great Britain (1707) and for the United Kingdom (1801).

The Baronets of the seventeenth and eighteenth centuries played a prominent part as Members of Parliament, sheriffs, magistrates or Lord-Lieutenants responsible for the militia, and as officers for the Army and Navy and parsons for the Church of England. They formed one of the most powerful and conservative elements in the state, and there was an element of truth in Disraeli's remark, which he put in the mouth of a caricature Baronet in *Sybil*, that 'the Reform Bill would never have been passed if the baronets had been organised', although it was meant as a joke.

Sir John Dashwood, the 4th Baronet, who was Member of Parliament for Wycombe from 1796 to 1831, was, like most Tories, strongly opposed to the Reform Bill of 1832, which extended the right to vote, and he got pelted with rotten eggs and apples in Wycombe for his views.

By the second half of the nineteenth century prominent men, especially in parliament, industry, commerce and medicine, were being awarded the title of Baronet and frequently went on to become Lords. Many were of humble origin but succeeded in founding dynasties and through their drive and enterprise helped to create the new wealth and employment which made Britain so prosperous. Many of them bought country estates and introduced new life and energy into the countryside.

Although the original Baronets were closely involved in military activities, baronetcies have seldom been awarded to war heroes. Marlborough's generals received none and only a few of Wellington's, and only Captain Hardy of the *Victory* was made a Baronet after Trafalgar. A few baronetcies were awarded to senior commanders in 1919 but none in 1945, although Marshal of the Royal Air Force Sir Arthur Harris, of Bomber Command fame, was subsequently made a Baronet in 1953 on the recommendation of Sir Winston Churchill.

Altogether nearly 3500 baronets have been created since 1611. The total today is slightly less than 1400 and includes more than a hundred living in Australia, Canada, South Africa and the United States. But no baronets have been created since 1964 and the title is likely to become extinct in the course of time.

THE
DASHWOODS

1

The Early Dashwoods

THE EARLIEST Dashwoods whom I have managed to trace are John Dayshwode, who was listed as a bowman in the Muster Roll of 1488 and lived in the parish of Iwerne Minster in the county of Dorset; and Richard Dashwood, who was appointed Chaplain in 1480 in the nearby parish of Tarrant Gunville. Both were almost certainly descended from an earlier Dashwood of about 1450 who was thus the common ancestor of the entire Dashwood family. At that time the family was concentrated not far from Dorchester in Dorset in a small area of two or three miles' radius called the Tarrants – Tarrant Hinton, Tarrant Monkton, Tarrant Gunville and Tarrant Rushton.

The Muster Rolls were drawn up to establish the number of active men and the weapons each could produce in case of military need. The Dashwoods listed from 1488 to 1569 were described as archers, bowmen, pikemen and billmen; they represented the élite troops of the Tudor and Elizabethan army and belonged to the class of prosperous yeoman farmers and minor gentry who founded the fortunes of so many leading families of the seventeenth and eighteenth centuries.

The name Dashwood seems to have been derived from 'De Asshewode' and means 'of or from the ash wood'. The early Dashwood Christian names were fairly conventional – Henry, John, Robert, George, William, Richard, Edward, Edmund and Samuel, although there was one called Hannibal.

From north-east Dorset the family spread to West Stafford in the south of the county, where the ancestors of the Dorchester branch originated. Edmund and Edward were wealthy mercers. Edmund is recorded as having contributed £20 in 1624 towards 'adventures to New England' which involved trading in Newfoundland, Virginia and Spain, and the following year his son, Francis, was apprenticed to Edmund's cousin John Blackford, who was directly involved in the adventure. Both were mayors of Dorchester: Edmund in 1632 and Edward in 1643 during the Civil War, when he played a prominent part in successfully fortifying the town against the Royalists.

Another relation, Robert, my direct ancestor, appears to have moved from Dorset to Monksilver in Somerset after 1569. He gave the Monksilver house to his son Samuel on the occasion of his marriage in 1598 and Robert built a new house at Rowden in the parish of Stogumber. This house still stands; on a stone over the door is the inscription '1603 RD'.

From Dorset and Somerset, where they were prospering as sheep and wool farmers and merchants, several of the Dashwoods set off to expand their fortunes in the City of London. By the mid-seventeenth century they had become well established and were members of some of the great City livery companies, principally the Saddlers', Brewers' and Vintners'. My ancestor, Francis, who was Robert's grandson, joined the Saddlers' Company in 1628. During the Civil War the livery companies suffered grievously from punitive demands for subsidies and merchandise from both the Royalist and Commonwealth causes. The Saddlers' Company was required to provide saddles for the cavalry and was in such dire straits that it had to cut back on all entertainment, and in 1643 had to sell nearly all its silver and gold plate. Francis took little part in the affairs of the Company and was frequently fined for not attending. He was presumably too engrossed with his own trading activities. But eventually, in 1653, he became Master of the Company and the following year presented it with a very fine silver-gilt loving cup, the first replacement of the Company's treasure and their only plate in late Tudor style.

Francis duly became an Alderman of the City of London in 1658. Alderman's Walk, which today runs off Old Broad Street past St

Botolph's Church, where he lies buried, was called after him, and Dashwood House, a vast modern office building, occupies the site of his town house which was pulled down in 1875. (Dashwood Finance Company, which occupies this building, has no connection with my family.) In 1663 Francis was one of those appointed to accompany King Charles II on horseback through the City and was required to be 'apparrelled with velvet coat and gold chain'.

From 1670 to 1684 the silk trade enjoyed a tremendous boom as a result of trade with Turkey. Francis was heavily involved in this and was also part-owner in 1669 of a 338-ton ship, the *Morning Star*. The silk, which arrived in bales, was sold through the East India Company. Some of the silk which Francis bought was sent to Macclesfield, a centre for making up silk garments and buttons where he and his son, also Francis, had a licence to trade. In gratitude he left a bequest of £100 in 1683 to the poor of that town – a large sum at the time.

Francis was joined by his two sons, Samuel and Francis, and the business grew rapidly so that by 1678 the young Dashwoods were among the leading silk importers in the City of London. That year they imported 45 bales of silk out of 139 sold and 40 of Floretta yarn out of 56. The following year this had grown to 189 bales of silk at 14s. per groat pound, 62 of raw silk at 16s., and 18 of Floretta yarn at 14s. 6d. This represented about one-third of the total silk sales made through the East India Company that year.

Alderman Francis's death in 1683 preceded a sharp decline in the silk trade; this was partly the result of the Dutch War and also of the unstable political situation which culminated in the flight of King James II and the seizure of the throne by William of Orange in 1688. It was at about that time that the brothers began to lose interest in the business and to turn their attention to politics. Sir Samuel, who was knighted in 1684 after being Sheriff of the City, represented the City in Parliament from 1685 to 1695, apart from a brief period after 1687 when he was removed by James II for his opposition to the King's efforts to re-establish Catholicism and, in particular, to the Repeal of the Test Acts, which banned Roman Catholics from the Houses of Commons and Lords, the Army and other official positions.

Samuel and his brother Francis were both prominent members of the East India Company, the former becoming Vice-Governor in 1700; and both were members of the Vintners' Company of which Samuel became Master in 1684 when he gave the Company two magnificent silver-gilt loving cups. It was to renew this family connection that I was allowed to become a Member of the Livery in 1956 and to hold a reception after my marriage in 1957 to Victoria de Rutzen. The Company even allowed Sir Samuel's cups to be used for the toast and we sang the rousing Vintners' Song which Sir Samuel had written for the Company. The verse was sung by my old friend Sir Edward Boyle, then Parliamentary Secretary for the Ministry of Education, and all the guests joined in the chorus: 'Come, come let us drink to the Vintner's good health'.

In 1702 Samuel became Lord Mayor of London and, besides entertaining Queen Anne at the Guildhall, staged a splendid pageant. The pageant is recorded in the Court Minutes of the East India Company.

On his return from Westminster, the Mayor was met at Blackfriars Stairs by St Martin, patron of the Vintners, in rich armour and riding a white Steed. The generous saint was attended by twenty dancing satyrs, with tambourines; ten halbardiers, with rustic music; and ten Roman Victors. At St Paul's churchyard the saint made a stand, and, drawing his sword, cut off half his crimson scarf, and gave it to some beggars and cripples who importuned him for charity. The first float was an Indian galleon crowded by Bacchanals wreathed with vines. On the deck of the grape-hung vessel sat Bacchus himself, 'properly drest'. The second float was the chariot of Ariadne drawn by panthers. Then came St Martin, as a bishop in a temple, and next followed 'the Vintage', an eight-arched structure with termini of satyrs and ornamented with vines. Within was a bar, with a beautiful person keeping it, with drawers [waiters] and gentlemen sitting drinking round a tavern table. On seeing the Lord Mayor, the bar-keeper called to the drawers:

> *Where are your eyes and ears?*
> *See there what honourable gent appears!*
> *Augusta's great Praetorian lord – but hold!*
> *Give me a goblet of true Oriental mould.*

In this period trading almost ground to a halt, but there were some interesting new developments. Sir Samuel made his first purchase of Bengal raw silk in 1685, a trend which was to continue for several years, and in 1700 the Dashwood frigate of 375 tons was despatched to Amoy in China under Captain Marmaduke Roydon. The *Dashwood* had on board £40,000 of gold bullion and goods, including woollen goods, for China and £7500 of bullion for use of the officers and men. On the return journey the ship was loaded with porcelain. A bill of 1702 describes such a consignment:

24th March, 1702
Chocolate cups, custard cups, coffee cups, plates, boats, painted dishes, tea cups, Sancta Marias (26 @ 5/– total), nests of sugar boxes, tea pots, rose water bottles, green bottles, Lyons, Griffins, Geese, Dogs, Images, Square pots, Chamber pots, Swans, Rabbits, Parrots, Patch boxes, Salvers, Muggs, Rowl waggons, red and white chocolate cups, Japan plates, Buffaloes, Parrots, Cocks, Eagles, Dutch families, 46 Pulpits with Padres, Cranes with candlesticks, Men on Dogs, Men on Lyons, Rabbits on Stands, Partridges, blue and gold cups and wrestlers.

There were also small purchases of seersucker, as well as Bengal and China raw silk and chests of china.

In 1696 the Court of the East India Company gave permission to its agent in Madras, Elihu Yale, 'to return to England with goods including cabinets, etc.', and in 1704 there was a dispute between Sir Samuel, Sir Francis (who had been knighted in 1702) and Mr Yale over a 'Parcell of Goods brought home on the Phoenix'.

Their Dashwood relations had also flourished. Francis's brother William became, in 1667, a fellow Alderman and Master of the Brewers' Company. He and his half-brother George farmed the Revenue of Ireland and collected the Excise and Hearth money in England in return for a substantial cash payment to the Crown. The former was a method of collecting ready cash through an indirect tax on beer and the latter a tax on the number of people in a household. When King William of Orange landed in 1688, it was George's son, Sir Robert (created a Baronet in 1684), who is said to have put up £100,000 to pay the troops; our crest carries the words 'Pro Magna Charta' signifying the family's support for the Glorious Revolution of 1688.

With their mounting wealth, the Dashwood brothers now began to turn their attention to acquiring land and building grand country houses set in parks which they proceeded to lay out and embellish. So it was that in 1698 Sir Samuel and Francis bought West Wycombe in Buckinghamshire from Alderman Thomas Lewis, who was married to their sister Elizabeth. Alderman Lewis had acquired it in 1670 from Charles Dormer, Earl of Carnarvon, when the fortune of that staunch Royalist family suffered heavily through the Civil War and the death of the first Earl who was ambushed on his way home after the Battle of Newbury by a solitary Roundhead trooper. Francis duly bought out his brother's share for £15,000 and proceeded to change the face of his new estate. He pulled down the Dormers' Elizabethan house which stood near the village and built one of red brick half-way up the hill – the nucleus of the present house – and built or improved many of the houses in the village. He probably also created a small lake from the streams in the valley.

Sir Robert too had bought land and lived at Northbrook near Oxford. His grandson, Sir James, built the great house at Kirtlington in 1746; it was described as the second largest in the county after Blenheim Palace, and his estate was so large that he could walk on his own land all the way from Kirtlington to Banbury, a distance of seventeen miles. Alderman George bought Heveningham Hall in Suffolk in 1714 but it was sold at his death in 1748. Sir Samuel's son Samuel married Anne Bateman, granddaughter of Sir Robert Chaplin, and lived at Well Vale in Lincolnshire where he laid out the park in great style with a delightful church and temples about the grounds.

By the end of the seventeenth century the Dashwoods' successful trading ventures were coming to an end. Sir Samuel and Francis were slowly falling out with each other and exchanged letters complaining about the slack trade and the division of expenses. Their business interests were concluded in 1704.

Sir Francis had, in the fashion of the time, greatly improved his position by marriage: first to Mary, the daughter of Alderman John Jennings of Westminster; secondly to Lady Mary Fane, the daughter and co-heiress of the 4th Earl of Westmorland; thirdly to Mary King, the niece of Dr John King, Master of the Charterhouse; and finally to Lady Elizabeth Windsor, daughter of the Earl of Plymouth.

At his death in 1724 he was succeeded by his son, Francis, by Lady Mary Fane, and it was he who transformed West Wycombe and added so much colour to the Dashwood name.

2

The Exclusive Clubs

THE DILETTANTI SOCIETY

TWO YEARS after his father's death in 1724, it was decided to send young Francis, who was then eighteen, off on the Grand Tour of the Netherlands, France and Italy, with a tutor. The choice of the latter had been a problem. The Earl of Westmorland, who was devoted to his nephew Francis – a feeling which was reciprocated – was his guardian, and took a keen interest in his education. He was, however, a Jacobite sympathizer, hoping for the restoration of the Pretender, Prince Charles, along with the style and elegance of the Stuart court in place of the heavy trappings of the Hanoverian one. To provide a tutor who could be relied on to support this view meant having a Catholic rather than the more natural choice of a Protestant, and unfortunately Lord Westmorland made a bad choice. The tutor turned out to be over-zealous and humourless, and the harder he tried the more he antagonized his young charge, driving him to ridicule the more superstitious practices of the Catholic Church.

Anyone who has had governesses will know the feeling.

Francis made numerous visits to Italy, sowing his wild oats and imbibing culture. Horace Walpole, alluding to the young man's numerous love affairs, said that he had 'the staying power of a stallion and the impetuosity of a bull'. Walpole went on to describe a visit to the Sistine Chapel in St Peter's whither Francis had been taken by his tutor to watch the special scourging ceremonies. Penitents were given small token whips with which to beat themselves as a mark of repentance. Francis thought it all very absurd. So he disguised himself as a night watchman and joined the congregation. Suddenly from under his cloak he drew out a stout horsewhip and cracked it up and down the aisle. In the dim candlelight the poor penitents thought the Devil himself had appeared and were frightened out of their wits.

During a later visit, in 1730, on the death of Pope Clement XII, Francis played another practical joke in the form of a mock assembly. In the words of a spectator, 'Never in my life have I witnessed anything so mad and so original. The leading part was taken by the chevalier Dashwood, one of the most amusing men in the world, who dressed himself up as an aged Cardinal, and imitating the trembling voice of Cardinal Ottoboni, intoned oremuses which were certainly not in the ritual.' He added that 'this cursed Huguenot had a repertory of licentious songs against the Papacy.'

During these visits to Italy Francis met other young Englishmen who were also on the Grand Tour. The English could often be found at Lady Mary Wortley Montagu's, who enjoyed playing the part of generous hostess to this medley of adventurous young men. Many of them had, however, a more serious side, and began to acquire a deep interest in Italian art and architecture, especially of the Roman period. So the idea gradually evolved of forming a dining club to promote the love of art, and, in about 1731, preliminary meetings were held in Italy. Bartolomeo Nazari, a Venetian painter, was commissioned to record the event in a series of almost identical paintings. They show the interior of a ship's cabin off the coast of Genoa with five men round a table studying a map. Besides the ship's captain, three of them are thought to be Sir Francis, Lord Middlesex and Lord Boyne, and one of the other figures could possibly be Lord Carlisle or Sir James Gray, who was to become secretary of the Society. One version of this painting is still at West Wycombe, another is at Castle Howard, which belonged to the Earl of Carlisle, and Lord Boyne has a third.

On their return to England, the young men gave formal substance to the idea with the founding of the Dilettanti Society in 1732/3. (The Society celebrated its jubilee in 1783.) Horace Walpole said of the Society: 'the nominal qualification is having been in Italy and the real one being drunk; the two chiefs are Lord Middlesex and Sir Francis Dashwood, who were seldom sober the whole time they were in Italy.' This stricture can be taken with a pinch of salt. Walpole was an abstainer; the members certainly drank heavily, but this did not deflect them from their main aim which was to encourage appreciation of art.

Members of the Society were required to have their portraits painted, and Sir Francis was duly painted by George Knapton in 1742 as a Franciscan monk, San Francisco di Wycombo, toasting a naked Venus. The painting, which is rather unattractive, now hangs, along with those of many other members, at Brooks's Club in St James's Street, London.

Sir Francis played the leading part in all the Society's activities. Besides choosing the Roman toga and crimson dress for the president and the dress of Machiavelli, the celebrated Florentine, for the secretary, and putting up many of his friends for election, Sir Francis was entrusted with negotiating the purchase from the Duke of Chandos of a site on the north side of Cavendish Square for a permanent home for the Society. The building was to have been designed as an exact replica of the Temple of Augustus at Pola in Istria; this was later changed into a plan for an Academy of Art with a Grand Council Room and wings to house academies of architecture, sculpture and painting. Sadly the project was abandoned, but the sale of the site, which was also entrusted to Sir Francis, made the Society a handsome profit. Sir Francis was continually suggesting schemes to further the cause of the Society in England. One such proposal in 1761 was 'to procure the first and best casts of the principal statues, Busto's and Bass Relievs, great or small, in order to produce something from this Society that may be beneficial to the publick.'

But much more important was the support he and other members of the Dilettanti Society gave to the highly successful publication in 1762 of *Antiquities of Athens* with its series of superb drawings by

James Stuart and Nicholas Revett. (It was this that led to Stuart's being dubbed 'Athenian' Stuart.) This publication was a milestone in drawing attention to the paramountcy of Greek classical art and inaugurated the 'Grecian Gusto' craze which swept the country. It was indirectly through this, many years later, that Lord Elgin retrieved the remains of the marble frieze from the Acropolis in Athens, thus ensuring its preservation for future generations.

Fired by the success of *Antiquities of Athens*, the Dilettanti Society next turned its attention to promoting a similar scheme for Asia Minor. Sir Francis became chairman of the committee which planned and financed the expedition undertaken in 1764 by Richard Chandler, Nicholas Revett and William Pars. On the successful return of the expedition in 1766, the Society immediately decided to publish a selection of drawings of the most important buildings in a magnificent series of volumes entitled *Ionian Antiquities*. Sir Francis was designated to present the first copies to the King and Queen in 1770.

In gratitude for all this, the Dilettanti Society gave Sir Francis a finely engraved and sculptured gold snuffbox in 1772. Until her death in 1973, this was in the possession of Mrs Starkey, who was directly descended from his illegitimate son, Francis, but it subsequently vanished and has not so far been traced.

The Dilettanti Society still flourishes. It meets for dinner every three months at Brooks's Club, and in May 1987 held a dinner at West Wycombe attended by the Prince of Wales, an honorary member of the Society. Its membership is as distinguished as in those earlier times, including many who are trying to preserve Britain's heritage: Lord Gibson, past chairman of the National Trust; Lord Normanby, chairman of the National Art Collections Fund; and owners or tenants of their family homes, Lord Anglesey (Plas Newydd), Lord Egremont (Petworth) and Lord Faringdon (Buscot). The Father of the Society is Lord de l'Isle (Penshurst), the Painter of the Society John Ward RA, and the Secretary Sir Brinsley Ford.

The officers still wear their traditional elaborate dress, but only for the election of new members. On such occasions the original quixotic and amusing ritual — no doubt it was thought up by Sir Francis himself — is still observed and remains a secret.

Recently the Society has sought to revive its ancient tradition of patronage and to support some of the many causes connected with our artistic heritage. It has, for instance, made grants towards the restoration of 'Athenian' Stuart's Temple of the Winds at Shugborough, of Giuseppe Borgnis's copy of Guido's painting of Aurora, the sun goddess, in the ceiling of the East Portico here at West Wycombe, and of monuments, pictures and sculptures in Venice. It has plans to make grants that will enable someone who is interested in Greek architecture and sculpture to visit classical sites and museums in Greece and Asia Minor. But this cannot compare with the major contribution which the Society made between 1762 and 1914 to the neo-classical movement in this country.

THE DIVAN CLUB

Sir Francis's next club was formed to commemorate a tour of the Ottoman Empire which he must have made by boat in the late 1730s, about the time of Lord Sandwich's visit, also by boat, which took place in 1738–39.

Sir Francis's tour embraced Constantinople and Smyrna, which had had long connections with the family's silk business, Ephesus, Palmyra and Baalbek, as well as the Great Pyramids and the Sphinx at Giza. Like Lord Sandwich, he brought back an Egyptian mummy (which my grandmother the Dowager Lady Dashwood gave away to the Tottenham Museum in 1912) and a model of a Turkish mosque. Subsequently he had himself and his wife sculpted in marble as sphinxes. He also bought books on Turkish costumes and customs, some of which are still in the library at West Wycombe.

Adrien Carpentiers and George Knapton were commissioned to paint a series of portraits of Sir Francis in about 1745 as 'Il Faquir Dashwood Pasha' wearing a gold brocade shirt, richly encrusted with jewels, a dark blue cloak edged with ermine and a jewelled turban; of his half-sister Mary Walcot as 'Sultana Walcotonia'; of Lady Mary Wortley Montagu; and of Fanny Murray, the celebrated courtesan. All the women are shown wearing similar gold dresses with ermine wraps and jewelled tiaras. Lady Mary had been in Constantinople as wife of the British Ambassador; she had been responsible for introducing into England in 1721 vaccination against smallpox which had been used with success in Constantinople. It is possible that the others had accompanied Sir Francis, although it is unlikely that they would have undertaken visits as far afield as Palmyra and Baalbek since robbery and murder posed a constant threat in these parts.

Recently I bought a painting entitled *Lady Dashwood of West Wycombe*, of Lady Ellys whom Sir Francis married in 1745. It shows the sitter in a similar gold costume; implying that she, too, must have visited the Ottoman Empire. It is quite possible that there are portraits to add to this list of other members of the Divan Club which have not yet been identified.

The Divan Club must have been started informally shortly after their return, since Mary Walcot died in 1741 and the formal founding took place at The Thatched Tavern in St James's Street on 8 January 1744. The qualification for membership was 'that none but such as can prove that they have been in the Sultan's Dominions be qualified to be chosen into this Club.' The founder members were Sir Francis, Lord Duncannon and Lord Sandwich.

Lord Sandwich and Lord Duncannon (later Lord Bessborough) were painted by Knapton in Oriental costume and with turbans, which they no doubt wore at the Divan Club meetings.

Lord Sandwich was chosen unanimously as Vizir on the first day. This position carried the right to name the 'Reis Effendi', or president, for the next meeting. The first three to occupy that position were Mr Edgcumbe, Lord Duncannon and Sir Francis, whilst Mr Frölick was appointed 'Hasnadar', or secretary, for the year. It was also agreed that the 'Society be called by the Name of the Divan' and that the 'Harem be a standing toast of the Divan'. A fine amounting to one 'Funduclee' was to be levied for absence from office and the minutes were recorded in a book entitled 'The Koran'.

The original list of members was as follows:

Sir Francis Dashwood
Lord Duncannon
Mr Edgcumbe
Mr Fanshaw
Sir Everard Fawkener
Mr Frölick
Lord Granby
Mr McKye [or Mackie]
Dr Pococke
Lord Sandwich
These were augmented by subsequent elections:
Sir Henry Calthorpe
Mr Edward Wortley
Mr James Nelthorpe
Mr Edward Vernon
Mr William Hewett
Mr Petre
Mr Wood
Mr Anson
Mr Maccartney
Admiral Anson
Captain Bonfoy
Captain Edgcumbe

There is no record of what transpired at the meetings, but Fanny Murray is shown in the painting with one bare bosom and nipple — surely a pun on the word 'Sultana' — and it is unlikely that the activities were wholly intellectual.

The last recorded meeting of the Divan Club was on 25 May 1746. Lord Sandwich, 'Il Faquir Sandwich', was Vizir and Mr Edgcumbe 'Reis Effendi'. The only other member to attend was Lord Duncannon.

Mr Blackwood was 'introduced on declaring his intention of going to Turkey when opportunity shall offer and Lord Sandwich according to Law paid his Harrack' (admission fee). It was then declared that 'the Divan stands adjourned from this day to the first Sunday in December'. No more was heard of it.

THE LINCOLN CLUB

Another club founded by Sir Francis was the Lincoln Club, which met at Dunston Pillar, outside Lincoln City.

Sir Francis had various estates in Lincolnshire; his seat was at Nocton, which belonged to his wife through her previous husband, Sir Richard Ellys. On his land at Dunston near Lincoln, in 1751, Sir Francis erected a great column, 92 feet high, called the Dunston Pillar, 'the only land lighthouse ever raised'; it had a large octagonal lantern on top and was 'of great utility' in guiding travellers across the heath. The lantern was lit regularly until 1788 when it was no longer needed, as the roads had been improved and the old heath converted into 'one of the most beautifully farmed parts of Lincolnshire'. The lantern crashed to the ground in 1809 and was replaced by a statue of King George III, which was in turn removed in 1939 as it was a hazard to low-flying aircraft.

At the foot of the column Sir Francis created a bowling green and plantations and erected two small stone pavilions. Later a two-storey building with a dining room was added. It was described in a letter from the Rev. William Wroughton, vicar of Welbourn, to Lord le Despencer, in 1766, as:

the Vauxhall of his part of the world. The Bowling Green is the best and kept in the best order I have ever seen and the plantations are all in a very thriving state and will in a few years be the Paradise of Lincolnshire. It was used for the accommodation of parties resorting thither for amusement – tea parties, playing at bowls, quoits, etc. – with as many as sixteen or eighteen carriages there at one time.

Little is known of the membership of the Lincoln Club. In a letter of 3 September 1770, John King wrote from his seat at Ashby:

the Honor of your Lordship's letter gave us great comfort and reviv'd our drooping spirits, which was an Act of Charity, far beyond what our Fathers and Brotherhood received here, wish it was in our Power to pay our Obedience at Medmenham, but cannot at this juncture leave our Family; so in the mean time must pay all Obedience to the Pillar annexed, the present standard of Mirth to the Sisterhood, who are determined to exert their spiritualities there, as far as their present condition are able, for I assure your Lordship their spirits are willing but the Flesh is weak . . . Father Paul, Bro. Burton and Pil Levet, the Sisters with Curtois Novice and I Pil unite in proper duty and beg to subscribe myself like your Lordship's Most obedient faithful humble servant John King.

Curtois Novice was probably Mary, the daughter of the Rev. John Curtois of Branston, who married in 1749 Dr Willis of Greatsford – the doctor who cured George III of his insanity and ran a private boys' school and an asylum for 'afflicted persons of distinction and respectability' there. At one stage he had 'two little Dashwood boys' in his care, but later became involved in a long and acrimonious dispute with Sir Francis over the occupation of the house which Sir Francis had let him have free.

Now only the truncated half of Dunston Pillar remains to bear witness to what must have been one of the high social spots of the county in the eighteenth century.

THE HELL-FIRE CLUB

The Knights of St Francis of Wycombe, or the Hell-Fire Club as it was later called, was a natural progression from the earlier clubs but with the difference that it indulged in mock religious and sexual frolics.

During his visits to Italy, Sir Francis had developed an acute antipathy towards the Roman Catholic Church, and on his return had gone so far as to have himself painted by Nathaniel Dance as a Franciscan monk, by Carpentiers as Pope Pontius VII toasting the statue of Venus, by Hogarth as a Franciscan friar leering at a recumbent statue of Venus and with a halo round his head enclosing the face of Lord Sandwich, and, as already recorded, by Knapton in 1742 as San Francisco di Wycombo, again toasting the statue of Venus which can still be seen at West Wycombe.

It was but a short step to the founding of the Knights of St Francis of Wycombe, which was probably started in the 1740s when these portraits were painted and flourished until 1763, although it did not die out until 1774 or even later. That it outlived the Divan Club was due to the combined talents of Sir Francis as founder who provided a stream of original and entertaining ideas, and of Paul Whitehead, the steward, who was adept at running it. Boswell described Whitehead as 'a member of a riotous profane club in 1738', and Whitehead was elected in 1744 to the Sublime Society of Beefsteaks where he may first have met Sir Francis. It was from among these clubs and societies, the Dilettanti, the Divan, the Beefsteak and Whites', as well as the House of Commons and neighbouring landowners, that the members of the new order were drawn.

A letter to Sir Francis from George Bubb Dodington (Lord Melcombe Regis) on 5 October 1745 is quite explicit about his particular interest at the time.

Your letter in praise of regularity charms everybody that I have read it to, and we are all in love with your agreeable Defence of that Steady Course you are in, of employing 20 of the 24 hours either upon your own Belly, or from thence, like a Publick Reservoir, administering to those of other People, by laying your Cock in every private Family that has any Place fitt to receive it.

The original meetings are said to have taken place in the George and Vulture Inn in the City. (With its eighteenth-century boxes, it is still today a pleasant place for City lunches.) Some early meetings were also held in the members' houses, Sir Francis's in Hanover

Square and at West Wycombe, Bubb Dodington's at Hammersmith, Sir Walter Stanhope's at Eythrope, Sir Thomas Stapleton's at Henley and perhaps also at Cliveden which was leased by Frederick, Prince of Wales, until his death in 1751.

The Caves at West Wycombe cannot have been used for meetings of the Knights of St Francis at that date since the excavation work started in 1748 and continued until 1754. It is possible, however, and indeed highly likely, that Sir Francis arranged a triumphal masquerade party in the Caves to mark their completion and included among his guests many of those who attended meetings of the Hell-Fire Club. He considered the building of a new temple or folly to be a good pretext for throwing an inaugural party, and these were invariably on a lavish and spectacular scale with, for instance, cannons firing in mock sea-battles on the lake or ancient rituals enacted by nymphs and satyrs wreathed in leaves and grapevines.

As the club flourished, Sir Francis cast around for a meeting place which would provide luxury and seclusion. What better, he concluded, than the ruins of the old Cistercian abbey at Medmenham, only six miles away from West Wycombe on the river Thames near Henley?

At the time all that was left of the abbey and surrounding buildings were some columns and walls and a few broken statues, to which, in 1595, the owners, the Duffields, had added a large E-shaped house of red brick and stone taken from the ruins. Sir Francis immediately set about improving this dilapidated Elizabethan house and the ruins, possibly with the help of Nicholas Revett, the architect who was destined to play such an important role in recording the major architectural remains of Greece and Asia Minor. A cloister with five or six arches and a ruined tower were added. Behind the cloister was the chapter or common room, 'fitted up with the same good taste and the glare of light is judiciously excluded by the pleasing gloom of stained glass, chiefly coronets, roses and portcullises.' The ceilings were decorated with fresco paintings by Giuseppe Borgnis, who had been brought over from Italy in 1751 to work at West Wycombe and who lived in a small house with a large studio a few miles from Medmenham just outside Marlow.

The chapter room was hung with forty prints of the kings of England; a piece of paper was stuck over the face of Henry VIII 'as a mark of their dislike to him for destroying monasteries'. These prints almost certainly came from the collection of the antiquarian Sir Richard Ellys at Nocton House in Lincolnshire whose widow, Sarah, Sir Francis had married in 1745. There were also ninety small prints of monks and nuns, four paintings by William Hannan of the house and gardens at West Wycombe, and two prints of Sir Francis as Lord le Despencer and of the painter William Hogarth.

Round the walls were pegs for hanging the dress of each brother, which, according to Walpole, consisted of 'a white hat, white jacket and white trousers whilst the Prior has a red hat like a Cardinal's and a red bonnet turned up with coney skin: each peg was marked with their Christian name and place of abode.' Thus Sir Francis was 'Francis of Wycombe' and Wilkes 'John of Aylesbury'.

The room was furnished with musical instruments, backgammon tables, chess-boards and cards. Against a wall was a bookcase; about thirty of the original books are still in the library at West Wycombe and provide a good idea of what was read. They were a mixture of humorous and satirical novels — *A Tale of a Tub* and *Gulliver's Travels* by Swift and the *Castle of Indolence* by James Thomson — of poetry by Pope, Congreve and Spencer, of love stories — *Les Aventures du Baron de Freneste* — and of religion — *Foxe's Book of Martyrs*, the life of the Virgin Mary and an ancient Bible. At the back of the latter were pasted most of the extant letters from members of the club. It is hardly surprising also to find a book on Rabelais, from whom the idea of just such a club originated, including the motto *'Fay ce que voudras'* (Do as you wish) which is inscribed in stone over the archway at the entrance to Medmenham Abbey and also over the fireplaces. This motto has often been quoted as encouragement to licentious indulgence, although this was far from its true meaning. Rabelais had taken it from a much more ancient source. When a young man asked St Augustine of Hippo, 'What must I do to be saved?', the saint replied: 'Love God and do what you like. For if with the spirit of wisdom a man loves God, then, always striving to fulfil the divine will, what he wishes should be the right thing.'

Some of these books belonged to Sir John Dashwood-King and some to John Clerke of Aston in Oxfordshire, but most of them were John Wilkes's; many have his own bookplate and handwriting in them. It was evidently he who acted as librarian, for we find Sir William Stapleton writing on 5 September 1761 in answer to an invitation to a chapter meeting:

> I unfurnished my Library at Twickenham last week and sent the pious books to Mr Deards [the bookseller] with orders to send them to George Street [where Wilkes lived]; if the Chapter think them worthy of the Abbey. I shall be extremely glad, hoping they will now and then occasion an extraordinary ejaculation to be sent up to heaven.

Next to the chapter room and the cloister were monks' cells and a tiny chapel built for private worship by the Duffields. One cell still exists beneath the staircase; it is very small and cramped and without a window. A wooden cot was kept in this cell and was shown to visitors in the nineteenth century. It was subsequently removed to a loft in the stables.

Off the common room was a dining room, which has a chimney piece also inscribed with *'Fay ce que voudras'* in the stone architrave. The east entrance from the garden has the same motto over the door. At the end of the passage were the words *'Aude, hospes, contemnere opes'* (Dare, O guest, to despise wealth).

On either side of the door from the anteroom into the large refectory are apertures with columns through which the company could be observed without the spectator being seen. At one end of the refectory stood a statue of Harpocrates, the Egyptian god of silence, and at the other the goddess Angerona – 'that the same duty might be enjoined to both sexes', that is to stress the oath of secrecy by which the brothers and sisters were all bound.

The rebuilding was carried out 'with so much taste and properly that when time shall have worn off all traces . . . when the ivy shall have continued its embraces and the mosses of various hues overspread the surface, some future owner will be disposed to class it with the more ancient pile.'

The gardens, which underwent a complete transformation, were described by John Wilkes as follows:

The garden, the grove, the orchard, the neighbouring woods, all bespoke the loves and frailties of the younger Monks, who seemed, at least, to have sinned naturally. You saw in one place, *Ici pâma de joïe des mortels le plus heureux* [Here the happiest of mortals died of joy] – in another, very imperfectly, *mourut un amant sur le sein de sa dame* [a lover dies on the bosom of his lady] – in a third, *en cet endroit mille baisers de flamme furent donnés, et mille autres rendus* [in this place a thousand kisses of fire were given and a thousand others returned]. Against a fine old oak was

   Hic Satyrum Naïas victorem victa subegit [Here the vanquished naiad overcame the conquering satyr].

At the entrance of a cave was *Venus*, stooping to pull a thorn out of her foot. The statue turned from you, and just over the two nether hills of snow were these lines of VIRGIL:

Hic locus est, partes ubi se via findit in ambas:
Hac iter Elyzium nobis; at laeva malorum
Exercet poenas, et ad impia Tartara mittit

[Here is the place where the way divided into two: this on the right is our route to Heaven; but the left-hand path exacts punishment from the wicked, and sends them to pitiless Hell].

On the inside, over a mossy couch, was the following exhortation:

Ite, agite, ô juvences; pariter fudate medullis
Omnibus inter vos; non murmura vestra columbae,
Brachia non hederae, non vincant oscula conchae

[Go into action, you youngsters; put everything you've got into it together, both of you; let not doves outdo your cooings, nor ivy your embraces, nor oysters your kisses].

The favourite doctrine of the Abbey is certainly not *penitence*;

for in the centre of the orchard is a very grotesque figure, *and in his hand a reed stood flaming, tipt with fire,* to use MILTON'S words; and you might trace out

PENI TENTO

non

PENITENTI.

In a small inlet off the river Thames close to the abbey, a boat was moored for river outings. It was probably similar to the one on the lake at West Wycombe, which had a small cabin of scarlet canvas with rectangular window openings. On fine days the sides were rolled up. The boat was propelled like a gondola by four men dressed in white with scarlet oars and was steered by a cox dressed in dark blue with gold braid and a tricorn hat. At the stern flew a large red ensign.

John Wilkes referred to the river outings in a letter to the Abbot, or Prior as he was variously called. 'When may I see you again steering along the Thames and fishing for the good Johnnies with a small hook or setting nets for really large fish? One may hope for anything – I shall say no more.'

Medmenham Abbey in the late eighteenth century.

Round Tar Island was leased by Sir Francis from Sir Thomas Stapleton. It lay about four miles from the abbey and was one of four little eyots or islands just below Cookham bridge. It has now vanished from sight, having become submerged beneath the water.

The front covers of the club's Cellar Book show an island with two little wooden huts, one thatched, against a hilly background. There is still an island about one mile upstream which has small huts on it and seems to fit this description. It is likely that these two islands were frequented by the brothers for picnics and outings.

What really took place in the abbey?

Numerous second-hand accounts appeared towards the latter part of the eighteenth century giving varying descriptions of the goings on, some of which seem to be completely fictitious and are not corroborated by any other sources. The original letters found at the back of the Medmenham Abbey Bible, together with several contemporary accounts, do however give a glimpse of what went on.

Twice a year, in March, June, August, September or early October, a chapter meeting was held, invitations being sent out by the Prior or Paul Whitehead, the steward of the club. For these meetings some sort of costume was worn. Portraits of the three Vansittarts, Arthur, Henry and Robert, which are attributed to Hogarth and are now at Shottesbrooke Park, show them in dark blue berets with floppy red cones like a clown's and the words 'Love and Friendship' on the front. They are however wearing ordinary three-quarter length coats, which was perhaps the dress for informal occasions; Walpole was quite explicit about the 'white jacket and trousers' which he claimed to have seen. Incidentally, the words *'Libertati Amicatiae que S'* (Sacred to liberty and friendship) also appear in a panel over the Arch of Apollo at West Wycombe and must have been as much the motto of the club as *'Fay ce que voudras'* found at Medmenham Abbey.

The chapter meetings were described in a book of 1779 entitled *Nocturnal Revels:*

They however always meet in one general sett at meals, when, for the improvement of mirth, pleasantry, and gaiety, every member is allowed to introduce a Lady of cheerful lively disposition, to improve the general hilarity. Male visitors are also permitted, under certain restrictions, their greatest recommendation being their merit wit and humour. There is no constraint with regard to the circulation of the glass, after some particular toasts have been given: The Ladies, in the intervals of their repasts, may make select parties among themselves, or entertain one another, or alone with reading, musick, tambour-work, etc.

The salt of these festivities is generally purely attic, but no indelicacy or indecency is allowed to be intruded without a severe penalty; and a *jeu de mots* must not border too much upon a loose *double entendre* to be received with applause.

The account goes on to describe the clothes worn and the admission ceremony. No vows of celibacy were required either by the ladies or the 'Monks', 'the former considering themselves as the lawful wives of the bretheren during their stay within the monastic walls; every Monk being religiously scrupulous not to infringe upon the nuptial alliance of any other brother.'

In order that the ladies should not have the embarrassment of unwittingly coming upon their husbands or acquaintances, they appeared masked and would not disclose their identity until all the members had 'passed them in review'. Should they recognize someone they did not wish to meet, they were allowed to retire without revealing themselves.

The description concludes:

Disquisitions of an amorous and platonic kind sometimes are introduced in which full liberty of speech is allowed, within the prescribed line of decorum. In case the topics should unexpectedly become too warm and passionate, the use of fans is allowed, to prevent the appearance of the Ladies' blushes; and under these circumstances, some females seize their opportunity for a temporary retreat with their paramours. The Monastery is not destitute of the aid of the Faculty, even of those who profess the chirurgical as well as the obstetric art; as the Ladies, in case they find it necessary, may make a temporary retreat from the world, and assure posterity with respect to the rising generation. The offspring of these connexions are stiled the Sons and Daughters of St Francis and are appointed in due order officers and domestics in the Seminary, according to their different abilities, or by drawing lots.

Sir Francis himself had several children. A son Francis was born in 1762 and may have been one of the two Dashwood boys who were reported at Dr Willis's school at Dunston in 1776. Francis was later enrolled as a lieutenant in the Buckinghamshire Militia and died in 1779. Another son, also called Francis, went to America in 1775. He became Postmaster in Jamaica; he was captured during the Revolutionary War and was later exchanged with two American Colonels. A third son named Francis was born in 1773 to his mistress, Frances Barry, who had also borne him a daughter, Rachel Frances Antonina, in 1770.

As in other fashionable clubs, the Sublime Society of Beefsteaks and the Dilettanti Society for example, meetings of the Hell-Fire Club were punctuated by frequent toasts as well as ribald poems and songs. In a letter to Sir Francis of 27 July 1761 Wilkes says: 'I already see your sides shaking with laughter and see you filling your nostrils with snuff: I already hear you solving riddles in your accustomed way; everyone shows their approval with applause.' Amongst the members were several leading poets and writers, notably Charles Churchill, who had shot to fame as the author of the *Rosciad*, Paul Whitehead (Poet Laureate) and Rupert Lloyd.

It was Churchill who coined the well-known verse about the club:

> *Whilst Womanhood, in the habit of a Nun,*
> *At Med'nam lies, by backward Monks undone.*

Wilkes, Thomas Potter, son of the Archbishop of Canterbury, and John Hall Stevenson were also prolific writers; it was Wilkes and Potter who collaborated in producing the obscene *Essay on Woman* which no doubt provided plenty of amusement after dinner.

After dinner, the twelve members and the Abbot, who was elected annually and took office from the beginning of October, repaired upstairs to the chapel where a mock religious ceremony took place. There is a hint of some such service in a letter from Sir William Stanhope: ' . . . my compliments to all your Brethren and assure them that they may have my prayers, particularly in that part of the Litany when I pray the Lord *to strengthen them that do stand*' (my italics).

Next to the chapel were some cells which, according to Horace Walpole, were fitted with cots and 'the brothers take their women there.' It seemed odd that they should have resorted to such cramped quarters when plenty of large spacious bedrooms were available. The Abbot was said to have had first choice of the ladies present.

The abbey was also used fairly regularly by the brothers for 'private devotions'. One or two used to go there for a night at a time and the Cellar Book records twenty-six such occasions during the four years 1760–64, including two which took place the night before a chapter meeting; the latter were attended by four or five brothers and were obviously to make arrangements for the chapter meetings.

The 'devotions' took place on Wednesdays, Thursdays, Fridays or Saturdays from July to October. John Wilkes was easily the most active with twenty such visits; others attending were Dr John Morton, Sir Thomas Stapleton, John Tucker, Sir Francis, Sir John Dashwood-King, John Norris, Dr Thompson, Francis Duffield and John of London (unidentified). Wilkes's most frequent companion was John Morton (John of Henley). His last recorded private devotion was on 6 September 1761, although he was still attending chapter meetings in 1762.

The brothers certainly did not drink excessively at these private devotions. Eighteenth-century bottles were smaller than those of today, and the usual consumption was one or two bottles of claret. Even when Wilkes was accompanied by another brother, they seldom drank more than one or two bottles of claret, one of port and perhaps one of calcavello. This last was a sort of sweet aperitif, popular with the ladies.

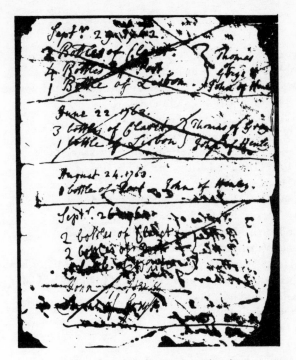

Extract from the Cellar Book, 1763–4.

These meetings provided an ideal opportunity for discreet rendezvous with ladies who did not wish to be identified. (It would, after all, have been so much more convenient to have resorted to the numerous 'convents' and 'nunneries' which existed in London, for similar purposes.) John Armstrong referred to 'the Sisters' in a letter to Wilkes of 20 December 1760: 'Well, but I hope you don't shave all — nothing below the chin — at least I trust the Sisters are excused from any ceremony of this kind.'

No list exists of all those who went to Medmenham Abbey. Over the whole life of the club, which was at its most active for about fifteen years from the early 1750s until 1764 and lasted until 1774 or even later, the twelve members must have changed through resignations and deaths, and many others would have taken part briefly out of curiosity. The following list gives the members during the club's heyday until 1762; it has been compiled from the two remaining Cellar Books and from letters and other sources.

Sir Francis Dashwood, Lord le Despencer
Paul Whitehead, poet and Steward
The Earl of Sandwich, First Lord of the Admiralty
Lord Melcombe Regis, politician
Sir Thomas Stapleton of Greys, near Henley
Sir William Stanhope, MP for Buckinghamshire
Thomas Potter, son of the Archbishop of Canterbury
Sir John Dashwood-King, MP and landowner
Dr Thomas Thompson
Francis Duffield, owner of Medmenham Abbey
John Tucker, MP for Weymouth
John Norris, don at Magdalen College, Oxford
Arthur Vansittart of Shottesbrooke Park, MP
Sir Henry Vansittart, Governor of Bengal and MP for Reading
Robert Vansittart, Regius Professor of Civil Law at Oxford
Charles Churchill, Poet
Robert Lloyd, Poet
George Selwyn, MP
John Wilkes, MP
Sir John Aubrey, MP
Dr Benjamin Bates of Aylesbury
William Hogarth, Painter
John Hall Stevenson
Edward Lovibond
Mr Clarke of Henley
Dr John Morton, MP
Richard Hopkins, MP

Wilkes was to become much the most famous of these men. He had come to know Sir Francis following his appointment as High Sheriff of the county of Buckinghamshire in 1754 and Member of Parliament for Aylesbury in 1757 when his friend, Thomas Potter, another member, gave up the seat for him. Two years later, in 1759, Sir Francis was appointed first Colonel of the Buckinghamshire Militia which had been formed following the outbreak of the Seven Years War in 1756, and he arranged to have Wilkes as his second-in-command.

In 1760 Wilkes was elected to the Hell-Fire Club and immediately took to the life at Medmenham Abbey with enthusiasm and even played an active part in running the club. In 1762 he wrote to Sir Francis: 'I feast my mind with the Joy of Medmenham on Monday and hope to indemnify myself there for the noise and nonsense here', and to Churchill: 'Pray remember the ghost for me tonight and next Monday we meet at Medmenham.' To Lord Temple he wrote of 'coming from Medmenham Abbey where the jovial monks of St Francis kept me up till four in the morning.'

Besides being in charge of the library Wilkes was also commissioned to procure silver for the use of the Order, including some silver cups in the form of a woman's breasts. But, in typical Wilkes fashion, he omitted to pay the silversmith, Mr Hemings, the £20 with which he had been entrusted so that the latter was driven to publicize his case in the *Public Advertiser*. Wilkes also provided the abbey with silver candlesticks, one of which he unsuccessfully sought to recover after his expulsion from the Order.

It was Wilkes who was responsible for the row which broke out in the club in 1762–63 and which caused a major breach between Wilkes, supported by Churchill and Hall Stevenson, and the rest of the members led by Lord Sandwich. But for this it is doubtful if anything would ever have been known about the revels at Medmenham Abbey.

The rift was instigated by the appointment of Lord Bute in 1762 in place of the Pitt–Newcastle administration. Wilkes was a staunch supporter of the latter – indeed his patron was Lord Temple, Pitt's brother-in-law – and like Temple, he strongly disapproved of the peace treaty reached by Bute to end the Seven Years War. Wilkes likened the Peace of Amiens to the 'Peace of God which passeth all understanding'. Actually, the terms of the treaty were probably more favourable than Wilkes and Pitt were willing to admit, and certainly public reaction in France was hostile to it.

Wilkes had also discovered during the summer of 1762 that William Hogarth was about to publish a hostile caricature of Pitt and Temple. In No. 17 of the *North Briton*, 25 September 1762, Wilkes launched an attack on Hogarth, who had been appointed sergeant-painter to George III, with the words 'I think that this term means what is vulgarly called housepainter.' Hogarth, in revenge, produced cartoons of Wilkes and Churchill, both of whom had been his close friends and cronies at Medmenham Abbey. Wilkes was shown with his wig shaped to look like the Devil's horns and with a satyr's expression on his face, and Churchill as a bear clutching a pint of porter with his dog Trump pissing on a copy of the *North Briton*. On seeing the cartoon of Wilkes, the King exclaimed 'That Devil Wilkes', an epitaph which clung to Wilkes thereafter. Churchill, in turn, hit back so viciously that his attack was said to have brought about Hogarth's premature death in 1764.

Wilkes's assault then shifted to a series of venomous articles in the *North Briton*, a publication which he had started in June 1762 with Charles Churchill and with contributions from Robert Lloyd. These attacks reached a crescendo with the publication of No. 45 of the *North Briton* in April 1763. In it Wilkes insinuated that King George III was participating in deliberately misleading the country about a treaty which was against the national interest, and that there was a plot to promote the interests of Scotland at the expense of England with the secret intention of replacing the reigning Hanoverians with the Jacobites. He went on to suggest that Lord Bute was having an affair with the Queen Mother, which naturally infuriated the King. The Government was finally stung into action and issued warrants for the arrest of those concerned in the publication of this 'seditious libel'. Wilkes was duly arrested and thrown into the Tower of London and his house was ransacked by Government agents.

Wilkes's friends, including influential politicians such as Lord Temple and William Pitt, were horrified at the arrest of a man without trial on a general warrant and after forced entry into a private house, although Pitt disapproved of 'all these sorts of papers, the *North Briton*, etc.' And when the case came to court, Lord Chief Justice Pratt ordered Wilkes's release. Parliament, however, took a different view; it resolved that the 'privilege of Parliament does not extend to the case of writing or publishing seditious libels' and sought to overturn the verdict. Pratt stood firm and his ruling, that general warrants were illegal, except in cases of treason, established in England the rights of the individual against general warrants – a very important principle of freedom.

Wilkes had by then become a popular hero and martyr, and the cry of 'Wilkes and Liberty' was to be heard everywhere.

The situation seems to have been further inflamed as a result of a practical joke which Wilkes played on Lord Sandwich at the Hell-Fire Club.

[Wilkes] had contrived the night before to bring into his cell a great Baboon which he had provided for the occasion. When the brotherhood retired to their cells after dinner, to prepare for the ceremony, he availed himself of the office of keeper of the Chapel, which he then filled to convey this creature, dressed up in the phantastic garb, in which childish imagination cloths devils, into the chapel, where he shut him up in a large chest, that stood there to hold the ornaments and utensils of the table, when the society was away. To the spring of the lock of this chest he fastened a cord, which he drew under the carpet that was on the floor to his own seat, and there brought the end of it through a hole, made for the purpose, in such a manner that he could readily find it; and by giving it a pull, open the chest, and let the Baboon loose, whenever he pleased, without being perceived by the rest of the company.

At the chosen moment, Wilkes pulled the cord and out popped the wretched animal which leapt on to the shoulders of Lord Sandwich, who, feeling the shock and seeing the animal grinning horribly at him concluded that the Devil had obeyed his summons in good earnest and had come to carry him bodily away. The harder he tried to shake off the poor creature the tighter it clung, whilst Sandwich cried out: 'Spare me gracious Devil: spare a wretch who never was sincerely your servant. I sinned only from vanity of being in the fashion; thou knowest I never have been half so wicked as I pretended: never have been able to commit the thousandth part of the vices which I have boasted of . . . leave me therefore and go to those who are more truly devoted to your service. I am but half a sinner . . .'

This story appeared in 1766 in a publication entitled *Chrysal or the Adventures of a Guinea* which purported to describe the adventures of a gold guinea as it travelled from one man's pocket to another's. The whole book is, however, inaccurate in almost every detail, and the chapel at Medmenham, which measures 21 by 19 feet, is rather small to accommodate thirteen participants and a baboon in a box without its presence being patently obvious.

According to the last descendant of the Vansittarts, it was another member of the family, George, a guest at the abbey, who took his brother Henry's baboon to the abbey in a bag and let it loose during the ceremony, causing pandemonium among the members. There may be some truth in this story since a baboon was kept at Medmenham Abbey for a time; it had been brought back from India by one of the members, Sir Henry Vansittart, the Governor of Bengal.

Lord Sandwich certainly hated Wilkes and went to great length to ruin him. It must be remembered that, lecherous as he no doubt was, Lord Sandwich was a most capable and industrious First Lord of the Admiralty, a position he occupied for a total of sixteen years between 1747 and 1781, which included the period of the Revolutionary War with America. It was largely due to his strenuous and efficient reorganization of the Navy that Britain was able to take on single-handed the principal sea powers of the world, France and Holland, and despite some failures to secure a final and triumphant victory at the Battle of the Saints in 1781, which enabled peace to be reached on reasonable terms.

At the height of the Wilkes scandal, Lord Sandwich insisted on taking a leading part in the Government campaign to have Wilkes expelled from the House of Commons so that he could be arrested for publishing the 'seditious libel' in the *North Briton*. Lord Sandwich took it upon himself to draw the attention of the House of Lords to another publication attributed to Wilkes, the *Essay on Woman*. This was a parody of Pope's *Essay on Man*. The original version of the parody had caused much amusement at Medmenham Abbey and had been enjoyed by Pitt himself. Subsequently it underwent considerable amendment and was turned into a most indecent but hilarious poem with obscene footnotes ascribed to Dr Warburton, the Bishop of Gloucester. The latter had been dragged in because he had carried out a revision of Shakespeare in which he had changed original words of the great poet and had inserted lines of his own. To make matters worse, Thomas Potter, who was responsible with Wilkes for the *Essay*, had previously had an affair, in 1756, with the bishop's wife and she had produced a child by him, to the bishop's rage and indignation.

Whilst the House of Commons was debating the Wilkes affair, Sandwich insisted on reading out the *Essay* in the House of Lords. After each stanza he apologized for shocking the assembled Lords and suggested stopping, but the Lords insisted on hearing the whole poem and shouted, 'Go on – go on!'

Sir Francis who, as Lord le Despencer, was listening to Lord Sandwich in the House of Lords was deeply shocked at his old friend's behaviour and commented that he never expected to hear 'Satan preaching against himself'. The public took the same view and nicknamed Sandwich 'Jemmy Twitcher', after the character in *The Beggar's Opera* of whom the highwayman, MacHeath, declares,. 'that Jemmy [a member of his own gang] should peach me I own surprised me.'

It seems more likely, however, that Sandwich's behaviour was prompted by the fact that he had discovered that Wilkes was about to publish a most venomous article about him in the next issue of the *North Briton* and decided therefore to beat Wilkes to the draw.

The outcome was that in January 1764 both Houses of Parliament voted that Wilkes, who had left for France to recover from the wound he had received in a duel, should be expelled.

In due course, in 1767, Wilkes returned to England but he was immediately arrested again and sentenced to prison for three years. During that time he conducted a courageous and incessant campaign from prison against the legality of general warrants, unlawful entry and the right of Parliament to make the final choice over which candidate had won an election, and finally for the freedom of the press. In spite of being in prison, he continued to stand for Parliament and was elected by overwhelming majorities on four different occasions. Each time the House of Commons voted his opponent the winner but, eventually, justice and sense prevailed and Wilkes was allowed to take his seat.

Wilkes had not confined his attacks to Lord Bute but had also launched a diatribe against Sir Francis, attacking in particular his excise levy on cider in the Budget of 1763 and pouring ridicule on his old friend by divulging some of the 'secrets of the Convent'. However, he was bound by an oath of secrecy; he had already fought three duels in one of which he had been severely wounded and wanted to avoid courting further challenges from his fellow brothers, so he confined himself to describing the erotic gardens, there and at West Wycombe, since they could hardly be concealed from public view. It is likely that much of the information which was published anonymously years after this episode was leaked by Wilkes, aided and abetted by Robert Lloyd and John Hall Stevenson, to periodicals such as the *Morning Post, Morning Herald* and *Public Advertiser.*

Sir Francis stopped attending meetings of the Hell-Fire Club as

John Wilkes promoting the cause of liberty.

he wished to avoid Wilkes, but Wilkes was keen to make it up and 'desired their common friends at the Abbey to represent to Sir Francis the nature of such an institution in which politics had not the least concern, that the brotherhood there was us'd to sacrifice to mirth, friendship and to love, never to fortune, nor ambition.'

Chapter meetings and 'private devotions' still continued during 1762, 1763 and 1764. John Tucker, MP for Weymouth, wrote to Sir Francis on 11 August 1764: 'My heart and inclinations will be with your Lordship and your friends at Medmenham at the next Chapter, but I am cruelly detained here by the sickness of my Brother – I pray you will present my fillial Duty to our holy Father and fraternal love and respect to the pious Brotherhood to whom I wish all possible Joy Spirits and Vigour.'

On 22 March 1766, however, Tucker wrote: 'I was last Sunday at Medmenham and to my amazement found the Chapter Room stripped naked.' Evidently, Sir Francis had decided that the time had come to remove all traces of incriminating evidence, including even the prints of the heads of kings and nuns and the pegs for the clothes with the brothers' names above. Perhaps he feared the political reaction which confirmation of the newspaper articles might have caused and hoped that the gossip would all die down and be forgotten.

According to tradition, the club took to meeting, after the 'break-up' at Medmenham Abbey, in the Caves at West Wycombe which Sir Francis had had excavated in 1748–54. But I have not managed to find any evidence for this, apart from a paragraph in Mrs Lybbe Powys's diary. Following her visit to West Wycombe and the Caves in 1796 she wrote:

Near the middle of the excavation there is a small pool which is now crossed by stepping stones, but formerly it is said it would only be passed in a boat. The excavation terminates in a large lofty circular cavern with a vaulted roof in which is a hook for suspending a lamp or chandelier. Here according to local tradition the Hell-Fire Club occasionally held its meetings.

Chamber's *Book of Days* for 1863–64 repeats the above

description, adding that the pool was called the Styx. Later writers enlarged on the theme, one asserting that it was in the end chamber that 'the Wycombe wenches lost the last vestiges of their innocence.' Even if this last observation contains an element of truth, it is inconceivable that the members of an exclusive society, bound by laws of secrecy and accustomed to comfort and luxury, would have resorted to a place with the entrance in full view of a public road and in damp and chilly surroundings. I have no doubt, however, that Sir Francis used the Caves for occasional parties, just as I have done myself.

The Hell-Fire Club did not collapse in 1763 but continued to function at Medmenham Abbey for another ten years or more. The Cellar Book of 1769 contains accounts of two 'private devotions' held by Francis of Cookham (Francis Duffield) and John of Henley (Dr John Morton, MP). And in a letter of 19 August 1770, Sir Francis wrote from his estate in Montgomeryshire to Lord Sandwich inviting him to another meeting at Medmenham.

Montgomeryshire
Millenden   Aug 19th 1770

My dear Lord,
I receive your rebuke with respect, for I do acknowledge I write most shamefully like a man of quality — I rec'd your's yesterday morn at Aberystwith in Cardiganshire. I was very glad you decyphered mine so as to understand our meeting at Medmenham is appointed for the 28th instant if you will do me the friendship to come to West Wycombe on the 27th yourself, Father Paul and I will march to Medmenham the next day. I mean on horseback. John Secular will clean your shoes, I can for once tend your sheets so you need not take much thought for the morrow.

Your Lordships most affect.
Le Despencer.

But the days of the Order were nearly over, and when Paul Whitehead, the steward, died, an inventory was taken. This, dated 15 October 1774, listed the wine then in the cellar, Lisbon (sherry), rum, port, hock, claret and Dorchester beer, as well as 29 pewter plates, 27 knives and 29 forks, 24 wine glasses and some teacups and saucers.

Even that did not signal the end, however, for in the *Morning Post* of 1776 it was reported that

> the order of the Franciscan Society at Medmenham Abbey being nearly demolished J — Y Twitcher (Lord Sandwich) who is almost) the only surviving member of that Club (formerly called the Hell-Fire Club) is determined to restore it to its original glory; in consequence of which intention we hear that he has taken down the circumnavigator [i.e. Sir Joseph Banks who had sailed round the world and was President of the Royal Society of Arts] and Dr Salamander [a pun for Dr Solander, the botanist] in order to initiate them into that Society.
>
> Another report stated that the Duke of Kingston and the Marquis of Granby had also been enrolled as members.

Little more is known about members of the club at this date but it is highly probable that Benjamin Franklin went to Medmenham Abbey. He was in England from 1757 to 1762 and from 1764 to 1775 and became a close friend of Sir Francis's during the latter period. Both were members of the Society for the Encouragement of Arts, Manufactures and Commerce founded in 1754 and had been elected Fellows of the Royal Society, Sir Francis in 1746 and Franklin in 1756. By 1767 they were certainly on friendly terms; Sir Francis was supplying Franklin with a special variety of oats for testing in America and Franklin was dining with the joint Postmasters-General, Sir Francis and Lord Sandwich, who were, of course, the leading lights in the Hell-Fire Club.

Franklin's first recorded visit to West Wycombe was for two weeks in October 1772 when he was much involved with the revision of the new Prayer Book which he helped Sir Francis to produce. On 6 July 1773 he stayed at West Wycombe on his way to Oxford to attend the installation of Lord North as Chancellor on 8 July (recording of the latter: 'we dined, supped and breakfasted together [at West Wycombe] without exchanging three sentences').

At Oxford he shared rooms in Queen's College with Sir Francis and stayed again on the return journey.

The following month, on 3 August, Franklin wrote from West Wycombe:

I am come hither to spend a few days — I am in this House as much at my Ease as if it was my own; and the Gardens are a Paradise. But a pleasanter thing is the kind Countenance, the facetious and very Intelligent Conversation of mine Host, who having,been for many Years engaged in publick Affairs, seen all parts of Europe, and kept the best Company in the World, is himself the best existing.

He was back again at West Wycombe, whence he wrote on 25 September an account of the famous 'King of Prussia hoax' (described on page 214) which he had perpetrated on the guests at breakfast, and he spent part of August the following year, 1774, there too.

Franklin's visits could easily have coincided with a chapter meeting and it is inconceivable that he would have been kept in the dark about Medmenham Abbey. Furthermore, he, like Sir Francis, had a keen and active appetite for women of all ages — hence his advice to a young man on taking a mistress.

You should prefer old women to young ones. Because they have more knowledge of the world and their minds are better stored with observations, their conversation is more improving and more lastingly agreeable ... Because there is no hazard of children ... Because through more experience they are more prudent and discreet in conducting an intrigue ... Because in every animal that walks upright, the deficiency of the fluids that fill the muscles appear first in the highest part. The face first grows lank and wrinkled; then the neck; then the breasts and arms; the lower parts continuing to the last as plump as ever; so that covering all above with a basket, and regarding only what is below the girdle, it is impossible of two women to know an old one from a young one ... Because the sin is less. The debauching a virgin may be her ruin and make her for life unhappy . . . Because the compunction is less. The having made a young girl miserable may give you frequent bitter reflection; none of which can attend the making an old woman happy . . . and lastly, they are so grateful. This much for my paradox. But still I advise you to marry directly.

Franklin would have been in his element at Medmenham Abbey, with the songs, ribaldry, practical jokes and amorous pursuits. Following his return to America, he wrote from Philadelphia on 3 September 1775: 'We have a little musical club at which catches are sometimes sung and heard with great pleasure, but the performers have only a few old ones. May I take the liberty of requesting your Lordship to send me half a dozen of those you think best among the modern? It would add to the happiness of a set of very honest fellows.'

John Wesley, the great preacher and founder of the Nonconformist Church, was also reported as visiting Medmenham in 1774. Wesley had been a wild and dissolute young man in his Oxford days but later in life, after parting from his wife, he had undergone a spiritual transformation. However, a letter published in the *Morning Post* of 1777 and signed 'Sting' questioned how genuine this was; it contradicted Wesley's statement (in his second Calm Address to the Americans) that 'he attends no great man's table.' This, says Sting, is a 'falsehood'; a few months ago Wesley 'was revelling with some of the religious at Medmenham.'

Wesley certainly seems to have been a friend of Sir Francis's. According to the latter's daughter, Rachel Frances Antonina, her father shared with the younger Wesleys, John and Samuel, a common interest in organ music and Sir Francis, indeed, installed a very fine organ in the church at West Wycombe. The Wesleys' father, Samuel, was the Rector of Epworth not far from Sir Francis's estates in Lincolnshire, and both Samuel and his son Samuel were members of the Spalding Society. Sir Francis had close personal ties with several members of the society, which corresponded regularly with the Society of Antiquaries in London of which Sir Francis was a member.

Wesley could easily have gone as an inquisitive guest to Medmenham but certainly not as a member of it; by that date the activities of the club must have been fairly innocuous, so that he might have concluded with Dr Benjamin Bates, the oldest survivor of the club, that the stories about it were 'scandalous and sarcastic fabrications'.

An Inventory Kitchen Furniture &c. at
Medneham Abby. Taken Oct: 15: 1774 ——

2 Copper Boyling Potts and
one cover ————
1 Fish Kittle Strainer
and Cover ————
2 Frying Pans
3 Copper Sauce Pans
and one cover
1 Copper Tea Kittle
1 Spitt
Fire Shovel & Poker
2 Tin covers for Dishes
1 Tin Dredging Box
6 Pewter Dishes
2 Doz & 8 Pewter Plates
2 Brass Candle Sticks
4 Tin &c with Nozzles
and &c without

2 Doz & 9 Knifes
2 Doz and 5 Forks
1 Pair of Snuffers
1 Coffee Pott
1 Coffee Mill
2 Chinice Candle Sticks
3 Glass Decanters
2 Dozen wine glasses
9 Tumbler Glasses
Some few Tea cupps and
Saucers &c ——
4 Battle Stands
5 washand basons
5 Table Cloaths
1 Doz of Doylies

Part of the 1774 inventory for Medmenham Abbey.

Sir Francis continued to lease the abbey from Francis Duffield until 1778, and the latter sold it with his land in 1779 to John Morton, who had been a good friend to the Duffield family.

In its heyday, the Hell-Fire Club had certainly indulged in mock religious ceremonies at the annual election of the Abbot for the ensuing year and also at the initiation of new members. But the main purpose of the club was, as Wilkes aptly put it, that 'a set of worthy, jolly fellows, happy disciples of Venus and Bacchus, got occasionally together to celebrate woman in wine and to give more zest to the festive meeting, they plucked every luxurious idea from the ancients and enriched their own modern pleasures with the tradition of classic luxury.'

Medmenham Abbey also provided a secret place for meetings between members and ladies who wished to remain anonymous – and have remained so to this day. There is not the slightest evidence that members worshipped the Devil. This is a myth which gained currency during the nineteenth century and has continued to do so.

During the nineteenth century, Medmenham became a popular place for tourists but it slowly decayed until 1895, when it was bought by Robert Hudson, the soap manufacturer, who spent a fortune restoring it. The walls were covered in wooden panelling and the ceiling divided into Gothic-type panels so that no trace of the original frescoes survived.

Today the whole place has a most delightful and romantic appearance. The cloisters and ruined tower and the restored brick and stone house of the Duffields give a charming effect and the panelled rooms provide a cosy, relaxed atmosphere. The gardens are reminiscent of the description by Wilkes, but without the erotic follies: 'Beautiful hanging woods, soft meadows, a crystal stream and a grove of venerable old elms near the house with the retiredness of the mansion itself, made it as sweet a retreat as the most poetic imagination could create.'

3

Expedition to Russia

S OON AFTER the founding of the Dilettanti Society, Sir Francis
set off, in 1733, with George, Lord Forbes, on a visit via
Copenhagen to Kronstadt and St Petersburg (Leningrad).
Forbes was responsible for negotiating the Anglo-Russian Treaty of
1734, Russia's first commercial treaty with a European power.

Sir Francis was probably the first to include a visit to Russia in
the Grand Tour. He kept a fascinating diary which provides the
earliest as well as the most detailed and accurate account in English
of St Petersburg just after Peter the Great's death in 1725, as well as
the only known contemporary account in English of Copenhagen
after the Great Fire of 1728. Many of his observations are as relevant
today as they were in 1733. 'It must be the extreme cold, and a very
hot sun for ten weeks of the year, that must operate to the decay of
all bodys, and is evident in their brick and stone houses, though I
must add, that bad workmanship does likewise greatly contribute –
going pretty much to decay.' The same factors are, no doubt,
responsible for the badly fitting doors and poor plumbing which are
common features of modern apartments in Leningrad and Moscow.

Sir Francis's description of the Summer Palace on Admiralty
Island – 'where the Czarina lives at present, is a long building of
wood, one storey high, there are large apartments, and it looks very
well for the season, it was entirely built from the ground when she
came to Moscow, in six weeks time' – seems to refer to the little
Summer Palace which stands to the east of the Hermitage. But since

this is a two-storey brick building in the Dutch style, it seems that it must have been built in place of the original house which Sir Francis saw in 1733 and cannot, as many guide books suggest, have been occupied by Peter who died in 1725. The only other explanation would be that Sir Francis mistook the Summer Palace for the small wooden house which Peter had built in 1703 on the opposite side of the Neva near the St Peter and Paul fortress; but this seems improbable.

As for the Winter Palace which joins the famous Hermitage Museum, the fine house left by Admiral Apraksin to the Czarina had just been demolished and was being replaced by 'two monstrous great wings – it will be very large when finished, but not a piece of much Architecture.' He was not to know that Rastrelli, who had been brought from Italy at the age of sixteen to join his father, was to transform this vast edifice into a triumph of the Baroque and one of the greatest splendours of this fabulous city so aptly described as 'the Venice of the North'.

On the opposite bank of the Neva, which could only be crossed by one 'good handsom bridge built on boats or in boats run by the Government as were the public houses and production of alcohol', was the fortress of St Peter and Paul with the tall glittering golden spire of the church of St Peter's; inside the church lay the coffins of Peter and Catherine, draped with golden cloth.

Just to the west lay Vassilyevski Island where the colleges for Foreign Affairs, for War and for Commerce were congregated, together with Prince Menshikov's splendid red painted palace which had just been converted into a training academy for four hundred young cadets; they were obliged to stay there from the age of six to twenty-one.

The nobility were likewise obliged to live in St Petersburg whilst the Court was in residence and many of them suffered much hardship, since they were away from their estates and unable to procure enough income, which was often rendered in kind, for their needs.

And no one was allowed to travel abroad without a permit.

Many of the noblemen were sent by Peter to serve as 'ship carpenters and to be quartermasters and gunners' mates'; he himself set the example by serving as a common sailor and soldier and even 'stood centinell in the coldest nights'.

Vassilyevski Island had 'long rows of large houses that look well on the outside but almost all unfurnished and most uninhabited.' It also boasted a 'Rarity Chamber' which had a display of all parts of the human system preserved in spirits, as well as babies at different stages of growth and sections of the female torso which can still be seen in the Gynaecological Institute. Besides these, it had Peter's hat, boots, coat and sword which he had worn at the Battle of Poltava, with the hole made in the hat by a musket ball still clearly visible. And a 'very fine telescope of Sir Isaac Newton' possibly built by Ferguson, the chief of three mathematicians brought out by Peter from England in 1698.

Sir Francis provides very full details of all the different Russian regiments, which amounted to about 200,000 men. These included the Cuirassiers in blue with buff waistcoats and on small horses less than fifteen hands high (smaller than most English hunters), the Dragoons on even smaller horses which were ideal for covering the huge expanses of territory, and the foot-soldiers in green edged with red, and with 'white Cocards in their Hatts'.

He did not think much of their arms which were heavy and cumbersome, but considered them 'as fine looking soldiers as ever I saw' — not much different from the tough-looking and disciplined men of the Guards regiment who take part in the May Day parades.

Peter had converted many of the monasteries and hospitals into quarters for soldiers, just as today these buildings are used for secular purposes such as storing grain or as restaurants.

Sir Francis felt much sympathy for the poor, who were obliged to undergo four fasts of six weeks annually; these 'kill great numbers in a year One would think the Devill might have spared that invention of this Country, where the poor people are So very miserable in the best of times, perhaps there is no Country where the Papas (or Priests) not even in England, gett drunk so frequently as in this Country, and that mostly with Malt Brandy.'

Punishments were equally severe. For murderers,

. . . a Hook that is drove in betwixt their ribbs, bearded, and in that manner they are hung up by a Gibbett, till they dye . . . The Canute (or Torture) is given generally, to make people confess . . . they tie the malefactors hands behind, and then draw him up to a Gibbett, so that his Arms are twisted back, and the Shoulders dislocated, then the hangman comes with a long whip and flogs them upon the back, and takes the Skin off every Stroke . . . after this, least the woulds should fester, they pass a red hot iron in the wounds.

He had heard from Henry Nye, a shipbuilder, 'how he saw a hundred and fifty bleeding heads of the rebellious Strelites, just cut off that lay before the door of a little wooden house, where the Czar was, perhaps, sayes the Czar to him, the world may think me a Tyrant for this, but did I not act in this manner I should be quickly as one of these.'

At the Alexander Nevsky Convent, where Sir Francis attended the funeral of the Duchess of Mecklenburgh, he noted the absence of musical instruments in the church and the cannon firing whilst the procession wound slowly round outside. In the handful of churches which are still allowed to function in Leningrad and Moscow, the powerful unaccompanied singing is still a remarkable and pleasant feature of the Russian Orthodox service and makes up happily for the absence of an organ.

Outside St Petersburg, Sir Francis visited the palace of Peterhof and was much impressed by its charming cascades and the two small Dutch garden houses, Mon Plaisir and Marly, although he was astonished at the poor condition of the many fine pictures.

The road south to Moscow had been surveyed by two of the mathematicians, Ferguson and Gwyn, whom Peter had brought over from England. Unfortunately the surveyed route missed the steeple of St Peter's by 4 versts (about 4000 metres) and one of the surveyors shot himself in the head.

The diary includes a good deal of other information, about pay in the army, the method of taxation, the leading members of the Administration and the relationship of the Royal Family. It shows Sir Francis to have been well informed and discerning, and provides a wide-ranging commentary on contemporary life in Russia.

Sir Francis was 'well contented' with his journey and thought it 'very much worth any curious man's while going to see and to stay for three weeks or a month but after once curiosity is satisfied, I think one would amuse oneself better in more Southern Climates.'

Horace Walpole dismissed this visit with the remark that Sir Francis went to a masquerade ball 'accoutred like Charles XII in hopes of captivating the Czarina'. It seems a most ill-chosen and unlikely fancy dress, since Charles XII had been the arch enemy of Peter the Great and had already been dead for fourteen years. But I can well believe that Sir Francis took immense trouble to appear in a magnificent and eccentric costume and became acquainted with the Czarina Anne. He brought back prints of her and of her coronation in the Cathedral of the Resurrection in the Kremlin and of the fantastic fireworks and illuminations which followed.

Sir Francis's connections with Russia did not end there.

Catherine the Great must have known about and been impressed with West Wycombe, for views of Sir Francis's house and gardens were included in the dinner service made for her by Wedgwood in 1773 and there were, and still are, three of the delightful paintings of West Wycombe by William Hannan hanging in her small boudoir in her palace at Tsarskoye Selo (now called Pushkin).

The architectural style of the gallery which Cameron added to the palace is also highly reminiscent of the Colonnade at West Wycombe, and so is her English garden, with its temples, bridges, grottoes and statues. Catherine had sent her Russian architect, Neyelov, and his son to England to study architecture in the 1760s, so both they and Cameron might have been aware of Sir Francis's work at West Wycombe.

4

The Public Life of Sir Francis

FORTY YEARS IN PARLIAMENT

THE REVELS at Medmenham were an amusing distraction for Sir Francis from his very active political life as a Member of Parliament for twenty years (1741–61) and as a member of the Government for a further twenty years (1761–81), and from his passionate interest in art and architecture, which chiefly found expression in embellishing his house and the landscape at West Wycombe.

As a politician Sir Francis was known as an Independent, which meant that he stood for the interests of the country without regard to party pressure, working towards closer attention to the wishes of the voters and the reduction of the power of the Monarch and Court party.

In 1747 he published *An Address to the Gentlemen, Clergy, and Freeholders of . . . Great Britain*, which sets out his philosophy and 'country party doctrine'. 'Man – has a natural Right to be free. By Freedom is not nor can be meant, that every Individual should act as he lists, and according as he is swayed by his own Passions, Vices or Infirmities: but Freedom is a Right every Man has to do what he will with his own, conformable to Law; is a Right every Man has to be judged impartially by his Equals and to have his Property secured to him as his Posterity' – an illuminating interpretation of the Rabelaisian motto *'Fay ce que voudras'* which he had placed over the entrance to Medmenham Abbey.

The *Address* then lists his political proposals: to reduce the life of Parliament from seven years to an annual or triennial one, to create a militia to replace in peacetime the standing army, and to reduce considerably the number of Army and Navy officers in Parliament. He also wanted parliamentary candidates to enter into a covenant with their electors to abide by their wishes, an undertaking similar to that required today of Labour MPs who are obliged to submit to readoption before each election.

The purpose of reducing the life of Parliament was to ensure that MPs took more note of the wishes of their constituents; the proposal for an annual election would have been hopelessly impractical although it was quite well supported by country members. The span of Parliament was eventually reduced from seven to five years, as it is at present, by the repeal of the Septennial Act in 1911.

The reduction and abolition of placemen, including officers who owed their allegiance to the King, was designed to curb the power of the Court party in Parliament – an issue which was only partially settled by the Great Reform Act of 1832.

Sir Francis, with Pitt's support, had presented a Militia Bill to the House of Commons in 1745, but it was not until 1757 that a similar Militia Act, incorporating most of the principles of this earlier Bill, was passed. The main difference was the size of the militia, which was reduced from the original number of 118,000 officers and men to 32,000. Two years later, in 1759, the Bucks Militia was formed with Sir Francis as its colonel; it consisted of a regiment of ten companies, a total of 560 men, and was the equivalent of today's Territorials.

In that same year, 1757, Sir Francis played a leading role in the House of Commons in trying to save the life of Admiral Byng. Byng had been court-martialled when, believing himself outgunned and outnumbered, he had withdrawn from Britain's base on Minorca. Sir Francis was largely responsible for orchestrating the campaign which culminated in the King's agreement to delay procedures so that members of the Court of Enquiry could confirm that Byng was guilty of misjudgement but not of cowardice. In the face of determined interrogation in the House of Lords, however, they lost their nerve and retracted what they had previously said, and the unfortunate admiral was duly shot on the quarter-deck of his own ship.

In Parliament, Sir Francis was an active member for more than thirty years of the committees dealing with the repair and building of roads and bridges, the establishment of turnpikes throughout the country, improvements to London and Westminster, and draining and navigation. His Poor Relief Bill of 1747 was designed to encourage voluntary public works to relieve the unemployed, and soon afterwards he set an example himself by building a new road between West Wycombe and High Wycombe and rerouting the Oxford road which had previously taken a wide detour up a sunken hollow – not infrequently the scene of armed hold-ups. Only recently two boys with a metal detector found eighteen sixteenth-century gold coins worth £10,000 hidden behind some loose chalk blocks in the side of this old road.

Sir Francis was highly regarded by his fellow-MPs, and as the most prominent of the Independents his support was frequently sought. He advised Frederick Prince of Wales on numerous occasions in 1747 and joined Bubb Dodington in his efforts to form a united opposition. On one such occasion in 1755 Henry Fox wrote to Sir Francis that he understood 'the Admiralty would not be agreeable to you' and offered instead 'an Employment that shall in your own Eye and that of the world be at least as good.' His reason for rejecting these offers was his determination to remain Independent and impervious to party pressure.

In 1761, however, Bute finally persuaded him to become Treasurer of the Chamber. Sir Francis accepted because he believed that the new king, George III, favoured the principles for which he stood, especially concerning the militia. The following year, 1762, Sir Francis was made Chancellor of the Exchequer.

Bute's Government was formed specifically to negotiate peace after seven years of war, a policy which was vehemently opposed by the two most powerful politicians, Pitt and Newcastle. They believed that the run of brilliant successes on land and sea against the French could be repeated and that further crushing victories would seriously disable France and act as a deterrent to future aggression. They tended to ignore the heavy costs which this policy would involve.

Considerable progress was made with the negotiations, and the presentation to the Commons by Sir Francis of the Preliminary Articles of Peace in 1762 was well received, the Government having a majority of 213 to 74. The Peace Treaty of Paris was duly concluded on 10 February the following year.

The budget of 1763, being the first one post-war, had to pay for the aftermath of seven years of war. In order to raise the extra revenue which was required, Sir Francis considered three alternative measures: raising the cider tax, an increase in the stamp duty on insurance policies and bills of lading, and a stamp duty on tickets of admission to public entertainments. He decided to drop the two last, presumably because he felt it was impractical to impose more than one new tax. Two years later, however, in 1765, George Grenville decided to implement the second of these, and in 1770 Lord North proposed the third, but although it was approved by Parliament he abandoned it in the face of opposition.

There were already two taxes on cider – an excise tax of 6s. 8d. a hogshead and malt duty of 4s. Sir Francis proposed an additional tax of 10s. a hogshead on cider sold, to be paid, as were the existing duties, by the retailer.

Following the debate the sum was reduced from 10s. to 4s., but the tax was to be collected from the maker instead of the retailer. This system was preferred by the Revenue since it was simpler, easier to assess and to collect and more difficult to evade. Malt and candles were levied in the same way and there seemed good reason to draw a parallel between makers of beer and makers of cider. At the same time a system of compounding and exemptions was introduced, as with the malt duty, to relieve small private consumers and the poor.

The Bill was passed in both Houses with comfortable majorities and the tax proved to be financially profitable, bringing in £141,293 over the three years 1763–66; so that by drastically reducing expenditure and slightly increasing taxation, the annual deficit was reduced from £49,742 in 1763 to £12,758 in 1765.

Sir Francis's mistake, however, was to introduce a measure which was likely to arouse the sort of political storm which Sir Robert Walpole had bowed to thirty years earlier in 1733. Pitt seized the opportunity to launch a deadly attack on the Administration. He pointed to the danger of admitting excise officers into private houses. The emotive power of excise, which was regarded as an 'engine of tyranny', was so great that the fiscal advantages of the tax were virtually disregarded in the exploitation of the measure for party political purposes, and the issue brought together again the formidable combination of Pitt and Newcastle. The cider counties were in uproar and the support of many Tories as well as Newcastle men was forfeited.

In point of fact, the Bill was a greater triumph for Bute than the Peace Treaty had been, yet he chose this moment to resign. His reasons were quite clear. He had been appointed by George III primarily to bring about a peace treaty and he had the King's 'solemn Promise to be permitted to go out when Peace was once attained'. He also had a considerable distaste for party politics and he felt that by retiring he would be removing the main bone of contention in the Administration and leaving a capable ministry under different leadership. Sir Francis was disappointed at Bute's decision and as surprised as were Bute's opponents and supporters. He himself had much more experience of politics than Bute and was not unduly perturbed by the antics of Pitt and Newcastle.

On Bute's resignation Grenville took over as First Lord of the Treasury, and since he was a commoner he also took the office of Chancellor of the Exchequer from which Sir Francis had resigned. Sir Francis was appointed Keeper of the Great Wardrobe.

The short period of Sir Francis's tenure of office as Chancellor of the Exchequer – ten months only – was packed with important administrative changes. He 'disapproved the practice of perquisites and Gratuitys, a practice so shamefully extorted from the Livery servant up to the Chancellor', and pressed for the abolition of fees which were payable to the Deputy Clerk and the Office Keeper in the office of the Treasurer of the Chamber, to be replaced by fixed salaries. He instigated the process which resulted in 1782 in the abolition by the Treasury of 'fees, gifts, gratuities and payments by individuals' who were thenceforth to be paid by fixed salaries — thereby introducing one of the cardinal doctrines of reform that all public servants should be paid entirely and only by fixed salary.

He also objected to the custom whereby Receivers of Taxes held on to money before paying it into the Exchequer and instituted a series of investigations into twenty-eight Receivers-General, which culminated in the issue of warnings to four that 'if they do not make immediate payment into the Exchequer of the publick money now actually in their hands, they will be superseded without further notice.'

At the same time searching enquiries were made into the operations of the Commissioners of Taxes in order to assess their performance with regard to their own costs and the amount of taxes recovered over the previous fifteen years.

Sir Francis is seen to have been a competent Chancellor of the Exchequer who set in motion reforms which were to have beneficial and far-reaching effects. He believed that political considerations should not be allowed to override administrative ones and that patronage and party should not dominate the political world.

Although Grenville managed the Treasury and the House of Commons competently, the King was not satisfied with him and after making an unsuccessful approach to Pitt, was obliged to fall back on Lord Rockingham. The latter, to the King's annoyance, insisted on removing several of Bute's friends from office, including Sir Francis (by then Lord le Despencer). It fell to Lord Egmont to convey the decision to the latter:

> I never till this day felt repugnance in the Execution of the King's Commands . . . it is improper of me to make any comment of my own upon this unpleasing Occasion farther than to express my personal concern to your Lordship in ye strongest Manner; Nor can I presume to say more in His Majesty's Name, than to assure your Lordship that notwithstanding this Event you may depend on the Continuance of his Regard, as for one whose services he knows to have been faithful and Sincere.

Under Rockingham both the cider tax and the Stamp Act were

amended, the former being increased from 4s. to 6s. and placed on the retailer as Sir Francis had originally intended.

Rockingham was urged by the King and by others to give office to Sir Francis and six others from Bute's administration 'as the most able men in Parliament' to strengthen his position; but failing, or being unwilling, to do so was removed from office. The King then sent for Pitt, once again naming Sir Francis and three others 'he wanted brought into office' - and Pitt 'said he did also'. Pitt had previously gone out of his way to praise his old friend, saying: 'Had I been employed, he is one of the first persons I should have endeavoured to keep.'

In the event, Pitt did nothing until the end of the year when he appointed Sir Francis Joint Postmaster-General. In the fifteen years he had known Sir Francis in the House Pitt had been impressed by his independent standing and consistency. He valued Sir Francis's part in strengthening his ministry, especially in the House of Lords whither Sir Francis had gone as Lord le Despencer.

POSTMASTER-GENERAL

The Post Office sounds rather a dreary enterprise. Still, it had two distinct and important advantages — it collected revenue and it was a potential source of political patronage which enabled politicians to reward supporters through the granting of lucrative jobs. Also of course it performed a major public service in the carriage of mail.

Sir Francis's tenure of office started at an important moment, for the Post Office had just taken over control of all its services which had until then been put out to contractors. For the first time, it directly administered the Inland Post, the Foreign Letter Post, the Penny Post and the Bye and Cross Roads Letter Post; it also had a network of more than four hundred post towns.

In line with his previous attempts to uproot corruption in the

Treasury, Sir Francis pursued a policy of reform which aimed to remove the right of appointment to the position of local deputy postmaster from Members of Parliament. Thus he refused Lord North's request to renew a contract with a useful supporter of the Government for the provision of packet boats and insisted that Franklin's successor as Deputy Postmaster-General of America should reside there. But he was not always successful in resisting demands from MPs over the appointment of local postmasters.

Among other improvements which were introduced during Sir Francis's tenure were a six days' post between England and Ireland in 1767, optional prepayments on letters sent abroad, the reform of the system of collecting letters from London Receiving Houses in 1769, and the establishment of a Penny Post Office in Dublin in 1773. He also took a keen interest in experiments with a new type of mail-cart in order to provide speedier and safer carriage of letters and to replace the system of 'postboy on horseback', and, as a result, the first mail-coaches were introduced in 1784 (three years after his death).

But other comprehensive reforms which the Post Office was very anxious to introduce were thwarted mainly because the Treasury was too heavily occupied with the troubles in America. These reforms were embodied in a Memorial in 1772 and included the delivery of country letters to the persons to whom they were addressed instead of to the nearest post office, the exemption of mails and expresses from the payment of tolls, the regulation of the privilege of franking and of orders for newspapers enjoyed by MPs, the extension of franking to senior officials of the Post Office, the application of the postal laws to Ireland and to America, the simplification of the method of charging letters, and proposals for new postage rates.

The privilege of franking and ordering of newspapers was open to much abuse and loss of revenue to the Post Office, and it was apparent that the only effective way of preventing abuse was to persuade MPs to relinquish that privilege. But political considerations were overwhelming and it continued until 1839.

It is evident that during his fifteen years in office as Postmaster-General, from 1766 to 1781, Sir Francis's aim was to ensure that the appointment of administrators of public offices should no longer be a means of obtaining political support. His views were, therefore, in close alignment with those of Pitt who subsequently introduced so many similar reforms. In the words of Benjamin Franklin, 'he has reorganised the postal services of England and provided something like a national postal service.'

PLAN OF RECONCILIATION

During his term of office as Postmaster-General, Sir Francis embarked on two other noteworthy projects, a Plan of Reconciliation with the American colonies and the revision of the Book of Common Prayer.

In 1769 and 1770, with William Strahan, he made a serious attempt to find the basis for a compromise with the American colonies in order to defuse the inflammatory situation caused by the imposition of new taxes which were not acceptable to the colonists, and which were to lead eventually to the outbreak of war.

Strahan had written to Benjamin Franklin on 22 November 1769 to ascertain the changes in general terms which might satisfy the colonies whilst still preserving the honour of Britain and her supremacy over the Dominions. In particular, Franklin was asked whether the repeal of all the duties except those on tea would fully satisfy the colonists and if not, whether a return to the status quo before the passing of the Stamp Act would suffice. His answer to both questions was in the negative.

He was also asked for suggestions for any other way of 'terminating these difficulties' which would neither be repugnant to His Majesty and ministers nor encourage demands for still further concessions.

Franklin, who greatly admired the British parliamentary system and fervently believed in the future of a great British Commonwealth of Nations, replied at length with reasoned arguments on each specific point; he clearly hoped that with goodwill and moderation on both sides, a settlement would somehow be reached.

The following year Sir Francis approached him with a revised Plan of Reconciliation, to which Franklin replied, on 22 July 1770: 'I heartily wish your Lordship would urge the Plan of Reconciliation between the two Countries, which you did me the honour to mention to me this morning. I am persuaded that so far as the Consent of America is requisite, it must succeed. I am sure I should do everything in my power there to promote it.'

But the plan evidently conceded too much to the colonists and proved unacceptable to the Ministry, so nothing further came of it.

THE REVISION OF THE PRAYER BOOK

Following this abortive but well-meant effort at conciliation, Sir Francis took upon himself the revision of the Book of Common Prayer for the Church of England for which he had completed the first draft by 1772. This may seem rather surprising, given his well-publicized antagonism to Catholicism and all the pseudo-religious antics at Medmenham Abbey. But it would be wrong to conclude that Sir Francis did not believe in Christianity; on the contrary, he declared himself to be a Protestant of the Church of England who 'holds in highest veneration the doctrines of Jesus Christ.' And in reality the Medmenham rites would have been much more stimulating and exciting for a believer than for an atheist or agnostic.

It was a period, too, when widespread dissatisfaction was being expressed over the contents of the Prayer Book and the Thirty-Nine Articles to which all clergymen in the Church of England had to ascribe.

Thus in 1766 Archdeacon Blackburne had pressed for reforms,

especially the removal of the requirement of subscription to the Thirty-Nine Articles, and his Petition for relief from this requirement was presented to the House of Commons in 1772. The Bishop of London also led a group of clergy in urging Archbishop Cornwallis to review the Liturgy and Articles 'in order to amend . . . those parts which all reasonable men agree stand in need of amendment.'

Bills were also presented to Parliament in 1772 and 1773 to extend the degree of toleration to Dissenters. Both passed the Commons with ease but were rejected by the House of Lords. Sir Francis voted with the minority against rejection and clearly believed in the Whig principle enunciated by his friend Lord Talbot that 'no person ought to suffer civil hardship for his religious persuasion.' He even went so far as to accompany Benjamin Franklin to the opening of the first Unitarian Chapel in London in 1774 by Theophilus Lindsey, who observed that Sir Francis understood the financial difficulties facing an independent chapel and 'subscribed handsomely towards indemnifying us for the expense of the chapel.'

Sir Francis submitted the first draft of his Prayer Book to Franklin in 1772 and wrote in the margin: 'Dr Franklyn is desired to add, alter, or diminish as he shall think proper anything herein contained.'

Franklin's role was, in fact, limited to amendment of the Catechism and the Psalms. He reduced the Catechism to two questions, What is your duty to God? What is your duty to your Neighbour? He made selections for reading and for singing from the Psalms, many of which were on the same subject and repeated the same sentiments and imprecated in the most bitter terms 'the vengeance of God on our Adversaries, contrary to the spirit of Christianity which commands us to love our enemies and to pray for those that hate us'. He also collaborated in the Preface, although most of this was the work of Sir Francis.

Sir Francis advocated replacing the one long service, 'which may suit the person who officiates', with three shorter ones at 9 a.m., 11 a.m. and 1 p.m. and limiting the sermons to 'a moderate length'. The First Lesson from the Old Testament was omitted on the grounds that it was 'an accurate and concise history and may more properly be read at home.' (His initial reason was more supercilious. 'It is a Jewish Book very curious, perhaps more fit for the perusal of the learned than suited to the capacitys of the general illiterate part of Mankind.')

The Nicene and Athanasian Creeds were also omitted and only those parts of the Apostles' Creed 'that are most intelligible, and most essential' were retained, so that it was to read: 'I believe in God the Father Almighty, Maker of Heaven and Earth: And in Jesus Christ his Son, our Lord. I believe in the Holy Ghost; the Forgiveness of Sins; and the Life everlasting. Amen.'

Similar cutting took place in the marriage ceremony; in the service for the visitation of the sick, especially 'when the afflicted person is very weak, and in distress'; in the order for the burial of the dead, 'to preserve the health and lives of the living — for numbers standing in the open air with their hats off, often in tempestuous weather . . . may be dangerous to the attendants'; in infant baptism and Confirmation; and in the Commination all cursing of mankind was totally expunged.

As a result the Prayer Book, which was considered by many to be far too long and full of repetitions, was reduced by almost half, the aim being to make it clear, short and intelligible and to remove all remnants of Catholicism; it was based on Sir Francis's definition of Protestantism which stood for liberty of conscience, toleration, reason and common sense.

It was hoped that this would encourage attendance at church by excusing the old and sick from sitting for hours in a cold building, especially in winter, and by attracting 'the younger sort' and business people who lived not far from the church. The intention was 'not to lessen or prevent the Practice of Religion but to honour and promote it.' Not a word had been altered in the remaining text, not even the substitution of 'who' for 'which' in the Lord's Prayer — 'altho' it would be more correct' and has, of course, taken place in the latest revised Prayer Book of 1965.

Inevitably such drastic cutting affected doctrine. In the Common Service, the old Elizabethan formula that was, and is still, in use embodied two ideas, that Christ is present in the consecrated elements and that the Eucharist commemorates His death. The abridgement put sole emphasis on commemoration; 'Take and eat this, in remembrance that Christ died and feed on Him in thy heart with thanksgiving. Drink this, in remembrance that Christ's blood was shed and be thankful.'

The Prayer Book was printed in September 1773 and sold by the publisher Wilkie in St Paul's churchyard. Little interest was aroused, some copies being given away, a few sold and the rest becoming waste paper. Franklin concluded that 'In the Prayers so much was retrench'd that Approbation would hardly be expected.'

But that was only part of the reason. According to W.B. Willcox,

The Prayer Book had proved to be resistant to change even in periods of spiritual turmoil, and in the 1770s the 'fat slumbers of the church', in Gibbon's phrase, were not yet disturbed by the twitching of reform. Even if they had been, the Abridgement did much more than 'retrench'; for the orthodox the process of condensing amounted to evisceration because it struck at the core of doctrine: the Holy Ghost virtually disappeared from the Trinity and the mediating role of Christ was reduced almost to vanishing point. Such innovations could not be expected to impress the faithful. The God of their tradition, a far remove from the simplified deity of the Abridgement, proved to be immune to simplification.

Nevertheless, their revision of the Prayer Book was to play a much more significant role than either Sir Francis or Franklin anticipated.

In 1783, after the end of the war with England, it was necessary for the Episcopalian Church in America to delete from the Book of Common Prayer references to the King, Parliament and other English institutions. There was too a widespread desire to go further than this, to avoid long and useless repetitions, shortening the service for the relief of both clergy and congregations. The Prayer Book which was printed in 1786 by the General Convention of Protestant Episcopal Churches was similar to Dashwood's. The Athanasian and Nicene Creeds were both omitted and the Preface exactly mirrored his sentiments. It was not, however, adopted for fear of schism, and the revised version which was finally used in 1789 was a compromise. The Athanasian Creed was not restored and the Nicene Creed was made optional. In drawing it up, the authors had paid close attention to Dashwood's version and through Granville Sharp had informed themselves fully of its contents.

Dashwood's parting shot was a characteristic one. He could not refrain from suggesting reform of the method of remunerating the inferior clergy and replacing the 'odious and vexatious as well as unjust method of gathering Tithes in kind which creates animosity . . . to the interruption of good harmony and esprit . . . between the Rectors and their parishioners.'

5

The Next Fifty Years

S IR FRANCIS, the 2nd Baronet, died in 1781 leaving no legitimate heir but two natural children, Rachel Frances Antonina, who was eleven, and Francis, eight, both by his mistress, Frances Barry.

His successor to the baronetcy and to the family estates in Buckinghamshire was his half-brother, John, who had added the name King in order to comply with the will of his uncle, Dr John King, Master of the Charterhouse. Dr King and his brother, Colonel Thomas King, both left John handsome legacies which included land in Lincolnshire and Wales.

Frances, or Fanny, was a high-spirited intelligent girl who had become very proficient in Hebrew and went so far as to publish a learned treatise on the language. She deeply resented her illegitimate status, claiming that her father and mother had been legally married and assuming for herself the title of Baroness le Despencer, which had legally passed to Sir Francis's sister, Lady Austen.

Both Fanny and her brother Francis had been well provided for. Francis had inherited the fine Jacobean house and estate at Hall Place in Kent which his father had bought from his sister, Lady Austen, as well as the valuable contents of her father's house in Hanover Square. These were sold by Christie's in 1786, and it is apparent from the catalogue that the house must have been one of the most elegant and sumptuous in London at that time, with its profusion of beautifully inlaid satinwood card tables, marble-topped tables with carved and gilt frames, superb pier and chimney glasses, 'the frames profusely ornamented and finished in rich burnished gold', paintings by Raphael, Veronese, Guido Reni, Carlo Dolci and Marco Ricci, numerous heads 'from the antique modelled at Rome', and life-size statues of two river gods, a lioness, a dancing fawn, a Venus de Medici and the Laocoön. Dealers flocked to the sale, and extremely high prices were fetched.

Francis married Lady Anne Maitland, the daughter of the Earl of Lauderdale, in 1793; shortly afterwards they left for South Africa, taking with them their smart English carriages and exceptionally fine porcelain, for Francis to become Receiver of Revenue and later, from 1809 to 1814, president of the Lombard Bank in Capetown. But the marriage was not a success: Lady Anne with their two sons returned to England in 1819, and Francis came back alone in 1825; he died in Scotland three years later. Hall Place was eventually sold and his descendants moved to Radway in Warwickshire, where they still live. Radway is a small picturesque village overlooking the steep hill down which the Royalist cavalry had charged at the battle of Edgehill – the first major engagement in the Civil War in 1642.

The Westmorland houses and estates, which included the splendid Palladian villa built in 1719 by the fourth Earl of Westmorland at Mereworth Castle in Kent and their family home at Apthorpe in Northamptonshire, passed to Sir Francis's cousin, Sir Thomas Stapleton, and thence to the Earl of Falmouth, whose descendant still has the title of Lord le Despencer.

Sir John Dashwood-King was the son of the first Sir Francis by his third wife, Mary King, daughter of Major Charles King who lived in Ireland. John lived at Halton near Aylesbury, a house which his father had left him, and married in 1761 Sarah Moore, the direct descendant of Ann, only sister of the poet John Milton.

Like his half-brother Sir Francis, John was a member of the Hell-Fire Club and attended the meetings at Medmenham Abbey regularly throughout his life; he was also, from 1753 to 1761, Member of Parliament for Bishop's Castle, a pocket borough which returned two MPs and was controlled by his brother-in-law John Walcot of Bitterley in Shropshire. The other seat was won by Lord Carnarvon, John Walcot's cousin. This proved to be an expensive activity as the burgesses of Bishop's Castle, who had the vote, expected to be entertained lavishly by the candidate and during the 1753 election consumed 1781 gallons of ale and £56 worth of other 'lickquors'. Many leading families who indulged in the game of politics lost a fortune, and it was said of Sir John that 'he might well wish that he had never seen Bishop's Castle.'

Much of John's time was spent on his estates in Wales where he served as High Sheriff of Montgomeryshire in 1777. His house there at Aberirieth was described as 'even more beautiful than that at West Wycombe'. It was set in spectacular country of which he said 'steep hills – rocks – precipices and torrents are the grand features which excite and claim attention.' Cemmaes Hill nearby provided him with grouse shooting whilst the river Dovey teemed with salmon. A few miles to the north-west was Cader Idris, the highest mountain in North Wales except for Snowdon 'which is nine feet higher.'

John also took a keen interest in his estates at Willoughby, Welton and Dunston in Lincolnshire, where he continued the policy of draining and enclosing the land and converting it from useless bog into good farmland.

His impact on the house and estates at West Wycombe was minimal. Everything there was in pristine condition and his interests lay elsewhere; in any case his tenure was short-lived as he died in 1793.

His death marked the end of an era, for his eldest son by Sarah Moore, another Sir John, the 4th Baronet, had few of the qualities or the vices of his fun-loving and cultured half-uncle, Lord le Despencer – not entirely surprising as the blood of the Puritan poet John Milton flowed in his veins. He did, however, have a passionate love of country pursuits which he had acquired on his father's estates in Buckinghamshire and in Wales.

After his marriage in 1789 to Mary Anne, the daughter of Theodore Broadhead of Monk Bretton in Yorkshire, Sir John continued to live at his hunting lodge at Bourton-on-the-Hill which is set amidst the most beautiful rolling Cotswold hills in Gloucestershire.

It was at Bourton that his eldest son, George, was born in 1790 and there also that he set about establishing his pack of harriers which were to become famous for the exceptional sport they provided. Initially, however, he hunted with private packs of fox hounds belonging to his neighbouring friends such as the Leighs of Addlestrop Park, Sir Charles Cockerell at Sezincote and the Hon. George Annesley at Bletchingdon near Oxford, and at Eyford which belonged to Thomas Dolphin. His diary of 1794 also mentions hunting with Ward, presumably the celebrated John Ward, who is known as the 'father of foxhunting' and started the Bicester and Warden Hill hunts.

At that time hunting was undergoing dramatic changes. In earlier times, it had been conducted on foot with bloodhounds which were slow and cumbrous, the aim being to run the exhausted quarry to ground. Hares were the most popular quarry; they were plentiful and more predictable than the elusive fox which was liable to take off for miles in any direction. Sometimes there were so few foxes that they were trapped by keepers elsewhere and sent in a bag to be released in the foxhunting country.

Sir John wrote to his son John:

I have a Fox for you which was caught yesterday morng. It would have been sent by last nights Coach; but the Coachman (on complaint of ye passengers) refused to carry it; therefore I desire you will appoint a day early in the week for a person to meet my man at ye Angel in Oxford; Sind has brought a Badger for Geo. which shall accompany the Fox. My hounds are so very slow they dwell so long upon ye scent that I have no sport and cannot kill – I wish you would get me a Couple of harder running hounds and send as soon as possible.

The countryside, too, was undergoing changes as it became enclosed with hedges and fences which called for horses capable of jumping them. And it was discovered that, instead of taking these obstacles from a walk or gentle trot, jumps could be approached at a canter or even a gallop, which added further excitement to the sport. Men like John Ward and Hugo Meynell in Leicestershire were setting a style of hunting which swept the country and has remained in fashion to this day.

Sir John had similar objectives in mind but concentrated on hunting the hare rather than the fox, possibly because the former was abundant and ensured constant sport. He was greatly assisted by, amongst others, George Annesley (later Viscount Valentia) who had his own pack at Bletchingdon and John Gage at Wytham, also near Oxford, and the Dymokes of Scrivelsby in Lincolnshire. (The Rev. John Dymoke was the hereditary 'champion of England'. The duties of this office involved riding into Westminster Hall at the beginning of the Coronation banquet and three times issuing a challenge to anyone who disputed the title. The Sovereign then drank to the champion from a golden cup which became the latter's property. Other perquisites of the office included an elaborate suit of armour, a well-caparisoned horse and 20 yards of crimson satin.)

George Annesley had to retire to Devonshire because of ill-health and wrote to John at Bourton in about 1794:

I have selected a few of the favourites which I beg your acceptance of so in a couple of years you can form a pack of your own. I know of no person who has as good a right to them. I wish some of my puppies which I loved may be small enough for you – should you like to have old Emperor to breed from – the father of Blemish – he is a most excellent bred hound by the Duke of Grafton's Dancer out of his Garland. He was a famous hound but he is now near deaf and blind – he is at your Service provided you will destroy him after you have made what use you please.

Annesley urged him 'for God's sake inoculate your puppies with vaccine matter – a certain preventation against the distemper', surely one of the earliest instances of inoculation.

Lewis Dymoke and Colonel Dutens were both scouring Lincolnshire for hounds and horses for Sir John and both procured additions for his pack in 1796, so that by the end of the century he had built up a first-class pack of harriers. Amongst those who wrote congratulating him on his hounds was J. Byng; he also thanked him 'for permitting me to wear your uniform – pray give me a pattern or size of your Button BH' (which stood for Bourton Hunt).

Charles Gore wrote from Chapel House in Oxfordshire, which belonged to Henry Dawkins, of a splendid hunt. George Dashwood, Sir John's brother, who was in the Coldstream Guards, had had 'a disagreeable ducking' when he fell in a ditch full of water and Sir John had missed seeing 'one of the completest Hare chases I ever rode to – we found near Great Tew, the whole of it was without a single check or double, we pressed her with a very high scent about seven miles – run from scent to view and killed handsomely.' Evidently hares did not go round in a large circle and return to base as they tend to do nowadays.

Some of Sir John's friends disapproved of this new style of hunting. J. H. Apperley's son wrote in about 1790: 'my father desires me to remind Mr Dashwood he wears the Bourton uniform but disapproves of hunting hares with foxhounds and foxes with greyhounds.'

The hounds were kept at West Wycombe where as many as 70 couples of whelps were sent out daily for walks. At the beginning of October they were despatched to Bourton. About 18 couples were hunted almost every other day and in 1811–12 the bag was 71 brace of hares which included 7½ brace at West Wycombe.

Sir John sent some of his hounds to the Prince of Wales. G. Leigh wrote from Crichel in Dorset in about 1795: 'the couple of Beagles His Royal Highness had from you turn out very well – we have had some very good sport with them since their return to Critchell.' And Sir John wrote in 1799 lamenting 'being unable to come to Crichel – I should be happy to avail myself of your Royal Highness kindness towards me but my pack is now complete as I would wish and my choice of whelps as promising as I could desire.'

He had also made a name for judging horses and helped to select horses for the Prince of Wales and for King George III. The *New Sporting Magazine* went so far as to describe him as 'certainly the best master of Harriers England ever saw and one of the best judges of horses.'

Unfortunately in 1800 his wife, Mary Anne, became rather too friendly with the Prince of Wales; Sir John took great exception to this, making her sign a three-page declaration swearing that she had not committed adultery with him, had not corresponded with him except for two instances which she had admitted and one other about hounds, had not met him except at Mr Walker's and Sir G. Heathcote's or received messages from him via Miss Belle Pigot.

Despite Mary Anne's protestations, Sir John pushed her off to his house at Bourton, whence she wrote on 15 March 1801:

Sunday   Bourton

My Dear Dashwood

The change in your conduct towards me is quite sufficient torment for me to endure without any addition indeed so little comfort do I expect from your letters that since I have been ill I very often keep them by me some time without opening them – your reproaches are very ungenerous I have never acted in any way towards you to deserve such a total change in your conduct towards me and if you will not believe this after all the earnest and repeated assurances you have had from me I repeat I had much rather not live with you as long as you as my protector treat me in such a way at least that makes life supportable.

Had I been fortunate in a Mother I wd long since have flown to her for protection every one has their faults and I have say I have mine but give me leave to ask you if you have ever devoted one hour to my amusement or comfort. I stay at home and take care of your Children indeed I now consider myself in no other light than head Nurse in your family.

Enough of this miserable. I am miserable.

Poor Mary Anne – one cannot help but sympathize with this attractive woman, deserted for months on end by her sports-loving husband.

Meanwhile, his old father, the 3rd Baronet, was enjoying life at West Wycombe. The vicar, Richard Levett, wrote to John on 31 January 1793:

We have had three Balls, Shrimptons, Sir John's and your Humble Servants; attendants between 30 and 40, dinners from 12 to 15 couple, and, would you believe it, I cut a caper amongst them till one o'clock in the morning, when we all retired to Elegant Suppers, sung till between 3 and 4; your sister Lechmere stay'd at the ball at Sir John's till past 12 o'clock when she retired to her room, and in three hours produced a fine boy, named John, both well.

Later that year, however, old Sir John died and it was John's turn to inherit.

The year 1794 must have been a hectic one for John and Mary Anne. Besides taking on West Wycombe, he was becoming involved in politics, having stood unsuccessfully at Wycombe as a candidate for Parliament in 1790.

Until the 1730s the two seats at Wycombe had been controlled by the Duke of Wharton who lived at Winchenden in Buckinghamshire, and had subsequently fallen under the control of Lord Lansdowne whose estate bordered the small town of about two hundred houses on the southern side. Sir John owned the manor of Bassetsbury, to the east of Wycombe, and rented all the rest of the land there from the Dean and Chapter of Windsor. He also owned all the land at West Wycombe to the west of the town. Encouraged by the majority of those burgesses who lived locally, he set out to break Lord Lansdowne's monopoly of the two parliamentary seats which relied mainly on the support of burgesses from outside the town.

In the election of 1794 Sir John was only narrowly defeated by 29 votes to 22, and following a compromise he was returned for Wycombe with Lord Wycombe as his fellow Member in 1796; he went on to represent the constituency until 1831. Also in 1794 he had qualified as a magistrate and proceeded to play a very active role in the County Court at Aylesbury and also at Wycombe. He showed himself to be both compassionate and moderate in the dispensation of justice. In those days punishments were very severe, even for modest crimes, with the penalties for burglary or assault ranging from transportation (for both men and women) to hanging. Sir John sent several petitions to the Lord Chancellor pleading for mitigation of the death penalty and frequently visited the men in the condemned cells. He recorded on 4 March 1828 how he 'saw Saunders first time after his condemnation and prayed with him.' Two days later he was back in the gaol praying with Saunders, who was hanged for burglary on 21 March. Besides drawing up rules for the gaol, he sometimes had to lecture the prisoners, as for instance those 'in the Datchet ward who had been throwing Bone and Coal into the female ward.'

Life at West Wycombe was not proving to be to Sir John's liking, however. To begin with he embarked enthusiastically on the park and gardens and called in Humphry Repton in 1795 to advise on improvements to the landscape. Repton found the gardens, especially the lake, overgrown and obscured by large trees. He also objected to numerous features which he considered ridiculous, such as the spire on top of the tower of a folly which from far off was intended to look like a church and was called St Crispin's after the patron saint of shoemakers (one of whom lived in the folly), and the statue of William Penn which Sir Francis had placed on top of the Sawmill in the park. These were soon removed, as were the statues of Venus and Mercury from Venus's Mount, which perhaps Sir John and Mary Anne considered to be unduly erotic.

Repton made further visits – two days in 1798 are recorded, for which he charged 10 guineas plus travelling expenses of £2 12s. 6d., and again in 1799. He set his proposals out in his customary Red Book but this, sadly, has disappeared. We only know from his introduction to the *Theory of Landscape Gardening* about some of his plans for West Wycombe; these included making a much longer and more impressive driveway sweeping round the lake and approaching the house from the south side with its impressive double colonnade. None of these proposals was implemented, however, and the landscape remained more or less as Sir Francis had planned it in the mid-eighteenth century with the help of Thomas Cook.

For Sir John, West Wycombe had great disadvantages. It required a large staff to maintain. Sir Francis had kept 33 servants from which a skeleton staff of 9 were left to look after West Wycombe; the latter included 'a sailor Weldern who was paid £12 a year, Harry the groom' and Thomas Young for the landscape and woodlands; when Sir Francis took up residence in the summer these were supplemented by his butler, Davis (£20), Edward Hounsum his valet (£18), three footmen as well as a housekeeper and cooks and maids, all from his Hanover Square house. Stewards were left in charge of Mereworth Castle in Kent, Dunston in Lincolnshire and Oak End near Iver. The total cost was £1232 a year, 'besides Liverys and losses by their neglect'.

Sir John could hardly afford such an establishment. Furthermore, the country round West Wycombe, which consisted of the steep Chiltern hills and was heavily wooded, was not much good for his style of hunting; it certainly did not compare with the flat grassland in the Vale of Aylesbury round Halton and the rolling Cotswold hills of Bourton. As John Gage wrote to him in 1809, 'I know you are longing for Bourton – it is a pity you dislike your part of Bucks so much.'

Sir John would have liked to sell West Wycombe and made a serious effort to do so in 1806. At that time he wrote to his eldest son George, who was at Eton:

> The Duke of Somerset has expressed a great desire to purchase the house and estate and the price given him is two hundred and fifty thousand pounds – which sum will enrich us enough to make us quite comfortable as we would wish to be. Your sanction to a part of this business will be necessary. Of course your interest will remain – excepting that the Estates will be to be found in a less disagreeable country than that about West Wycombe with a less expensive house upon them.

Luckily George did not agree with his father.

So West Wycombe was leased periodically, and Sir John spent more and more of his time at Halton. This he set about enlarging and improving with the help of an architect, J. Rhodes, whilst the well-known London firm of Gillows was used for supplying and fixing curtains and japanning chairs. From Halton Sir John would go foxhunting all round the Vale of Aylesbury with packs belonging to John Drake of Shardeloes at Amersham, the Rapers of Amersham, the Duke of Grafton and also with the King's Staghounds.

There was also plenty to do at Halton, which was well stocked with game; during the winter season if Sir John was not hunting he went out shooting almost daily with his younger sons John and Henry or with neighbours whom he invited. The bags were modest, from two to eight brace of pheasant and a few hares and rabbits and the occasional partridge. On one such occasion he accidentally shot John in the head and some weeks later John missed a rabbit which was being chased by his father's dog and shot the dog instead. Sometimes they were joined by the ladies when coursing with greyhounds, netting rabbits or fishing in the canal which had to be periodically cleared of mud. One cannot but be impressed by the enormous amount of physical energy which such men expended in the course of a day when covering long distances on horseback or on foot. No wonder the younger sons of the gentry made such good material for the Army and Navy.

Thus Halton gradually replaced Bourton as the main interest in Sir John's life, whether he was directing the planting of trees and woodlands, the building and repairing of cottages and farm buildings or the construction of a new boathouse, the breeding of his horses or the harvesting of his crops. Now and then he called in at various 'patients' with eye troubles and to them he dispensed a special eye salve.

He also went regularly to Wycombe to meet his chief political supporters such as Joe Shrimpton, Samuel Welles, Robert Wheeler, Thomas Clarke and Samuel Rotton, influential aldermen who were determined to uphold the independence of the borough. Frequently he timed such visits to collect rents from the Corporation of Wye which leased land from him at Bassetsbury, and from his other tenants.

Usually on his way there and back he stopped at West Wycombe to have a look at work on the estates, as for instance repairs to the Colonnade or the enlargement of the kennels at St Crispin's. Thus in 1822 he went to see the erection of a new iron fence along the drive and the removal of Venus's Mount, where the Temple of Venus had previously stood.

In those days, before the coming of the railways, social life in the country revolved round local friends and neighbours, many of whom were in the church or legal profession. Then there were visits which usually lasted a week from his relations, especially Augustus and Brinckley Broadhead, the Hon. Augustus Berkeley and Anthony St Leger (his two sons-in-law), the Lechmeres of Steeple Aston and the Walcots of Bitterley in Shropshire, as well as close friends from the sporting world, such as J. H. Apperley (Nimrod).

Periodically, Sir John set off to call on his hunting friends, Lord Abingdon and John Gage at Wytham, Lord Redesdale at Batsford Park, Sir Charles Cockerell at Sezincote, and Lord Northwich at Northwich Park (Lord Northwich's family, the Rushouts, had bought from the first Sir Francis the house which he had built in Wanstead; two of its Palladian temples still survive but are obscured by development).

Sir John also made regular annual visits in August to his estates in Wales and Lincolnshire. For the former his route took him via Worcester, where he called on Dr Wall at the china works, and Eastnor Castle in Herefordshire, ending up at Hopton Wafers and Bitterley, the Walcot homes in Shropshire; there he saw friends such as Colonel Newport, Mr Rock and Sir Edward Blunt, and called on Sir Tyrwhitt Jones at Stanley Hall, Lord Forester, and the Gresleys at High Park. In Lincolnshire he stayed with friends, including Mr Vyner and the Dymokes, and dealt with the running of his estates.

His love of horses also involved Sir John in racing in a modest way, and from 1811 to 1835 he entered horses at Aylesbury, Cheltenham, Northampton, Epsom and Goodwood. But his horses did not have the success of his hounds. Of five horses which he owned between 1819 and 1838 only The Little Master came in second at Aylesbury in 1819, whilst in 1833 Cinderella came third in the Goodwood Stakes at Goodwood and in October that year won at Epsom.

From 1796 until 1831 Sir John represented Wycombe in Parliament as a Tory. He took his duties seriously, attending regularly when the House of Commons sat – usually from January to March and then continuously in May, June and July. He travelled back and forth from Halton to London by one of the regular coaches, usually Wyatts, but also on the Bicester or the Buckingham coach. The journey took about two hours, not so different from the time it takes today from door to door by public transport. Sometimes he had to sit on the box if the coach was full, and that could be cold and unpleasant.

Sir John was typical of the country MPs who tended to take an independent line, voting on the merits of each issue without having any strong allegiance to a particular party. Basically Sir John was a Tory, a friend of diehards like Lord Chandos, but also of Mr Peel whose major reforms of the penal system between 1822 and 1830 commanded his support. In the disturbances caused by high food prices after Waterloo, his windows in Baker Street were smashed by the mob and in 1831 he was booed, hissed and pelted in Wycombe for his opposition to the Reform Act which was to enlarge the franchise and give more people the right to vote. As a result he decided not to fight the election of 1832 and retired from parliamentary politics just as Disraeli, whom he met for the first time in June that year, was entering the political scene at Wycombe.

In London Sir John did not live in the Hanover Square house which had been let on a long lease but in a house in Baker Street. His life in London was much the same as at Halton, with family and friends dropping in for drinks and dinner, visits to friends for parties, levées, presentations to the King and Queen at St James's, the Prince Regent at Buckingham Palace and dinners at Clarence House. Among the close friends with whom he and his wife Mary Anne met for dinner were Lady de Saumarez, the Duke of St Albans, Lord Chandos, Sir Charles Cockerell, Lady Cosby, Lady Rushout, Sir Francis Burdett and Mrs Coutts at Richmond. At a party given by the Duke of St Albans, the famous Madame Pasta sang. Mary Anne was a close friend of the Duchess of St Albans and went off to stay with the latter at the Hôtel Meurice in Paris.

On other evenings Sir John would play cards or listen to someone playing the piano or singing. Sometimes he took his wife and daughter, Elizabeth St Leger, to the Haymarket and to the Theatre Royal, Covent Garden, where he had a box. The theatre was run by Charles Kemble, brother of the famous actress Sarah Siddons. In 1828 Sir John and Elizabeth saw 'a New Musical Farce called the Invincibles' and two months later 'a Comedy the Inconstant' in which Charles Kemble played one of the leading parts. The theatre was heading for trouble, however, and had to be closed down in 1829, almost ruining Kemble. Rescue came in the form of his daughter Fanny, whose performance at the age of nineteen as Juliet the following year brought the house down, and who went on to one success after another. Lady Dashwood offered Fanny the use of one of her handsome veils which she declined, although 'I am very glad you are coming to see me'.

In fact, the relationship blossomed and Mrs Kemble with her other daughter Adelaide (Totti) stayed at Halton with Sir John several times and was also invited to his Baker Street house, where in 1835 'Lady Dashwood read Fanny Kemble's narration', her memoirs as the wife of a plantation owner in Georgia which enraged the Southerners in America but gained considerable popularity in England.

The declining years of Sir John's life were in marked contrast to what had passed. First of all his second son, Edwin, who had been in the Royal Horse Guards, became seriously ill and in 1835, after an eighth attack of delirium tremens, died in Paris where he had gone to live with his family. On hearing the news his father, who seldom recorded his feelings in his diary, wrote that he 'was ill all this day.'

Worse was to follow. His youngest son, Henry, had gone into the church and had become vicar of West Wycombe in 1832, although he spent most of his time in a house on his father's estate at Halton. Unfortunately he took rather too close an interest in the opposite sex and his behaviour obliged the Bishop of Lincoln to ask for his resignation. Soon afterwards, in 1846, he died, and his father wrote: 'he was naturally of an amiable disposition and was an excellent scholar but his habits were in many respects far from being commendable.'

For Sir John this must have been a bitter blow. He himself took religion very seriously. He read the Bible regularly at home and attended church every Sunday morning and evening either at Halton church, which he had rebuilt in 1805, or at Weston; when in London he went either to the Park Street Chapel, North Audley Street Church or South Audley Street Chapel, always listening attentively and critically to the sermon.

Sir John's beloved daughter, Lizzie St Leger, died in August 1846 and his granddaughter, Amelia Story, the following year. He himself was facing ruin, mainly through buying up land near Halton and West Wycombe and thereby incurring heavy debts. (This was akin to the policy adopted by the Duke of Buckingham who wanted to help deserving tenants, but the idea ruined him and resulted in the great sales at Stowe in 1848.) The principal and interest had to be repaid regularly by instalments, and failure to pay meant expropriation by the bailiffs. And so it was. His daughter Mary, whose husband had filched all her money and had had a baby by one of the village girls, came in 1847 to see him and found the bailiffs ransacking Halton and her stricken father living in an hotel in Berkhampsted. Later he moved to lodgings in Baker Street, but his faithful attendant Agnes Erskine, who had read him the Scriptures and taken such care of him, was no longer with him. His death in 1849 came none too soon.

6

The Progressive Tory

S IR JOHN's eldest son, George, the 5th Baronet, who succeeded in 1849, had rather a cool relationship with his father, partly due perhaps to the way his mother had been treated. They also differed over West Wycombe, which George loved as much as his father disliked it, and about politics, the former being a progressive Whig and Liberal and the latter a Tory of the traditional school, whose power rested on the ownership of land and who was opposed to any move to extend the right to vote.

Shortly after George's marriage to his cousin Elizabeth Broadhead in 1823, they moved into West Wycombe where he involved himself in the traditional country pursuits of hunting, shooting and fishing. The protection of game, especially fish, against poachers was a constant problem. On one such occasion George's keeper, Tregus, suspected that fish from the lake were being netted and, accordingly, set a spring gun with a wire across the water below the Cascade. George heard the sound of a gun going off during the night and learnt next day that the notorious poacher, Ben Burnett, and another man 'are lame both in the knees – they say it happened from cutting themselves with glass bottles.' He had also heard a report that 'that devil Burnett sold a trout to that Doctor I informed against – 16 lbs in weight, the finest fish ever been and from what I hear it was from our water.' The setting of guns and man traps to protect game against poachers was not prohibited by law until 1826 and I still have one of those man traps, which resembles a giant squirrel trap with a powerful spring and teeth to grab the poacher's leg.

George took part in shoots at Halton and West Wycombe but not as regularly as his father had. The bags were modest – a good day at Halton in 1830 produced 8 brace of pheasants, 3½ couples of rabbits and 1 partridge and at West Wycombe 20 brace of pheasants, 7 brace of hares and 3 couples of rabbits which were driven by ferrets. George also shot with friends like Lord Chandos at Stowe.

An attempt at robbing the coach in 1826 was described by George in a letter to his wife and caused much excitement.

> The guard had got down to do something to the coach when two men went up to the coachman and asked for some money. One got up upon the wheel and was threatening a gentleman on the box if he did not give up his money when the coachman drove on. The other was standing near the horses immediately fired a pistol and wounded one of the horses. The men then made no further attempt. Vearys people were called as one lady was dreadfully alarmed. The men were seen today on the road to Oxford.

Later in 1838 George was called out from a magistrates' meeting in Wycombe to deal with a battle on Radnage Common.

> Lord Waterford was there and I understand Lord Vernon. We could get no constables and arrived at the spot alone where 900 or more were collected. Sir W. Young read the Riot Act and might just as well have read his prayers. I happened to know many of the parties and told them how impossible it was we could allow it to proceed. We then got a constable and made him capture one of the men when the whole posse removed. I said we deserved three cheers for our conduct.

In 1831 Sir John had stood down as Tory MP for Wycombe, being firmly opposed to the Reform movement and the extension of the franchise. The following year George offered himself as a candidate for Parliament, tactfully not for his father's seat at

Wycombe but for the County of Bucks; he was an ardent supporter of Reform, describing his policy as 'economy and retrenchment in the public expenditure – the abolition of Slavery and of monopolies – Reform in the Church – the extension of knowledge by education – prompt and cheap justice – and diminution of capital punishments.'

A few years later, in 1837, George reverted to Wycombe and held the seat until his death in 1862. He had the support of the better class of voters in Wycombe and appears to have been a popular and conscientious MP with progressive Liberal views. Thus he supported the Government in their policy of increasing substantially the annual grant to the Maynooth seminary in Ireland. The seminary was the most important Catholic centre for religious education in Ireland and the Government hoped, by showing generosity and magnanimity, to lessen religious tension there. The proposal was violently opposed by extreme Protestants, and in 1845 George had received a requisition signed by 120 names at Wycombe 'requesting me to vote against the measure. The feeling is very great on the subject but still a greater number of respectable persons are in its favour.' He disregarded the request and was able to report 'some of the voters, liberals, who did not support the last election came over last evening with a very pretty present of a book to present to me from the Temperance Society – and stated they approved of the grant.'

George was much involved with Wycombe affairs and with the leading citizens of the town. Both he and his wife Elizabeth were on close terms with the Disraelis who lived two miles away at Bradenham, although one detects a certain coolness between George and the man who was to lead the Tory party and become Prime Minister. 'B. Israeli sat on the bench today evidently for some political object. They granted licences to everyone which formerly they used to object to,' he wrote to Elizabeth, and later, on 24 December 1843: 'Harman was here yesterday and informed me he was going to Bradenham with a Chancery writ against B D-L. He must be in a dreadful mess as to pecuniary matters and it seems she is kept as much in the dark as possible. I suspected there must be some strong motive for the quiet sojourn at Bradenham.'

Above: Sir Francis Dashwood, 2nd Baronet, as a Franciscan monk,
c.1735, and as a Member of Parliament about ten years later.
Below: West Wycombe. The Colonnade front in a painting by Thomas
Daniell, 1781. The Mausoleum can be seen on the hill behind.

Above: Dressed for the Divan Club – Fanny Murray as a Sultan and Sir Francis as 'Il Faquir Dashwood Pasha', c. 1745.
Below: This painting by Bartolomeo Nazari shows Lord Boyne, Lord Middlesex and Sir Francis (seated) celebrating the founding of the Dilettanti Society in a ship's cabin off Genoa, 1732.

Above: Sir George Dashwood, 5th Baronet and MP for Wycombe, and
(right) Sir Robert Dashwood, my grandfather, 1893.
Below: My mother, Helen Lady Dashwood, c. 1932, and my father, Sir
John Dashwood, as Assistant Marshal of the Diplomatic Corps.

*My sister Sarah, Ma, John, me and Pa, photographed at West Wycombe
by Cecil Beaton in 1933.*

A coach 'hold-up' during the 1953 Coronation celebrations at West Wycombe, and (below) an 'Underworld' party held in the Music Temple on the lake: (left to right) Roy Harrod, the Marchioness of Dufferin and Ava, Dick Smallwood and my father.

Digging the bypass tunnel in the Caves, 1954 – Les Lawrence, Jim Powney, me and Les's son. Right: My own building staff, Bob Forbes, Gerry Gillespie and Les Hilton, working on the Mausoleum, 1956.
Below: Miss Mavis McKnight, Ma and me removing the paint from the King's Room ceiling.

The Caves. A copy of Ulysses and the Lion, and the river Styx complete with fibreglass stalactites and stalagmites.

Above: My first wife Victoria with Georgina at Chipps, 1960.
Right: My wife Marcella modelling in the Blue Drawing Room
shortly after we first met.
Edward, Georgina, Marcella, me, Emily, Marco and Caroline.

The Disraelis continued to call at West Wycombe, however, and their financial straits did not affect their relationship with the Dashwoods. The following year, George wrote to his wife: 'the D'Israelis enquired yesterday thro' James when you returned and were anxious to know. I suppose this augurs another dinner.' And Mrs J. W. Disraeli wrote to Elizabeth: 'When I return I hope that . . . I may then have the pleasure of taking you by the hand. You are very kind to express any interest about my future. For some months Bradenham will be my home and I hope never to remove very far from it but it is difficult for James and I to realize all our plans in such a restricted circle.' In the event, Disraeli bought nearby Hughenden Manor in 1849, so Mrs Disraeli's wish was fulfilled, even if Bradenham was a far more elegant house. Hughenden had belonged for years to the Norris family who had been close friends of the Dashwoods, so George knew the house well.

The other principal landowner nearby was Lord Carrington, who had rebuilt a large house on the edge of the town and named it Wycombe Abbey and was consequently nicknamed 'The Abbot'.

Lord Carrington had been a friend of George's father and they had sat together regularly on the bench as magistrates. Both men were Tories of the old school and became very unpopular in Wycombe because of their stance against the Reform Act. George wrote to his wife that Lord Carrington was indulging in heavy bribing of the lower class of voters – similar to the criticism made by Lord Lansdowne against the Dashwoods when they were setting out to acquire political influence in Wycombe fifty years earlier. On another equally vital issue, the Repeal of the Corn Laws, which was carried by Peel in 1846, George and Lord Carrington were also on opposite sides, with George supporting Peel 'although I was not sent to keep Mr P in place.' He also supported free trade and the abolition of tariffs and in 1849 was invited to take the chair at a meeting held in Aylesbury by Richard Cobden, the leading exponent on the subject.

When the House of Commons was sitting, George, who attended regularly and took a keen interest in the debates, stayed in rooms in London which he rented. His wife, Elizabeth, whom he affec- tionately called Bower and to whom he was deeply devoted, spent much of her time in her mother's house at Brighton, as she suffered badly from arthritis and the cold. While in Brighton she went to the baths, and also to various quack doctors which alarmed her husband. George must have been lonely on his own in London, although he attended various dinner parties – with the Duke of St Albans, with John Cam Hobhouse, with Lord Melbourne – and continued to see old family friends, such as the Pigotts and Sir George Warrender and the Staniforths. In 1840 he attended a levée at Buckingham Palace and wrote: 'The Queen does not look so nice as last year. Her chops have become much larger as well as her Bust and it gives her a coarse appearance which she had not. He is exactly like the picture but is very deficient in animation but certainly good looking.'

Throughout his life until his father's death in 1845, George was short of cash. But in 1851 he sold the Halton estate to Nathaniel Rothschild for £54,000; the Rothschilds, on the advice of their Aylesbury solicitor, Mr John James, had wisely decided to concentrate their purchases of land in one area, north Buckinghamshire, and had soon acquired a substantial acreage of land there. Waddesdon was bought in 1847 from the Duke of Marlborough for £280,000 and this was followed by other acquisitions which included Ascot and Halton.

Also in 1851 the mortgagees foreclosed on the Welsh estates and George, possibly sensing the impending fall in land prices and in rents and farm incomes, disposed of the Manor of Bassetsbury and his lease of all the land there as well as his land in Lincolnshire. So for the first time in his life he had plenty of money, and immediately set about modernizing and redecorating West Wycombe. The house had barely changed since Sir Francis's death in 1781, although major repairs had been carried out to the Colonnade front by his father in 1834.

George possibly employed the London firm of Gillows, who had previously carried out work for his father at Halton. He was certainly influenced by the vogue for imitating the French, typified by the Rothschilds at Waddesdon and later also at Halton. The splendid painted ceilings, marble mantelpieces and door frames at West Wycombe were all left, but the walls and curtains of the principal rooms were completely redecorated. The marbled walls of the Hall were painted with a dark glaze varnish and the heads of the Roman emperors with their wall brackets were removed, to be replaced with huge seventeenth-century paintings of ladies in gilded frames. The Dining Room was hung with deep red damask on the walls and with dark red velvet curtains, and a heavily carved mahogany base was made to support the vast black and gold marble slab, which was recorded in the eighteenth-century inventory, together with small matching pier tables between the windows. The breakfast room with the statue of Venus de Medici in a niche was decorated in a dark Prussian blue flock with yellow-gold silk curtains, and two pairs of large mirrors took the place of the pictures with which two of the walls had been hung. The walls of the Music Room were covered with pink wallpaper richly embossed with a black and gold pattern, and ornate golden damask curtains were hung from poles above the windows in place of the mirrors which had covered the whole of the east wall; the room, though much smaller, must have originally been intended to look like the great saloon of mirrors at Versailles.

French furniture which George bought included suites of Louis XVI chairs and settees covered in Beauvais tapestry, vitrines with ormolu mounts, and a very fine Louis XIV Boulle centre table with torchères to match, which I sold in 1985. The effect must have been stunning; clearly the interior decorator who advised had excellent taste.

The heating and plumbing system also had to be altered; the underfloor heating of the hall was replaced with radiators, and two bathrooms and WCs were also introduced.

Sadly, it was his wife Elizabeth who reaped the benefit of these improved circumstances, for George died in 1862. He was buried in the church of St Lawrence on top of the hill, on the north side of the churchyard – a place normally reserved for miscreants – and not in the Mausoleum, possibly as a mark of his disapproval of Sir Francis and his associates.

Elizabeth lived on at West Wycombe for a further thirty years; she seems to have been a delightful person and, like George, took an active interest in the welfare of her parishioners. In 1869 she was approached by Disraeli about giving land for a new church at Downley on the outskirts of Wycombe, but replied that she did not consider it necessary as 'the people there are not so far from the church at West Wycombe as some of the Parishioners are from the Church at Hughenden.' Subsequently, however, she built a small private church, St Paul's, in the village at West Wycombe in 1875 in response to the needs of the villagers who lived at the bottom of the hill and objected to the steep climb to St Lawrence's at the top. The Wesleyan church in the village was not built until 1894 although John Wesley had a strong following in these parts.

Elizabeth continued a close friend of the Disraelis and in 1873 wrote to the Prime Minister:

West Wycombe Park.　　February — 24 — 73.

Dear Mr. Disraeli.

I was glad to hear from you, tho' I wish you could have written in a less desponding tone.

I am much touched by what you tell me, of the feelings entertained by your wife towards myself.

Your friends gave you good advice, when they asked you not to give up your position. I feel sure she would feel the same. She has often talked to me on this subject, and expressed how proud she was, of your brilliant career. I am convinced it would be her wish, you should continue it. This trial will be a bitter one at first, but when you remember her wish, you will be encouraged to pursue — and as time passes on, you will be glad you paid this homage to her Memory.

With regards to my going to town. I shall not be there until after Easter, that is, the last week in April. I shall be glad to see you at any time. I have lost so many friends in the last six months, it seems as if the last page in my own life, were before me.

　　Yrs. sincerely Elizabeth Dashwood

7

Down Under

SIR GEORGE was succeeded by his nephew Sir Edwin, the son of Captain Edwin of the Royal Horse Guards. Teddy, as he was called, and his sister Amelia were brought up in France where their father had died. He was sent to Monsieur Monades' school and evidently was not much impressed by the discipline, for his mother, in 1839, wrote: 'Johnny [Edwin's brother] will be rather shocked that there is no flogging – dry bread and confinements to the house in play hours are the punishments.' She contemplated sending him to the Royal Military College at Woolwich, but it appears that he actually went to a military academy in Germany. In due course, Edwin went out to India to join the 10th Regiment (the Lincolnshire Regiment) in time to take part in the Battle of Sobraon in 1846; this was the decisive engagement in the First Sikh War and has been described as 'one of the hardest encounters of which the annals of warfare in India afford any trace.'

The Sikhs had amassed a powerful army of 35,000 men and 67 heavy guns at Sobraon to cover an important bridge, formed of boats across the river just below the fort of Harrekee. They were confident of defeating the British since as well as being superior in number they were defending fortifications of considerable strength; the British force consisted of about 15,000 men of whom less than a third were Europeans.

Lieutenant-General Sir Hugh Gough, the Commander-in-Chief, aware that victory could prove decisive for the war, had to await the arrival of his heavy guns and ammunition. At last all was ready. The attack was led by the 10th Regiment, in which Edwin was serving as a lieutenant, together with the 53rd Regiment and with the 43rd and 59th Native Infantry Regiments between them, under the command of Brigadier Stacey.

Gough's men fell in at two o'clock in the morning, in silence and under cover not only of darkness but of a dense fog. The battle began at seven o'clock. Albert Lee, in *The History of the 10th Foot*, describes it thus: 'The rising sun rapidly dispelled the fog, when a magnificent picture presented itself. The batteries of artillery were in position, and the plain was covered with troops. Immediately the guns opened a heavy fire. The enemy suddenly realised their danger, then drums beat the alarm, their bugles sounded to arms, and in a few minutes the Sikhs were pouring shot and shell upon our troops'. The British army returned the fire for two hours, 'but all was in vain; the Sikhs stood unappalled.' So Gough ordered the attack to begin. First of all, Lane's Horse Artillery and Fordyce's and Horsford's batteries galloped to within 300 yards of the enemy's guns, thus covering the advance of Stacey's Brigade.

Then the Brigade advanced in line with the regularity of a parade movement, and were the first to reach the entrenchment. But every shot from the enemy's lines told upon the expanse of men, and the greater part of the division was driven back by the deadly fire of muskets and swivels and enfilading artillery. However the Tenth and their comrades were not to be put off and returned to the attack. After this, although the Sikhs gathered to defend the entrenchment, and pounded in a withering fire, the advance never ceased. Men fell at every step but still their comrades went on. The effect was disconcerting to the enemy.

On they went, in a silence unnerving to the Sikhs, until, in the words of Hookum Singh:

with a shout, such as only angry demons could send forth, and which is still ringing in my ears, they made a rush for our guns, led by their Colonel. In ten minutes it was all over; they leapt into the deep ditch or moat in our front, soon filling it, and then swarming up the opposite side on the shoulders of their comrades, dashed for the guns, which were still defended by a strong body of our infantry, who fought bravely. But who could withstand such fierce demons, with those awful bayonets, which they preferred to their guns — for not a shot did they fire the whole time — and then, with a ringing cheer, which was heard for miles, they announced their victory.

Edwin was leading the assault and Colonel Franks afterwards wrote to him:

Lahore
Feb. 28th 1847

My dear Dashwood,

I cannot allow you to depart for England on leave of absence particularly as I am aware that it is your intention on your arrival there to apply for an exchange to a Corps serving at home, without expressing to you in writing my sincere thanks for the gallant manner in which you conducted yourself at Sobraon on the 10th February 1846 — on that occasion the Regimental Color of H.M. 10th Regt. was by you planted the *first of the whole army* in the enemy's entrenchments and most nobly and devotedly defended until the bayonets of our brave comrades bore down all opposition.

I have also much pleasure in bearing testimony to the zealous and gentlemanly manner you have at all times performed your duty while serving under my command.

Pray accept my best wishes for your future success in life and
Believe me,
Very faithfully yours
F.H. Franks
Lt. Colonel Commanding H.M. 10th Regt.

Shortly after the battle Edwin returned home via Egypt to see his grandfather, Sir John, at Halton, who was slowly failing.

Traditionally, younger sons like him went into the services, the legal profession or the Church. Two of his brothers, John and Henry, had chosen the latter and numerous relatives were serving in the Indian Army. During the Indian Mutiny Captain A. J. Dashwood and his nineteen year old brother Ensign Charles Dashwood were cut off and surrounded in the Residency at Lucknow in 1857. Captain Dashwood died of cholera that year, and his brother was sitting sketching in the garden, recovering from an earlier wound, when a round shot exploded by him. Both legs had to be amputated and he died two weeks later, just before the relief column broke through and rescued the gallant defenders.

Edwin, however, had other plans, and after resigning his commission in 1848 he sailed for New Zealand, fired by reports from brother officers about the opportunities which this new country offered for sheep and cattle farming.

South Island, then known as Middle Island, comprised 46 million acres; it was larger than England and Wales combined and had only about two thousand inhabitants. The country was lightly wooded with fertile soil for ploughing, and there were vast areas of pastures, downs, plains and valleys superb for grazing. It also had other advantages: the natives were honest and intelligent and tended to look after rather than steal or injure sheep; there were no wild animals to hunt the sheep and no droughts, and the quality of the grass meant that much less land was required to support a sheep than in Australia. It was estimated that sheep and cattle farming could show a return of 30 per cent or even 100 per cent a year and that farmers could easily undersell the Australians.

Edwin had made up his mind to settle at Nelson, which lies to the north of the island in Tasman Bay. The settlement had only been established for ten years but it was seen as a gateway to the good grazing lands to the south and east; only recently Nathaniel G. Morse had been the first man to drive his sheep eastwards to the lush grazing area round Blenheim on the Wairau River, but no route had been discovered from Nelson to the Port Cooper plains and the port of Canterbury which lay 150 miles to the south-east.

On arrival Edwin immediately joined a party to reconnoitre possible routes from Nelson to Port Cooper. On their return he bought a farm at Motueka and a sheep station about seven miles from Blenheim up the Awatere River. It was here that another settler, Thomas Arnold recorded meeting him that November.

About two miles from the head of the inlet, I distinguished a small black speck which appeared to be moving round it. From the comparatively rapid progress which the thing made, I knew it must be a man on horseback riding very fast. Nearer and nearer it came, the only moving object in that great bare plain; nearer and nearer, till the eye could separate the horse from the man. A black horse, urged at a gallop over the stony path – the rider blue-shirted, crimson capped, with a long blue tassel waving in the wind. The strange figure approached, stopped. 'What, Dashwood.' 'Well, Arnold.' 'What have you got that odd Turkish cap on your head for?' Dashwood smiled, and lifted up his cap; his head was bald as a dervish's. 'Why on earth have you shaved your head?' It appeared – let it wound your delicate ears, my love – that having been obliged to sleep in a Maori ware [hut] for two or three days, he had been made the victim of certain pedicularian intruders, which, to extirpate, he had shaved his head.

Edwin's sheep were being shorn. The only building that he had yet erected was a large barn or shed, in which he and his shepherds slept, had their meals and sheared the sheep. There being no chimney, the fire was on the ground in the middle of the barn. 'His head shepherd cooked us some mutton chops, and made some tea; which, with damper and butter (an unusual luxury in the bush) made an excellent dinner.'

Soon afterwards they were joined by a party consisting of Major R. K. Newcome, Sir William Congreve, Morse and young Andrew Richmond, and after 'another attack had been made on the eatables and drinkables', they all decided to go down to the mouth of the river on Edwin's bullock dray to see Arnold off by boat.

The following year, Edwin decided to make a determined effort to find a route to Port Cooper, as this would enable the farmers at Nelson, who had a surplus of sheep, to drive hordes of them safely south where there was a ready market. At the beginning of April he set off with Captain E. M. Mitchell, who was on leave from the Indian Army, on a short reconnoitre of the terrain and then, on 22 April 1850, they began the major expedition. They were accompanied by an old whaler called Harris and each had a horse and a mule, carrying about 200 pounds, and a dog which caught them wekas (small flightless water birds) to eat. The plan was to follow the right side of the Waihopai River from Blenheim across the Kaikoura mountains to the Port Cooper plains and the port of Lyttelton (now Christchurch).

The journey was beset with difficulties and fraught with danger. Rocks and vegetation made the going extremely difficult and frequently forced them to make wide detours as they could not get through the solid phalanx of spear grass. Where the bush had already been fired by the Maoris the going was good, but there were gaps where they had to wade for miles along the edge of a shelf of rocks from which one of the mules slipped twice, 'spoiling all our biscuit'.

At one stage they encountered a most severe frost; 'never in England have I felt it so intensely cold. The banks and the rocks in the river were masses of immense icicles; and our clothes were frozen hard and stiff two minutes after we had taken them off.' They aptly called the gorge the 'Devil's Grip'.

Then they came out into a valley which they named after HMS *Acheron,* whose commander, Captain J. L. Stokes, was then charting the coastline with great accuracy. This valley is now known as Molesworth; about four or five miles wide, it consisted of 'easy low hills over which you might drive a cart,' so that 'Starvation Hill, the Devil's Grip and our enemies the prickles would be avoided.'

Some miles further on, however, they were forced back to the river route. During the night the horses and mules strayed off, and whilst Mitchell and Harris were retracing their steps six miles to catch them, Edwin discovered another valley to the west which Mitchell promptly named Dashwood Pass.

They crossed the Acheron River and continued south to the Clarence. As they were crossing the Clarence, which was much deeper than they had anticipated, Murray held up his shirt to stop his notebook getting wet and lost his compass – the only one they had, so that thereafter they had to rely on guess work. Having surveyed their position from the top of a nearby hill, they decided to leave the gorge of the Clarence and to follow a small branch of the

Hossack River which led to the Hanmer Plains and the Waiau River. In fording the Waiau's seven streams, Mitchell had a narrow escape from drowning; for he was suddenly swept off his feet and when he surfaced he 'perceived a trusty stick held out to me. Seizing it, I was dragged on shore by the same hand and the same stick that had once before done me the same good service – those of my friend Dashwood.'

Their route through the Waiau gorge was flanked with fern, toi-toi and manuka; the soil was very rich and produced flax of an extraordinary height and size. Captain Mitchell wrote in his diary:

Suddenly we burst upon the finest grazing plain I have ever seen in this or any other country. I know it is the fate of travellers to be accused of exaggeration; but I care not, as long as I call attention to the splendid inland plains. I will therefore attempt a description from the hasty observations I was enabled to take.

The plain surrounded by low undulating grassy hills backed by higher ranges – is bowl shaped, and contains not less than 260,000 acres (I believe much more). Two rivers, the Waihou and Hurunui, run through it parallel to each other, at eight miles distance. The grass is of the best description, and the soil in many places fit for cultivation. It has a perfect natural drainage, is well sheltered from all winds, has no swamps – but also I much fear, no wood.

The remainder of their journey was fraught with hazards, for they were overtaken by a violent snow storm and got caught in swamps 'over which no horse would venture'. After wandering for two days, starved from want of food and cold 'we had not had a fire since we started, not having any timber or matches, we shouldered our blankets and leaving our horses made through the swamp to Kaiapoi.' Eventually they reached the town of Lyttelton.

Captain Mitchell concluded his diary rather modestly:

And now, sir, in conclusion, I have only to add that Mr Dashwood and myself both regret our inability to furnish more satisfactory information of the country adjacent to that through which we travelled, but the loss of our compass in an utterly unexplored, and unknown, country, the shortness of the days, the continual thick weather, which prevented our seeing a mile before us for days, and the storms of snow, sleet, hail and rain, rendered that which may henceforth easily be accomplished in ten days, a difficult and laborious journey of six weeks.

Edwin made one further attempt to improve on the route by taking the left side of the Waihopai instead of the right, but we do not know how far he got.

Edwin must have felt very lonely at times, and he took to drinking heavily. In 1850 Constantine Dillon, who was appointed Civil and Military Secretary to the Governor Sir George Grey in 1848, wrote to his wife about Edwin, whom he found 'intelligent, agreeable and very gentlemanlike in his manners, language and appearance – but he is dreadfully addicted to drinking . . . he said that his father died of delirium tremens and that his uncle is put to bed in a state of drunkenness every night. In fact it is the family failing.' Dillon added that Edwin was living with another man's wife, 'a woman of the town in London before she married the mate of the ship she came out with.' When Dillon stayed with him, 'I spoke to him about his mother and when I mentioned his sister [Amelia, who had married Captain Henry Story, and who had died in 1847; he was related by marriage to Dillon's wife, Fanny] he was quite upset and I thought he would have cried outright. I felt for him very much. No man when sober is more liked.'

In 1852 Edwin successfully applied for pastoral licences over 250,000 acres between the Waiau and the Hurunui rivers, 'the splendid inland plains' noted by Mitchell, but the following year he disposed of this vast tract of land, which was some of the best grazing land in New Zealand and is today worth a fortune, to his agents, Henry Young and E. C. Minchin. He himself retained his house at Nelson, his three small farms at Motueka outside the town and 7000 acres at Bluff Run near Blenheim on the north-east coast, and then set sail for England to procure funds for further investment in New Zealand and perhaps to look for a wife.

He duly returned with his bride, Roberta Henrietta, the

daughter of Sir Robert Abercromby, who proved everything he could have hoped for. He also took back five valuable Merino rams which had been specially bred at Rambouillet by the French Government out of pure Merino sheep and had been selected, together with some rams for the Australian Agricultural Society, by a leading authority, S. B. Edenborough.

Edwin's life continued to prosper. Henrietta produced a son, Edwin, soon after her arrival in 1854. And the sheep were proving so successful that Edwin was able to acquire more land at Aorere near Collingwood further up the coast from Nelson. He enlarged his house at Motueka to thirteen rooms, which Henrietta had papered, and surrounded it with an orchard of three hundred fruit trees, paddocks put down to English grass, and fields of turnips, oats, tares and wheat.

As well as the sheep, Edwin had brought from West Wycombe pheasants and trout sperm frozen in blocks of ice; he released the pheasants at Motueka where they flourished and spread all round the neighbourhood. At the time there were only native bird species in New Zealand, and the early settlers were keen to increase the variety. Ten years later, however only a limited number had been imported. They were listed in 1864 as follows: 8 Partridges, 26 Blackbirds, 5 Thrushes, 17 Starlings, 7 Grey Linnets, 10 Goldfinches, 1 Robin, 5 Greenfinches, 3 Yellow Hammers, 1 Sparrow, 23 Chaffinches, 20 Larks, 2 Redpoles, 6 Australian Sparrows and 7 Black Swans.

Henrietta gave birth to a second son, my grandfather Robert, in 1857, and the same year Edwin had built a 10-ton schooner, *Ocean Sprite*. which he used to sail back and forth from Motueka to Collingwood and which he entered in the annual Nelson Regatta. He came third in the Nelson Challenge Cup in 1858 but, determined to win, he converted her into a cutter and it was reported that 'with a few judicious alterations and well handling, she cannot fail to prove a formidable opponent on a future occasion.'

But he had no chance to put her to the test. Word had reached him that his uncle, Sir George, was ill in England and that as heir to the baronetcy and the estates his immediate return was paramount. So he sold his house in Nelson, his farms and stock at

Motueka, as well as the *Ocean Sprite* and Henrietta's rosewood piano.

In September 1859 Edwin set sail with his wife, the two boys and a servant. In some respects he must have regretted the move. New Zealand offered great opportunities for developing sheep farming and acquiring large quantities of beautiful unspoilt countryside; moreover, he had prospered and had made many friends there.

West Wycombe doubtless gave him plenty of headaches, particularly as Sir George's widow, Lady Elizabeth, lived on for another twenty-seven years (in fact she was to outlive him); and he had to contend with the beginning of the great agricultural depression in the 1870s which was to have such a devastating effect on farming and bankrupt many landed families.

Although the West Wycombe estate of about 7000 acres had been left to Edwin, Lady Elizabeth was entitled to a substantial income, and under the normal provisions of a will at that time, she had also been left Sir George's personal chattels, jewellery, silver, furniture, wine and carriages. The other estates in Buckinghamshire, Lincolnshire and Wales had been sold a few years previously. All the land to the east of Wycombe, which had been rented for 150 years from the Dean and Chapter of Windsor, had been given up and the Manor sold, so that Sir Edwin was short of money and could not afford to send his younger son, my grandfather Robert, to a public school.

On his death in 1882 Edwin, the 7th Baronet, was succeeded by his eldest son, Edwin, who had gone back to New Zealand in 1874. Perhaps because of the slump in the sheep market, he removed to the North Island where he became gum buyer for Sir Edwin Mitchelson in the Kaihu Valley. The gum was 'Kauri gum' from the dead forests. It was used by manufacturers of paint, varnish and linoleum and for a short time offered a most lucrative occupation.

Edwin was a very good cricketer and played for the Wairoa team. He had inherited his father's weaknesses and, like him, was nicknamed 'Lord Dashwood'. However, in 1889 he married Florence, the daughter of Dr Frederick Norton, a highly respected doctor in Dargaville, and shortly afterwards, following the death of Lady Elizabeth, returned to take up his inheritance.

Beset by financial problems and with the agricultural depression in full swing, his first act was to raise £45,000 through a mortgage on the West Wycombe estate. But his tenure was brief and he died suddenly in 1893 at the age of thirty-eight whilst entertaining a party for the Aylesbury Races. My grandfather Robert, who was working in a solicitor's office, was the next to succeed, as 9th Baronet.

The outlook was much less rosy than he might have anticipated. For thirty years nothing had been done by Lady Elizabeth to maintain the house and lake, let alone the tenant cottages and farms. On his succession Lady Elizabeth's executors had just sold all the family silver and jewellery at Christie's – the catalogue occupied 14 pages – and were laying claim to the entire contents of the house; agricultural and cottage rents were plummeting and he had the £45,000 mortgage round his neck. Luckily the furniture and pictures had been left as heirlooms by Sir George, but Sir Robert still had to buy back from the executors all the rest of the contents. He also embarked on a costly legal battle, which he lost, over the large sums of money which Lady Elizabeth had received from the woodlands. He claimed that the trees which had been felled were essentially capital to which she was not entitled. Her lawyers, however, were able to show that the fellings were part of the normal practice of thinning which had prevailed for years in the Chilterns and which was designed to encourage the growth of the remaining stock of trees as well as natural regeneration. The proceeds from these fellings, therefore, represented income and not capital. The case, known as Dashwood v. Magniac, became a cornerstone for forestry law in Britain.

Sir Robert did have one unexpected piece of luck when he was left £30,000 by Mrs Meynell, an old friend, which enabled him to indulge briefly and unsuccessfully in horse racing.

So he cast around for ways of surviving. High Wycombe was beginning to grow through the prosperity of the chairmaking industry. There was a demand for his beech trees as well as for building plots, which he sold off along the main road. He also concluded a 99-year lease of the Hanover Square house and sold off its beautiful ceilings by Borgnis and wonderful marble chimney pieces by Cheere. He also tried to lease West Wycombe, but without luck.

At the same time he decided to tackle the problem of the old servants' wing which was highly inconvenient and expensive to run. His plan, which was eminently sensible, was to inser. dormer windows in the attic bedrooms of the house to make them lighter for the domestic staff; the windows would have been set back above the top Colonnade and therefore hidden from below by its roof. And the kitchen was to have been housed in a small service wing to be built outside the pantry, matching the unobtrusive bathroom wing which he did, in fact, build at the opposite end of the house.

The scheme was left in abeyance when Sir Robert died suddenly, like his brother, in 1908 at the age of fifty-one. Thus West Wycombe came through the Victorian era in a sense unscathed, whereas many other eighteenth-century houses were spoilt by vast additions which altered them beyond recognition. The trustees for my father, who was only twelve at the time, had neither the funds nor the inclination to do anything except try to hang on to the estate until he came of age.

This was a blessing in disguise. Our distant relations, the Dashwoods of Kirtlington near Oxford, had had a colossal estate which had slowly dwindled away until the house and park were finally sold in 1911 to a builder. Soon after the First World War the magnificent dining room was sold for more than Sir George had received for the entire property and was sent to America where it was re-erected as the Dashwood Room in the Metropolitan Museum, New York.

8

Pa and Ma

M Y FATHER, Sir John Lindsay Dashwood, was born in 1896. He was the eldest of eight children, five of whom died very young, leaving my father a brother, Robert, and a sister, Helen, known to us as Aunty Babs.

Pa had been a page at the Coronation of King Edward VII in 1902, the start of a long association with the Royal Family, for he served on the Royal Household as Assistant Marshal of the Diplomatic Corps for thirty-three years from 1933 until his death in 1966.

When war broke out in 1914, he joined the Argyll and Sutherland Highlanders and took part in the appalling campaigns of 1915 and 1916. On one occasion a brother officer, Captain Norman Colville, had been sent out to reconnoitre the German positions. A shot was fired at him so he fired back with his revolver. This tit for tat was repeated, but the German was a machine-gunner getting the range and when he opened up he shot off several of Norman's fingers. Dazed and in great pain, Norman was wandering hopelessly around, so my father went out and carried him back.

The battalion was almost wiped out at the Battle of the Somme, every officer being killed or wounded. My father's escape was due to his having dislocated his knee badly whilst playing rugger (at which he excelled) just before the battle started; an injury which caused him to use a walking stick for the rest of the war. He was then seconded to the Tank Corps and took part in Tank No. 716 in the first major tank attack of 1917. It was not the success which had been hoped for, but the idea was right as the Germans were to demonstrate when their Panzer divisions broke through and crushed the Allied armies in 1940.

My father's brother, Captain Robert Dashwood, known as Robin, was killed on active service in 1918, surrounded by Germans and firing his machine gun to the last. A letter to his mother from Corporal Wilson describes what happened and pays tribute to the Captain, who 'by his bright and cheery manner, kept up all our spirits . . . he was a hero all through, and a true soldier, afraid of nothing, and there was no false courage about him.'

When my father returned home in 1919, he found a dismal scene. Maintenance on the house, village and farms had been minimal for sixty years due to the lack of income caused by the agricultural depression, and more lately because of the shortage of skilled men who had gone off to fight. A survey of the house in 1909 had indicated that heavy costs would be involved in rectifying the situation. There was also the alarming mortgage on the estate.

Pa decided, therefore, to sell the house and the park of 338 acres with all the temples, most of which were dilapidated; he intended to sell the contents later. The auction was fixed for 19 July 1922. But no interested buyers appeared and, as there was only one offer of £10,000, he decided to cancel the auction.

A few months later he met and fell in love with my mother and by the end of the year they were married. Her arrival dramatically altered the situation, for she loved the house and struggled to keep it going; and although my father moved out five times in the course of the next forty years, her will prevailed and he always came back in the end.

My mother was christened Helen Moyra Eaton. She was born in Canada, the daughter of a regular soldier in the Royal Canadian Horse Artillery. Her father, Vernon, came from a farming family which had been flung out of Connecticut in 1779 for their Royalist views. At the age of sixteen he left to sail before the mast on a tea clipper out of Digby Harbour to the East Indies. When he had amassed enough money he put himself through the Royal Military College at Kingston in Ontario, and his two brothers followed him

By direction of Sir JOHN LINDSAY DASHWOOD, Bart.

BUCKS.

Within ten minutes' walk of West Wycombe Station on the G.W. and G.C. Joint
Railways, 2½ miles from High Wycombe Station and 31½ miles by road from London.

Illustrated Particulars, Plan and Conditions of Sale

OF THE

Very Valuable and Attractive

FREEHOLD COUNTY SEAT

KNOWN AS

West Wycombe Park

Dating from the Early XVIIth Century, and containing
Entrance and Central Halls, Magnificent Suite of Reception
Rooms, Sixteen Principal Bed Rooms, Four Bath Rooms,
Ground Floor Offices and ample Servants' Accommodation.

Stabling.   Garages.   Two Lodges and several Cottages.

FINE UNDULATING PARK.

WOODLANDS, LAKE and HOME FARM.

The whole extending to

Over   338   Acres.

For Sale by Auction by Messrs.

GIDDY & GIDDY

At the London Auction Mart, 155, Queen Victoria
Street, E.C.4.

On WEDNESDAY, 19th JULY, 1922,

At 2.30 precisely
(unless previously Sold by Private Treaty).

LAND AGENT ·   Mr. W. R. BUTLER, 15, High Street, High Wycombe.

SOLICITOR   ·   Mr. E. VERNOR MILES, 30, Theobald's Road, Bedford Row,
W.C.1; and 15, High Street, High Wycombe.

AUCTIONEERS' OFFICES:—

11a, REGENT STREET, S.W.1; and Maidenhead and Windsor.

Prospectus for the sale of West Wycombe Park, 1922.

there, so that by the time of the First World War there were three Colonel Eatons serving with their regiments.

He was described as a superb horseman and also excelled at skating, swimming and boxing. As a regular officer he was sent off on various missions, including the expedition under A. P. Low which travelled by dog team to make the first official map of Labrador.

During the Boer War he had taken his battery through some of the bloodiest fighting and ended up on General Baden-Powell's staff. Lord Roberts recommended him for the Military Staff College at Camberley, which he was the first officer from any of the overseas forces to attend. Subsequently he became Director of Military training in Canada from 1905 to 1911. In 1916, after serving at the front, he was recalled to train the Third Canadian Divisional Artillery before taking command of a brigade of artillery. He was mentioned in despatches in January 1917, and along with a great many Canadians he was killed at Vimy Ridge later that year.

Vernon's wife, Myra FitzRandolph, my grandmother, was descended from Alan Rufus, cousin of William the Conqueror and one of the commanders of the army which conquered England in 1066. She and her sister, Aunty Nell, were very proud of their Norman ancestry and took my mother on a special pilgrimage to Normandy in 1931 to unveil a plaque in the castle chapel at Falaise with the names, which included theirs, of the descendants of England's first Norman king.

Mainly because of religious differences, the FitzRandolphs, who were Nonconformists, emigrated from England. Edward, known as 'The Pilgrim', landed in Massachusetts in 1630 and settled at Scituate. Later he moved to Woodbridge in New Jersey where he became known as the 'Quaker financier of Woodbridge'.

The FitzRandolphs prospered and Edward's third son, Nathaniel, was chiefly responsible for establishing the College at Princeton, for he gave the ground on which Nassau Hall was built in 1754 – 55 as well as the original campus. The official seal of the university is patterned after his coat of arms, the huge main gates are known as the FitzRandolph gates, and his bones are buried in one of the quadrangles.

Unfortunately the Revolutionary War was disastrous for loyalists like them and they had to flee, losing their home and lands as well as contact with many of their relations. Their misfortune can be judged from sad letters written by Edward's grandson, Robert, some time after 1783:

Dear Brother James and Edward FitzRandolph, I now feel Very Desirous to know whether my Brothers, Sister Uncles Aunts and Near Relations and friends Remain in this life, as Many of them are far advanced in years and I hope If living are Making an Earnest Request to the Father of Mercys for an Admittance into that of his Glorious Kingdom when time to them Shall be no more, and my Desire is that I with you and you with me may be found Praying to God Almighty that He would be Pleased to give us of this good Spirit whereby we might be kept from all the Allurements and Defilements in this life as there are very many. O Poor Man Although Formed After a Most Noble Being may become the most Miserable of All Creatures . . .

On the back of this letter he had written: 'O The American War What Losses Crosses and Devastations hath it made for me Robert Fitz Randolph.' He then proceeded to itemize his losses, which included three farms, a plantation and numerous possessions 'plundered by the Rebles'.

The FitzRandolphs, or Randolphs as they then called themselves, who stayed in America continued to be highly respected, especially in Virginia and Alabama. Robert's granddaughter Sarah had married John Little, the Governor of Arkansas. My grandmother, Sarah's great-niece, left me a beautiful Chelsea tea service which had been given to Sarah as a wedding present.

Slowly Robert's descendants recovered and by the 1900s they had built up a successful lumber business in New Brunswick as well as owning the main stores in Fredericton. Shortly before the First World War, Granny and Aunty Nell were bought out by their brother and they followed Colonel Eaton when he came to England with the Canadian Army, so that my mother and her sister Evie received their education in both countries.

From an early age my mother had been blessed with remarkable gifts. She was pretty, intelligent, musical and good at games. In 1920 she won the Litton skating cup at Mürren and was one of the first women to have a go on the Cresta run at St Moritz.

Shortly after her marriage to my father, he was posted to the British Embassy in Brussels. He did not have time to attend to West Wycombe so he relied on my mother to make the house habitable, the immediate concern being to ensure the supply of water which had to be pumped from the lake and to redecorate the bedrooms. It was not a satisfactory situation, especially since the estate was being milked in his absence. So in 1927 he resigned from the Foreign Office and went to work for the stockbrokers Rowe and Pitman, just before the Wall Street crash. One of my father's colleagues faced disaster and committed suicide and my father was lucky to escape almost unscathed.

My father had learnt enough to realize that City life was not for him and in 1930 he returned to West Wycombe and set about repairing and modernizing the farms and cottages, which had barely been touched since 1862. He also took a lively interest in the management of the beech woods, working on the principle of taking out the worst trees thus encouraging the better ones to grow on. He had also been appointed Assistant Marshal of the Diplomatic Corps in 1933 and his duties, which involved looking after Ambassadors, took him frequently to Buckingham Palace and gave him enormous pleasure and satisfaction.

My mother threw her energy and considerable talent for organizing into the house and their social life. She had developed into a stunning beauty and was described by one columnist as 'the most beautiful brunette in London'. She was also listed in 1934 among the six best-dressed women, the others being the Hon. Mrs Reginald Fellowes, Mrs Simon Brand, Mrs Julie Thompson, Lady Castlerosse and Mrs Harriet Harriman.

So West Wycombe came to life, and to some extent the eighteenth-century scene was re-created. There were weekend house-parties, especially at Easter and in the summer for racing at Ascot and polo at Windsor, and in winter for shooting. Through the doors poured a galaxy of visitors. Heading the list were Queen

Mary, the Duke and Duchess of York and Princess Marina, Duchess of Kent; there were various foreign grandees, including Prince Otto Bismarck and his glamorous wife, Ann-Marie. Colleagues of my father included Lord Hardinge, successively Private Secretary to George V, Edward VIII and George VI; Gladwyn Jebb (subsequently British Ambassador in Paris and now Lord Gladwyn) and Bill Cavendish-Bentinck, now the Duke of Portland; then there were politicians like Alan Lennox-Boyd (later Secretary of State for the colonies and now Lord Boyd), Randolph Churchill, Sir Henry 'Chips' Channon, Lord Jowitt (Lord Chancellor) and Lord Winterton (later Father of the House of Commons); architects and connoisseurs such as Lord Esher (chairman of the National Trust), Lord Gerald Wellesley (later the Duke of Wellington) who designed a beautiful new church with a large copper dome just outside the park at West Wycombe, Claud Phillimore, the architect who restored No. 10 Downing Street, Sybil Colefax and Kathleen Mann (Lady Queensberry), both of whom had started their own highly successful and influential interior decorating businesses; landowners like my father's kinswoman, Lady Seafield, who reputedly owned 750,000 acres in Scotland, Lord Scarsdale, whose wonderful Adam house at Kedleston has recently been the centre of a great battle to save both it and its contents for the nation, and Lord Jersey, the owner of another great Adam house Osterley Park which has also become the subject of a major planning battle.

The musical world was represented by a string of conductors and composers, including Sydney Beer, Sir William Walton, Sir Malcolm Sargent and by pianists such as Artur Rubinstein and Eddie Sackville-West with whom my mother used to play duets.

Literary guests included Sacheverell Sitwell and Sir Jack Squire, who composed on 17 July 1938 a poem after a confession by one of the members of the house party that he had conceived a great admiration for the Begum Aga Khan – to be sung to the tune of *The Lost Chord*:

> *I've just come away from the Begum*
> *Begum she is fair to see*
> *I've fallen so hard for the Begum*
> *I'm right up a begum tree.*

The sun and the stars cry Begum
The woods all whisper her name
And the bees all hum Begum Begum
And the little birds sing the same.

The dreams that mock my broken nights
Are full of that lovely face
There's an ache in my heart like a begum boil
But oh, what a hopeless case.

I'd work like a slave for my Begum
But what's the begum use
Since I can't lay hold of an Aga Cooker
To cook the Aga's goose

As soon as that tyrant Moslem learns
That I am the Begum's beau
Next day you can bet your begum boots
She'll go where the bad niggers go.

For the Aga Khan as the Aga can
Will carry her over the sea
And she'll live and die with that fat brown man
And what will begum of me?

There was also a sprinkling of Guards officers and I particularly remember one, Peter Nicholson, who had been appallingly wounded in the war and limped painfully on a stick. He put up a good pretence of chasing me and my brother John and for some reason or other we nicknamed him 'Uncle Oojah'. Others were Johnny Drury Lowe and Sir Hugh Smiley of the Scots and Grenadier Guards respectively, and Sir Allan Adair who became a general and commanded the Guards Division during the Second World War.

My father had developed a brief interest in flying and took lessons at Hendon. One of his flying friends, Reggie Leslie, used to take him up from nearby Booker aerodrome and he crash-landed his two-seater plane on the lawn at West Wycombe. Another flying guest was Freddie Miles, inventor of the Miles Magister, a training plane used by many RAF pilots at the beginning of the war.

Sportsmen were represented by cricketers. Errol Holmes, who was captain of Surrey XI and had played for England, took a gigantic swipe at one ball which sailed right out of the ground when playing for Jack Squire's team against the village, but was then clean-bowled by the next ball. Lord Donegall and Lord Ronaldshay both excelled at squash and tennis, and Freddie Cripps, who had taken part in the last full cavalry charge in Mesopotamia in 1916, was a crack shot who helped to run the shoot.

To this heterogeneous crowd were added industrialists such as Sam Courtauld, who founded the Courtauld Institute and was the father-in-law of R. A. Butler, and bankers such as Sir Dougal Malcolm, Fellow of All Souls and chairman of the Chartered Company of South Africa; 'Old Dougie' stayed more than anyone else – over forty weekend parties.

Now and then my father tired of this hectic social life and took off to Canada, where in 1931 he went trekking in the wildest parts of the Far West with Mr and Mrs Sam Courtauld, and to South Africa where he stayed with Sir Ernest Oppenheimer.

He also took up sailing and raced at Bembridge with a distant relation, Jack Fane; they managed to come third in a Solent Sunbeam. He had a small yacht built which he appropriately named *Helen*.

The Second World War came as no surprise to either of them.

They had correctly gauged both the situation in Germany and Hitler's intentions. My mother had warned a Conservative meeting at Wraysbury in 1933 about German rearmament, and her speech was reported in the local newspaper.

The whole manpower of the country was being trained and drilled and every town and village resembled an armed camp. All the unemployed were in uniform and Nuremberg was like an army headquarters – flags flying everywhere, swastikas on all shop windows and even women were marching in detachments. At Cassel, the troops wore helmets, carried gas masks and full equipment. These splendidly trained men were certainly unarmed in accordance with the Peace Treaty but it took little imagination to realize how quickly munitions could be manufactured and every man fully equipped for war. The leaders maintained that this spirit of soldiery was only of peaceful intent but coming as she did from the peace-loving, unmilitary country, the pseudo warlike preparations all over Germany filled her with alarm.

So my father became a flight-lieutenant in the Balloon Squadron of the Auxiliary Air Force which formed part of the defences of London. The idea was to suspend steel cables from balloons to prevent dive-bombing of the city. He brought his unit to West Wycombe where they practised inflating their giant balloons in the field above the house.

My brother John was despatched to Canada with my grandmother and great Aunt Nell (much against my father's wishes), and I went off to Eton.

When the bombing of London started in earnest, hordes of evacuees passed through West Wycombe, so my mother organized free meals on the Colonnade. We children were sent off to pick blackberries for apple and blackberry pie for their lunches.

Ma qualified as an air-raid warden. She also started a working party of locals who made pyjamas and knitted pullovers and socks for the Armed Forces. She herself slept with a loaded shotgun under her bed with the avowed intention of 'taking at least two Germans with me if they come'.

In September that year an advanced guard from the National Trust arrived in the form of two secretaries, Miss Paterson and Miss Ballachey. They converted the Brown Drawing Room and my father's study into offices.

The Wallace Collection also arrived and took over the Blue Drawing Room and the Music Saloon which were used for storing pictures in racks. The curators moved into the damp and derelict old servants' wing.

Ma also took in various friends as paying guests. The first to arrive were Sir Horace and Lady Rumbold; he had been British Ambassador in Hitler's Reich. The were followed by Peggy Forbes-Sempill, a distant relation of my father's, Jim Lees-Milne of the National Trust and Eddie Sackville-West; Nancy Mitford popped in and out, staying for three months in 1941 and overlapping with her cousin Clementine, married to Sir Alfred Beit, owner of Russborough in County Wicklow.

Eddie Sackville-West was a charming, cultivated man. He was a very good pianist and used to play my mother's Bechstein piano in the hall, sometimes in a duet with her, so that the house rang to the sound of classical music. He disappeared for most of the day to his bedroom where I think he was compiling the Record Guide.

Eddie 'enjoyed ill health', as Nancy put it, and kept an array of small elegant snuff boxes on the table in front of his place, from which he carefully extracted pills to swallow at different stages of each meal. He was rather fastidious about the food and liked to prod the dish when Black was handing it round. Once, after a prod at a pudding, he announced, 'Collapsed apple, I presume,' which annoyed my mother as it was intended to be a flat apple flan. He loved getting a rise from her by exclaiming with glee, 'This calls for cream,' to which she replied, 'Don't be so silly – you know there isn't any cream.'

On one occasion Violet Trefusis came to tea. My mother had produced a pot of strawberry jam from her secret store known as Aladdin's Cave, which she had with foresight stocked with delicacies and vital supplies before the war began. Violet took a large spoonful of the precious jam and, after eating a little, left the rest on her plate. 'No,' said Eddie, 'that's not allowed. You must put it back in the pot'; as she didn't move, Eddie himself popped it all back.

He was also responsible for introducing the 'sitting stack'. To save Black collecting all the plates and tramping back and forth to the distant kitchen, Eddie insisted on everyone passing their used plates without getting up to one person to stack and then hand to Black.

The conversation at table was often hilarious, especially when Nancy and Eddie were there. Nancy was a great tease and nearly everyone came in for her butts sooner or later. She used the people she met as characters for her books. Anyone who has read *In Pursuit of Love* will recognize the similarities between Eddie Sackville-West and Davey, and Aunt Sadie and my mother.

In the evenings we all squeezed into the small Tapestry Room and Nancy read aloud extracts from books like Captain Scott's last expedition. This gave her the idea of naming the loo at the top of the house, which was terribly cold, the 'Beardmore' after the great glacier of that name.

My mother and Nancy remained devoted friends. My mother visited her almost daily when she was desperately ill in hospital in London. Eddie's and Nancy's deaths deprived her of two of her greatest friends, and she felt their loss deeply.

By 1941 the nursery had been taken over as a maternity and convalescent home for wives of serving Army officers, under Sister Simond, and the Dining Room had become a sort of restaurant. The centre table was used by the family and friends; tables in one corner were for the National Trust staff and in another for the convalescent mothers.

The following year we were pushed out of the Dining Room, which was needed to house the Witt Collection, and we retreated to the servants' hall.

A company of Gunners had taken over the old wing – much to the delight of our scullery maid, for we found written in large letters in chalk on the kitchen wall, 'Boys. Olive is here.'

By 1942 my father had been called back to the Foreign Office. His appearances at West Wycombe became less and less frequent and rather uncomfortable, as the only sitting room was the Tapestry Room and it was too small to accommodate house parties, so that when Pa returned he was annoyed to find the only armchairs by the fire occupied. Worse still, when he retired to his bed for his Sunday afternoon siesta, my dance band would be practising in the Masonic Room above his bedroom.

As if this were not enough, Ma then went to work in a local factory which made the wings for the Mosquito fighter plane. She used the pseudonym 'Mrs Wood' but made such a fuss about the filthy women's loos that she had to give up her job.

The entry of America into the war in 1942 brought the US 8th Air Force Headquarters to High Wycombe where they took over part of the well-known girls' school, Wycombe Abbey, originally the home of the Marquess of Lincolnshire. So, with RAF Bomber

Command nearby at Naphill, West Wycombe became a regular venue for senior RAF officers such as Sir Arthur 'Bomber' Harris and Sir Charles (later Lord) Portal, several of whom snatched a few hours of peace and quiet fishing in the lake and river, and for their opposite numbers in the 8th Air Force who were more inclined to play tennis or bridge or join in a duck shoot.

9

Getting Started

CHILDHOOD DAYS

I was born at West Wycombe on 7 August 1925 and was christened Francis John Vernon Hereward – Vernon after my gallant Canadian grandfather, and Hereward because a sooth-sayer predicted that I would follow in the steps of Hereward the Wake and be the rallying point for the ultimate defence of England!

My sister Sarah was christened Maud after the Queen of Norway, who was one of her godparents, but my younger brother John escaped any similar encumbrances.

We were brought up in the day and night nurseries until the Masonic Room became our nursery. This large room above the Music Saloon had only two high windows over the East Portico, through which we could just see the tree-tops and sky. Still, although the room was always rather cold and gloomy, we, as children, hardly noticed. Our day consisted of riding for an hour or two with the groom, Dudman, followed by French lessons until lunch time.

Our French governess was a swarthy dark lady called 'Mammo'; she was a tough disciplinarian and we all disliked her cordially. I thought she was particularly hard on my sister Sarah, so one morning, aged six or seven, I armed myself with a tiny toy saw and rushing into the room where Sarah was having her lesson tried to saw off Mammo's head.

We never took to any of our governesses and I don't suppose they liked us much either. One of our standard tricks was to take a boat to play hide and seek on Music Temple Island. We all hid and the governess had to find us. The moment she had disappeared round the Temple, we rushed out of our hiding places and pushed off in the boat, leaving the wretched woman alone on the island.

The nursery food was brought up by the footmen, Stanley and Henry, on large black tin trays. They had to carry it along the top passage from one end of the house to the other, and my brother John and I used to kick a football past them and try to trip them up. They took this in good humour, however, and after lunch they often came to bowl cricket balls at me on the lawn. Stanley also taught me to play the harmonica, or mouth organ as it was called, and it was this rather than our piano lessons which encouraged me later to tackle a variety of wind instruments, the clarinet, saxophone and trumpet.

John and I used to spend a lot of our spare time playing with the electric trains my father had given us. They were set up on a huge table made by the estate carpenter in the Gallery overlooking the squash court in the old servants' wing which was totally empty except for the servants' hall which was then used as the estate office. To reach it we had to walk through a long tunnel known as 'The Tube' to the main hall and then up the stone staircase. At the end of the first-floor passage was the room where an Egyptian mummy had been stored; the room had no windows and the door was often ajar, leaving a gaping black hole. There was something rather sinister about that room, and we used to run as fast as possible across the passage and into the train room, closing the door behind us.

Our chauffeur, Whatmore, was an ex-Rolls-Royce mechanic who used to make beautiful model cottages to go with the Basset-Lowke gauge 0 trains and carriages which came from a marvellous model train shop, Walker and Holtzapfel in Soho.

Both the train room and the room next door were stacked with books from the Library bookcases which my father had removed in order to take weight off the floor which was supported by rotten beams; they were very cold and damp, like the rest of the building.

Although John and Sarah and I rode every day, we never became proficient riders and knew next to nothing about looking after our ponies, as they always appeared groomed and bridled and ready for us to mount. But we had a lot of fun cantering round the place, although Blacky was too old to go fast and Browny had a nasty habit of racing off out of control. Dudman, the groom, who was over six feet tall and had been a heavyweight boxer in the Navy, once mounted this small pony. His feet almost touched the ground and although he pulled with all his might on one rein only, she ran away with him too. The worst incident occurred when with Sarah riding her she tore under the low branch of a tree and Sarah was half knocked out.

Aunt Babs, my father's sister, would have none of this. Whenever she came to stay she immediately took control and started shouting instructions at us, yelling, 'Don't pull on the pony's mouth – just feel it,' or 'Sit up, don't lean back. Stop pulling,' while the wretched animal shot off into the distance. She herself was an excellent horsewoman and hunted regularly with the Warwickshire where she kept a small riding establishment. She regularly won prizes at the Bath and West show for her Exmoor ponies which she bred and trained. Aunt Babs became an ATS Commandant during the war and must have sharpened up the girls' lives no end.

A few years ago my brother John took his wife, Harriet, and their children, Thomas and Rebecca, to stay with Aunty Babs. Noticing an odd colour in the milk, John said, 'I think there's something wrong with the milk.' So Babs took out a spoon and tried it. 'Oh dear, Maisy's still got mastitis.'

On a subsequent visit, Babs said to him, 'Do hope you like the roast lamb – straight off my farm.' 'Yes,' said John tactfully, 'delicious, but it's a bit high.' 'I know, darling. All my meat's been high for the last two years. I wish you'd have a look in the larder after lunch and see if anything's wrong.' When John inspected the larder, he found water dripping down the wall from the cracked loo cistern in the bathroom above.

My mother had a similar experience. She asked Babs if she could avoid using the first-floor loo as the stairs were rather steep. 'Just use the one through the drawing room.' 'I didn't know you had one there.' 'Of course I have – it's the gentlemen's.' Soon afterwards my mother came rushing back. 'There's a toad the size of the *Daily Express* in the loo.' 'I know, my dear. That's Genevieve – she's one of my pets. Been there for fifteen years.'

Last winter Aunty Babs rang me up. 'You haven't heard of my latest catastrophe.' 'No, what?' 'Well you know I always wash my feet in the bath before lunch and it's such a sweat climbing the stairs, I decided to do it in the basin in the gent's loo on the ground floor. Alas, alas, I got my foot stuck in the basin and it came away from the wall, so there I was standing on one leg in the middle of the loo with the other stuck in the basin. Luckily dear Pauline was outside in the yard and came to my rescue.'

At Christmas there was always a large family house-party. An enormous Christmas tree was put in the Music Room and decorated by my mother and the butler, Black. We were not allowed to see it until after tea on Christmas Day, when the candles were all lit and Father Christmas appeared through the Portico windows. This was usually a role adopted by my father who dressed up in the customary red coat and hood with a long white beard. He always enlivened the proceedings with all sorts of antics, tottering like a drunken man or an elderly cripple supported on my mother's arm. My step-grandfather, Captain Alexander Fraser, who had married my grandmother after my grandfather died, had to stand by the tree with a long candle snuffer to make sure the tree did not catch fire.

My mother also arranged children's parties for us and we used to dance 'Ring-a-ring o' Roses', 'Oranges and Lemons' and 'Sir Roger de Coverley' while she played the tunes on the piano.

On one occasion, when the two little Princesses, Elizabeth and Margaret, came, she arranged a circus in the room with miniature ponies trotting round a ring full of sawdust and with clowns and acrobats.

ETON, RABBITS AND JAZZ

When the war started I went off to Eton, my brother John having been despatched together with my grandmother and her sister to Canada.

My first year was not an unqualified success. I had lent a friend, Andrew Arbuthnot, 6*d.* to buy a chocolate bun in the school stores – Rowlands – but finding I had not got another 6*d.*, I tried to recover his bun. In the tussle, I pushed Andrew into a wicker wastepaper basket. The mêlée was observed by a master, 'Bloody Bill' Marsden, who was cycling past, and a day later Andrew and I received a short note from a cricketing swell, J. G. Mackeurtan. 'Please be outside my tutor's library at 5.45 next Tuesday.' So I spent the weekend rubbing rowing cream into my behind in anguished anticipation. On the appointed day Andrew and I were questioned and then each given six strokes. I am not sure which was worse, the waiting or the pain of the punishment.

A short time later I missed, or 'shirked' as it was called, a game of cricket in order to take my mother for a walk to see the Copper Horse in Windsor Great Park. So I was duly summoned by the Captain of the Cricket XI, the Hon. N. T. A. Fiennes (now Lord Saye and Seele) to appear outside POP* room at 5.45 p.m. a few days later. I again got six, but from a longer sixth-form cane.

Actually I thoroughly deserved both canings. I was in a small holding house of about twelve boys waiting for places to become vacant in C. J. Rowlatt's, a very grand and successful house, and as there were no senior boys to administer discipline in the holding house we were becoming unruly and out of control.

*POP or Eton Society was a self-electing group of about twenty-five of the senior and most successful boys. Some were elected automatically when they attained the top positions in the school, the Captains of the School, the Cricket and Football teams and the Rowing Eight; others because of distinction in other fields or simply because they were popular with the other members. They were responsible for maintaining discipline in the school and also had extraordinary privileges which included wearing grey sponge-bag trousers instead of the standard black, coloured waistcoats, stick-up white collars, buttonholes and sealing wax on their top hats.

A few weeks later a friend came round to my room in a panic saying 'I've just been caught by a member of POP throwing stones from the towpath at boats and I'm terrified of being POP tanned' (with a knotted cane used by members of POP). I sympathized with my friend, but when he had gone I transcribed the note which I had previously received from J. G. Mackeurtan on a piece of his own house's notepaper and got a friend to deliver it. The poor boy rushed to his housemaster, 'Bloody Bill' Marsden, saying, 'I don't see why I should be POP tanned. Several others were throwing stones and it is most unfair to single me out.' So I spent another anguished few days rubbing rowing cream ferociously into my behind, but, as luck would have it, Mackeurtan took it as a joke and nothing further happened.

After that I settled down happily and joined enthusiastically in school sports, especially fives, a handball game played in a three-walled court which was apparently originally played between the buttresses of the fifteenth-century chapel. Eventually, when I became keeper of fives, my language tutor Oliver van Oss advanced the theory that as I was so short-sighted I could not see the ball but went by its smell.

Another tutor, Lionel S. Fortescue, who was a terror to the boys, suddenly became passionately interested in rabbits. He managed to persuade all the forty-odd housemasters to contribute enough money to start a school rabbit farm. The idea was to feed the rabbits on the slops from the houses and for the rabbits to produce enough little rabbits to feed all 1100 boys once a week. The cricket practice shed on Agars Plough was taken over to house the 300 or so doe rabbits and the smaller number of bucks. Any boy who failed in his German or French work was given by Fortescue the option of writing out lines, mowing his lawn or working in the rabbitry.

I took an active part in the Eton College rabbit farm, and when not playing cricket, football or some other game, I cleaned out, fed and generally looked after the rabbits. One idea I conceived was to accelerate the mating process by tickling the does and then putting them in with the bucks, but it did not work.

Lionel Fortescue even gave talks on the BBC about the merits of rabbit-keeping as a means of producing more home-grown food. At the end of the Summer Half (term) Fortescue persuaded me to organize a rabbit show at West Wycombe in order to encourage the development of this new industry. So, with the help of William Bowles, the famous head groundsman of the playing fields at Eton, and two or three school friends, the show took place. We had a tent on the cricket field with rows of small pens for showing the rabbits, which turned up in crates from far and wide. In order to identify the rabbits we stuck labels in their ears, but they soon flicked the labels out with their paws and caused quite a muddle when they escaped from their boxes and crates. The show was in aid of the Red Cross and would have made a loss if Bowles and I had not won most of the prizes with our Flemish Giants, Blue and White Beverans and Chinchilla Gigantas and returned the prize money.

After it was all over Bowles asked, 'Could I possibly go shooting? I've never fired a gun in my life and I've always wanted to.' 'Certainly, I'll give you a gun and you can pot anything that moves.' So Bowles trotted off towards the wood above the house. Just before lunch he returned. 'How did it go?'

'Splendid — I've had a marvellous time and I got two cock pheasants.' This rather surprised me as the estate had been poached to death apart from one beat at Cookshall Farm where two old keepers, West and Low, were still patrolling. West had an iron hook in place of a missing arm and when faced by a poacher he would pull back the hammer on his old gun with his right hand and present the fearsome-looking hook with his other. So I asked Bowles where the pheasants were. 'I've left them by the dead oak tree in the field because I wanted you to have a look at them.'

John and I rushed up and found two of my mother's laying hens. 'What on earth happened?' I asked.

'Well, you said shoot anything that moves and I saw all these birds running around; they looked a bit like chicken but, as I have never had a proper look at a pheasant, I thought they must be pheasants. So I fired a shot into the ground. They all flew up in the air and two came down with my second shot.'

'Actually they're my mother's laying hens, but don't worry — we'll run them down to the butcher and get them plucked and we'll pass them off as pheasants. My mother will never know the difference.'

So John dumped them in the basket of his bicycle and left it on the Colonnade as the gong had just gone for lunch. My mother was looking out of the window and suddenly spied two pairs of legs sticking out of the basket.

'What's that?' she asked.

'Oh, nothing, Ma – just a brace of pheasants shot by Bowles.'

'Pheasants – I haven't seen a pheasant for ages. I must have a look at them.' Whereupon she shot out of the servants' hall, which we were then using as our dining room, and found her laying hens on the Colonnade.

No explanation would suffice – she seized Bowles by his sweater and shook the poor man, shouting, 'How dare you shoot my laying hens?'

A few years ago a party of visitors was going round the house, and there was Bowles himself. 'I hope you don't mind – I've brought the Mayor of Slough to see round. I told him it's the finest house in England. You know, I haven't been here since that unfortunate episode with your mother's laying hens. That was a right do.'

'Yes', I said. 'God, what a laugh; I always tell the story when I have to speak to an audience about West Wycombe. It usually brings the house down.'

'Well, I never told you what your father said. "Good show, Bowles, good show – first decent meal I've had for eighteen months. For God's sake go and shoot two more!"'

This wasn't the only shooting incident. My mother used to organize shoots, mainly for the duck on the lake and driven partridges on the Cookshall beat. That winter, 1942, she invited some of the senior officers of the American 8th Air Force stationed nearby at Wycombe Abbey. On the morning of the shoot a convoy of jeeps arrived, and out jumped General Ira C. Eaker, Brigadier Jingles Bubb, Colonel Jimmy Parton and other high-ranking officers. They were armed with an alarming assortment of shotguns and repeaters and looked a pretty lethal bunch. I explained the plan of action.

'You have to creep quietly round the lake and you'll find a stick with a number marking your stand. It's quite misty so you should be able to get into position without disturbing the wild duck. I'll go round this side of the lake with keeper Low and when you hear a whistle get ready and have a go at anything which comes over.'

So off they all went. Then, after a time, Low and I set off to put the duck up. Suddenly there was an outburst of firing – all hell seemed to have broken loose, and duck were flying round and round as they gained height. Then there was complete silence. 'Good God, someone's obviously got shot!' I shouted, and we both rushed round to see what had happened.

In fact, General Eaker had trodden on a wasps' nest and, in trying to get away through a barbed-wire fence, had got caught up in the wire. He was stung thirty-eight times and had to be rushed off to Wycombe hospital. Having been a tough cowboy, however, he personally led the first American bombing raid over Germany the next day. He told me also that a man once came up behind him in Jermyn Street with a knife and tried to stick him up. The ex-cowboy flattened him with a punch.

The rabbit farm was quite a success as I had no wages to pay and grew potatoes on a patch in the garden to augment all the grass and hay which I collected. I had a ready market, selling the meat to my mother at 1s. 8d. a pound and having the skins made into gloves which I sold for 25s. a pair.

Nancy Mitford, who was staying at the time, nicknamed me 'Scrubs' as she thought my dealings in rabbits were shady and prophesied that I would land up eventually in Wormwood Scrubs prison.

When I went back to Eton, Nancy and Clementine Beit volunteered to look after all my rabbits – which they did, although I think Clementine bore the brunt of the work. I had built rabbit hutches in tiers in one of the back sheds and also portable runs which were all over the lawn. Each doe rabbit was named and there was much consternation when everyone discovered we were eating 'Granny' at lunch one day. Nancy called one of the male rabbits 'Buck' after 'Buck' de La Warr (Lord de La Warr) because she thought both were excessively randy.

Back at Eton, I became heavily involved in the Eton dance band. This came about because I had been given a set of drums for Christmas and had taken lessons from Freddie Griffin, a drummer in the local dance band. I used to practise for hours in the Music Saloon to records on the gramophone, later trying to copy the style and breaks of famous drummers like Gene Kruppa. I had also bought for £12 a huge xylophone from the Hon. Gerald Lascelles, who was in my house at Eton, and later went on to buy a variety of instruments, including a trumpet, all of which I taught myself to play but not at all proficiently.

Humphrey Lyttelton, who was to become' world-famous as a trumpet player and leader of his own band, had started the first Eton dance band and occasionally allowed me to play the drums when the regular drummer was not available. When Humphrey left in 1941, I took over the running of the band which consisted of Christopher Hodder-Williams, a brilliant impromptu pianist, Timothy Jones (a Queen's Counsel) on saxaphone, Alex Benckendorf (grandson of the Tsarist Ambassador) on guitar, George Younger on double-bass and either me or 'Black' Pilkington on drums. Our signature tune was 'Whispering', but we also had a very catchy one composed by Hodder-Williams, 'Can't Keep my Mind off You'. The band eventually played at the first dance ever held at Eton in the school hall and also made a few recordings.

During the holidays I started my own band at West Wycombe. We wore green satin shirts with scarlet collars and cuffs made by my mother's working party. The band consisted of Harold Mead the church organist, Jack Why, who played the piano-accordian and was quite happy to continue indefinitely on his own when we were exhausted, Charlie Gerrard, a furniture-maker at Gommes factory, on trumpet, Bill Kingham, a railway worker, on the horn, Steve Stone, leader of the choir, on violin, and Major Arthur Ladenberg, a retired Hussars Officer, on the swanhee whistle. 'The Major' was encouraged by my father to accompany us to dances to 'keep an eye on the boy'.

'Francis and his band' had quite a good run. We played at a dance for Sarah's eighteenth birthday here at West Wycombe in 1941 and at various dances in aid of the Red Cross and other charities. Our greatest achievement was to be invited to play at RAF Bomber Command. During the interval the MC asked if I had any objection to the RAF band playing. This turned out to be Buddy

Featherstonehaugh and his sextet, the crack RAF Dance Band, and it made us look pretty small.

The noise and disturbance caused by my band practices in the Masonic Room were one thing, but the house was also getting rather spooky. On occasions I used to wake up in bed with the distinct feeling that there was a presence in my room. So I would turn on the light and say words to the effect of 'What do you want? Get the hell out of here.' And it seemed to work.

My mother, however, decided to take more dramatic action. She summoned our old vicar, Canon Harold Pickles, who had been appointed to the living at Woodstock by the Duke of Marlborough, to return and exorcise the house. So dear Mr Pickles held a service of exorcism in the Dining Room, witnessed by my mother and our butler, Black, and blessed some water for my mother to sprinkle round the house. She poured the holy water into an old Schiaparelli scent bottle marked 'H.W. [holy water] 1943', and the scullery maid, thinking it was a valuable scent, pinched it. So the ceremony had to be repeated. It seemed to work wonders as the ghosts vanished and have not reappeared.

THE WAR

By 1943 I was eighteen and the time had come for me to leave Eton. I had assumed that I would go straight into the Grenadier Guards and went for an interview at Wellington Barracks. To my dismay, I failed the medical test because of my eyes. So I had a general army medical test with a view to joining the County Regiment, the Oxford and Bucks Light Infantry; and failed again. I was then asked if I was interested in doing work of a highly secret nature, which involved foreign languages (I had won the top French and German prizes at Eton). Soon afterwards I found myself learning Japanese and cryptography on a crash course at Bedford. But I still yearned to be on active military service with all my old friends. One weekend,

Fitzroy Maclean was staying at West Wycombe and I asked if I could join his SAS unit in Yugoslavia, to which he agreed. So I said goodbye to everyone at Bedford and reported to Combined Operations HQ in London. There it was pointed out that I had had access to information of a highly secret nature and could not therefore be taken on. Back I went to Bedford with my tail between my legs.

Some months later, determined at least to be posted overseas, I managed to obtain a posting to Mauritius in the Indian Ocean. Unfortunately at the medical test I fainted when the blood sample was taken and was promptly declared unfit. This made me even more determined to go, and I insisted on another test. On this occasion I was next to a padre in a queue of soldiers so, to relieve the tension, I started chatting him up. 'I see you're in the Church. We've got a ghastly vicar at West Wycombe where I live. Which parish do you come from?' 'Actually, I'm the Archbishop of Canterbury,' was the reply, and it was only then that I noticed his black breeches and gaiters.

My route to Mauritius took me via Khartoum and Cairo. Our Minister Resident in the Middle East, Lord Moyne, had just been assassinated in Cairo but his ADC, Adam Hughes Onslow, to whom I had presented a letter from my father, took me to the palace for the night. It seemed like the Victorian world of General Gordon and the British Empire. The bedrooms were reached from a passage which ran round the inside of a large courtyard, around which sentries in red fezes were positioned at intervals. If one went to the bathroom during the night, they clicked to attention one by one. And at the local cinema, the whole audience stood to attention while the Governor-General's party took their seats.

When I got to Cairo I sent a similar letter from my father to Lord Killearn, our Ambassador to Egypt. I had just settled down for a nap in my room at Shepherd's Hotel when a messenger arrived. Outside was a Rolls-Royce and a motorcycle escort waiting to take me to the British Embassy.

I knew that my father had been in the Middle East several times but only learnt much later that he had been especially detailed to try to catch Cicero, the master spy who had passed to the Germans a good deal of information which had been sent to Sir Hughe Knatchbull-Hugessen, the British Ambassador in Ankara. Cicero was thought to be one of the employees at the Embassy in Ankara: the problem was to decide which one.

After the war, my father told me that one suspect had been 'put in the bag' and brought out but had proved to be innocent. Being convinced that the valet to Sir Hughe was Cicero, my father hatched a plot to catch the master spy. Sir Hughe was to go out to dinner, leaving his red despatch box on his desk whilst my father hid himself beneath the sofa. After an hour or so my father got rather bored, and also realized he had left his revolver in his bedroom. So he decided to lie on top of the sofa and pretend to be asleep. In due course the valet entered the room and after doing his valeting jobs left, so they were none the wiser.

The Killearns treated me regally, and a week later I arrived in tropical Mauritius, dressed in a tweed suit as all my clothes had gone to Calcutta by mistake. In fact a native was later apprehended walking off the harbour quay wearing my Eton Ramblers cricket blazer.

The work in Mauritius was interesting, and became doubly so when my boss fell ill and I was deputed to take over his work of editing the weekly report to London and Washington.

During my spare time I decided to start a Mauritian dance band. There was only one double-bass on the island but I managed to borrow this from the police band in Port Louis. The band consisted of Robert Muir on the piano, Bill Gray, clarinet, and Arthur Wilkinson, double bass, with me on the drums. We played at the Bastille Ball at Government House and were due to broadcast on Radio Mauritius, but on our big night the King's African Rifles were embarked at Port Louis for East Africa and the band folded up.

Soon after this, an appalling cyclone devasted the island. I was sharing a house with three Army Intelligence officers and three girls from the Foreign Office when the cyclone hit. The kitchen roof flew off with a loud bang and the house started shaking violently. Water poured through the ceilings, so we all sat on tables in the dining room wearing tin hats whilst I played my trumpet with anything from 'In the Mood' to hymns like 'Eternal Father, Strong to Save' and Purcell's 'Trumpet Voluntary'.

In the morning it was clear that the house would have to be evacuated, but as my ground-floor bedroom was virtually undamaged and there was no rent to pay, I stayed on with a Belgian officer, Captain Pierre Humblet.

Then a major epidemic of poliomyelitis broke out in the island, and I was one of the first casualties. This turned out to be a blessing in disguise, as I had had an interview with the K.A.R. a few days earlier and if I had been enrolled, would have been sent off to the Far East to mop up. Paralysed from the waist down, I was taken off to the local hospital. A week later, however, I woke up to find the paralysis gone. I had also had my appendix removed during that time, but I felt a terrific urge to get out of bed so I struggled into a basket chair in the sick room. This marked the beginning of my recovery. I sent for my trumpet and played it every day in bed. Boxes of sweets used to appear from other patients; I never knew whether it was to encourage me to continue to play, or to stop.

Weeks later, when I was again walking, I suddenly remembered the double-bass which had been left in the Army hut. All the strings had been eaten through by rats and the wooden casing gnawed. So I hired a Chinese boy to carry the double-bass and together we took the train to Port Louis. There we wandered round vainly looking for double-bass strings; but our luck was in for we found a small music shop which had the first consignment of strings since the war started, so I was able to return the instrument in reasonable working order to Police HQ.

Then a friend, Bob Shilling, who worked in the port and with whom I had played a lot of tennis, rang to say there was a job going as utility man on an American tanker. If I could make it in two hours, I could work my passage back to Lourenço Marques in Portuguese East Africa.

I packed and said goodbye in great haste and just caught the SS *Stevenson Taylor* as she was moving slowly out of Port Louis.

My introduction was not auspicious. The crew was from the slums of Chicago and very anti-British. The third cook, known as Heavy, said 'Have some mashed potatoes' and when I replied yes, he rammed the dish down on my head. A tanker has a very slow, gentle roll and I was soon violently sick. 'Heavy' advised me to eat some poached eggs covered with marmalade, and to my amazement this did the trick. He was surprised too and impressed as I had struggled on with my work, which was to clean out the officers' heads (lavatories) and make their bunks, so we soon became buddies – a great piece of luck as he was a heavyweight boxer, and before long we more or less had control of the situation below decks.

From Lourenço Marques I made my way to Johannesburg, where I had a terrifying experience. I was waiting in the Grand Hotel when a huge Australian soldier asked me to join him for a can of beer. No sooner had I sat down than he said, 'You're another god-damned bloody Yank. I hate all your bloody guts and I'm going to smash you to bits when you've had your beer.' He kept on clenching and unclenching his fists and I felt most apprehensive. I assured him that I was an Englishman but he refused to believe me, especially as I was wearing a blue American merchant navy jacket and jeans. So I said, 'Do you mind if I go to the loo?' 'No, but I'll be right behind you and if you try and run, I'll smash your bloody head in the pan.' Off we went, and when he was fully occupied I shot out of the door and ran as fast as I could out of the hotel.

My next boat from Capetown to London was full of RAF wives and babies. I had stocked up with crates of sweets for my family, bottles of brandy for my father, a dozen pairs of nylons for Sarah and twenty wrist watches to sell in London. When we got to Tilbury I arranged for an attractive blonde, Stella, to take the nylons through the customs and meet me at the Strand Palace Hotel in London. I had three bottles of brandy, one in each pocket of my camel hair overcoat, and the watches strapped round my arms. The customs man took one look at the crate of oranges and bananas which I had also bought in the Canary Islands and said, 'Give me half a dozen bananas for Christmas and I won't bother to search you.' What a relief. It was like the return of the Prodigal Son, and I dished the sweets round my family and the staff and sold the watches to Rossi, the head-waiter at the 400 Night Club. I went to meet Stella as arranged at the Strand Palace, but she failed to turn up and eventually sent me an envelope containing one pair of tattered nylons.

HOME AGAIN

When I got back, West Wycombe was more or less empty and felt like a deserted tomb.

The Wallace and Witt Collections and their guardians had gone, as had the National Trust staff, the maternity home, the paying guests and the soldiers in the old servants' wing. Only our semi-retired butler, Black, remained, and a daily cook, Mrs Green.

I went straight up to Christ Church, Oxford, as I did not require entrance qualifications having been eligible for the Gladstone Memorial Scholarship at Eton. I decided to read PPE (Politics, Philosophy and Economics), as Britain was clearly in a terrible mess and I felt duty-bound to go into politics and try to sort things out.

I still had my trumpet, and when King George VI came to dine at Christ Church to celebrate the college's fourth centenary, Sir Thomas Armstrong, the college Master of Music, asked me to play a solitary fanfare before all the six hundred students rose to sing 'Here's a health unto his Majesty', as I was the only trumpet player available. The rehearsals were not a success; my trumpet had been stuffed with port and mustard and I kept on hitting the wrong note, but on the night everything went like a dream.

When Queen Elizabeth II came later to visit the university the Dean decided that Christ Church would, unlike the other colleges, mark the occasion in dignified silence. This did not seem right, so I climbed on to the roof of Peckwater Quad and played 'Colonel Bogey'.

From Oxford the next step was somehow to get to America, as before entering politics I wanted to find out why American industries were so much more efficient than ours. So I decided to try for a Henry Fellowship. Two were awarded each year from Oxford and Cambridge and there were hundreds of applicants. When it came to the final choice, the selectors had a difficult job as short-listed candidates had all got blues at major sports, such as cricket or rugby, as well as firsts, whereas I only had a half-blue at Eton fives and a second-class degree. When the professors asked me about my other interests, however, they were so amused by my account of the rabbit farm that they awarded me this valuable Fellowship – $5000 for one year in America.

In the meantime, the situation at West Wycombe was deteriorating steadily.

Staff were continually coming and going, and when we heard suitcases bumping down the back staircase my father used to say 'That must be the new cook going – let's open another bottle of port.'

It got to the point when both my father and mother tried their hands at cooking. My father had kept a pig, as country householders were encouraged to do, and decided that the time had come to eat it. So he read up some cooking instructions in a French book which stated that every bit of a pig, from its snout to its trotters, could be eaten. So the pig was duly killed, and my father put on a white chef's coat and set about dealing with it. One lunch we had to eat part of the pig's stomach; the smell in the dining room was indescribable, but still my father insisted on working through the animal. Then he got hold of a recipe for hare pâté and spent hours making it. 'What do you think of the pâté de lièvre – I made it myself?' Actually it wasn't too bad.

My mother had some Cordon Bleu cookery lessons and produced one or two excellent dishes. She also got very keen on making marmalade. The trouble was the mess left in the kitchen, which we usually had to clear up. So we tried to deter her from this new activity by marking the marmalade pots 'Mrs Merryfield's No. 1' or 'Mrs Merryfield's No. 2'. Mrs Merryfield had been convicted of murdering her husband by putting arsenic in his marmalade, and this device was intended to discourage guests from eating the marmalade and hence to stop the cooking.

Eventually, I managed to find a cook and a maid through Bill Ofner who ran the Polish Brigade Dance Band, stationed near High Wycombe. Madame Krenikov was the widow of a Russian colonel and her attractive daughter, Nina, was an aspiring ballet dancer. To everyone's relief they arrived just before Christmas, but Madame Krenikov promptly fell down the back stairs and broke her leg. Moreover, they didn't speak much English and I was deputed by my mother to explain in faltering Russian to Nina that she was not to wear expensive scents when making the beds.

Some time after this, my father decided to move out of West Wycombe and into Chipps, which was about one and a half miles away on the estate. Chipps had been let to Lord Gerald Wellesley and Christopher Hussey in the 1930s and they had saved this semi-derelict delightful Queen Anne house from destruction. So the heating at West Wycombe was turned off and Madame Krenikov and Nina left to look after my father.

Apart from spending odd nights with him at Chipps, my mother stayed most of the time in her flat in London, and John and I picnicked during the holidays at West Wycombe. We often had lunch in the Apple Orchard tea rooms – known as the Love Nest because it was rented by Miss Donald (nicknamed 'the Duck') who was living there with Major Ladenberg, an antique dealer – in the village or in a pub, and occasionally joined my father at Chipps for dinner. Even that wasn't up to much as Madame Krenikov was a hopeless cook but a pleasant and presentable lady.

On one occasion my father asked me to organize a special menu for the writer Rebecca West and her husband, Henry Andrews. So, armed with my Russian dictionary, I explained what my father wanted. But it didn't work out as expected. Instead of borsch, the Russian cabbage and beetroot soup, the first course was a sort of beef bouillon; then instead of beef, the main course was pirozki, minced meat in a pastry with shredded raw cabbage; and the pudding, which was intended to be cream cheese, was a paste of solid whipped cream mixed with walnuts.

I also had to translate for Madame Krenikov all the household instructions, particularly the operation of the anthracite boiler; this meant demonstrating how to pull the damper out and push it in, which put my father into fits of laughter as the motions looked rather improper.

My father still attended at Buckingham Palace two or three days a week. On each occasion a taxi took him from Chipps to West Wycombe where Black helped to dress him in his full court uniform. Then the taxi took him to the palace. At the end of the day, the procedure was reversed and he landed back at Chipps. Despite all this he really enjoyed his duties as Assistant Marshal of the

Diplomatic Corps, and he looked resplendent in his full dress uniform.

On one occasion, when he had to go to Paris for the reopening of the British Embassy, a very grand French Duchess quizzed him with her lorgnette and remarked to his delight, '*Ah, comme il est charmant – tout à fait du dix-huitième siècle*' (How charming – right out of the eighteenth century). When he told us this story, we maliciously observed that she was a hundred years wrong, as he belonged to the Edwardian period.

To make life more convenient, my father bought an old 1933 Wolseley car; the glass in the windows had yellowed, the mudguards were painted white so that people could see him coming, and the exhaust fumes came up through the floorboards. It was known as the 'gas machine' or the 'political asset', as we felt no one would be envious of a family with such a car.

When it finally fell to bits he bought an enormous black Buick, but it seldom left the garage as he was terrified of driving it. So my mother used to place lumps of sugar on the bonnet, as if it were a horse. He soon got fed up with it and asked me to sell it, and I drove it around for a time. We did not realize that the accelerator had to be pumped before pressing the ignition so Jim Elton, our handyman, put a can of petrol in the glove compartment for priming the carburettor. As we went round Hyde Park Corner one day, the petrol burst into flames, shorted by the wires of the electric clock which had been removed. A taxi driver kindly put the fire out, and luckily a few days later I managed to sell it.

As West Wycombe was like a morgue, I suggested making part of the old wing into a squash racquets club and selling off the remaining half for building materials. My father gave his approval.

Then I said, 'What about converting the top floor of the house into furnished flats?' To my surprise he did not flatly reject the idea but wanted to discuss it with my mother. Eventually it was all agreed. 'Your mother wants to do it herself so you'd better leave it to her to sort out.' I waited for about six months and it became clear that nothing was likely to be done. So I decided to get things moving whilst she was abroad on holiday.

First the Masonic Room, which was to be the drawing room of

Flat No. 1, had to be cleared of junk. It was full of cardboard boxes filled with straw which had been sent with presents for Sarah's wedding and had been saved as they were in short supply. So with the daily, Mrs Elton, I heaved them out of the window to her husband James who had a tractor and trailer below.

In one corner there were two boxes marked 'Miss Sarah's dresses 1932'. So I rang Sarah and said, 'I've found some party dresses of yours when you were a little girl. What do you want me to do with them? I could try to sell them for you.' Sarah approved this idea.

In another box there was an old fur coat. Black took it out and shook it and a lot of moths flew out. 'I should burn it — it's only her Ladyship's second mink.' 'No, we'll bung it in the sale.' Another box contained two fur hats, so I put the lot on a table on the Colonnade and they were bought for £12 by visitors to the house. I sent Sarah a cheque for £12.

A few weeks later my mother reappeared from staying at the Embassy in Rome. 'I can't find my second mink coat and the astrakhan and mink hats which your father brought back from Teheran when he was with Anthony Eden. Do you know where they are?'

'Well I'm afraid I did sell an old fur coat and a couple of hats, but before you get too excited let me check and find out what's happened.'

Unfortunately soon afterwards my mother was looking out of the loo window over the kitchen and saw Mrs Green, the daily cook, walking up the drive wearing her mink coat and astrakhan hat. So Ma rushed down to the front door and tore them off Mrs Green. The poor woman was so frightened that she left immediately, and that was the last we saw of her.

But worse was to follow. I had sold the mink hat for £2 to a Mrs White who lived in Nottingham. So I wrote, returning the money and explaining my unfortunate mistake.

A few weeks later we were having breakfast when an envelope addressed to me arrived. Out fell the mink hat, but it had been cut into eight pieces to make a stole.

So I rushed round to the stable cottages where my old Nanny Marriot lived and implored her to sew it together. This was easier said than done. It took her months to do and when finished it was slightly lop-sided. But my mother didn't seem to notice. She used to ram one or other of the two hats down on her head and bang on my bedroom door shouting, 'Where are my diamond-studded evening shoes? I can't find them anywhere and I need them for the French Embassy tonight. You must have sold them too.'

My father used to sit on the Colonnade wearing his blue Tank Corps beret, quietly puffing at his pipe and enjoying every minute of all this.

Conversion of the top floor continued, however, and I soon had both flats let and the squash club well under way. So my father decided to abandon Chipps and return to West Wycombe. He also moved my grandmother and great aunt from Mill End farmhouse, which he had lent them, into West Wycombe. It was a very kind act, but it made his life much more difficult. 'Never, dear boy, do what I did and make the mistake of marrying three women at the same time.'

Still they were marvellous old ladies and full of sport. My grandmother occupied a bedroom at the top of the main staircase. Late at night, after we had been playing bridge downstairs, John and I used to creep up and very quietly open her bedroom door when she was reading in bed. Then we would crawl across the floor under her four-poster bed. Slowly we would raise the bed off the ground and tilt it to one side. This made the empty gin and whisky bottles, which she stored at the foot of the bed, roll on to the floor with a clatter. It must have been quite an ordeal but she joined in, imploring the dreadful ghosts to go away.

By her bed my grandmother had an electric bell to her sister's bedroom. So we used to press this, whereupon Aunt Nell came padding down the passage to see what all the commotion was about. At the first opportunity, John and I crept out of the room and ensconced ourselves in Aunt Nell's bedroom. On one such occasion she opened the cupboard door to put her slippers away but, as she could not find the customary gap, she started counting her pairs of shoes and rearranging them. Suddenly her hand alighted on a pair of men's shoes and, feeling John's ankles, she let out a great shriek. I think they both rather enjoyed these pranks, certainly more than our escapades with my Bentley.

I had bought the 1922 two-door coupé, which was standing in a field, for £50. John and I spent weeks stripping all the paint from the aluminium body and painting it black and maroon. It always started but only by swinging the handle, and the brake was very slow to take effect. When the painting was finished we decided to take my grandmother and Aunt Nell on a trial spin. Granny sat in the back seat behind me. The drill when we wanted to stop was for her to raise her knees to stop the front seat sliding backwards when I pushed the foot-brake pedal. It was a hazardous operation. Coming out of Stokenchurch there were some temporary road works but there was no time to slow down; suddenly I saw a man slowly crossing the road and when I pressed the horn (an electric bell-push which we had installed) nothing happened. Luckily he heard us coming and jumped out of the way just in time. Further on, the road descends down Dashwood Hill, and this gave me a chance to get the old car really moving. By the time we reached the outskirts of West Wycombe village we were hurtling along at 70 miles per hour and unable to stop as the brakes, with everyone pushing, were not up to the job. Eventually we came to a halt about half a mile beyond the village. Granny and Aunt Nell kept on saying, 'Don't you think we might go a little slower, darling.'

John sold the Bentley for £90, a welcome deal, but I suppose it would be worth a fortune today.

AMERICA

In taking up my Henry Fellowship in 1948 I chose to go to the Harvard Business School because this seemed the best and indeed my only way of finding out about America and why it was such a rich and powerful country. But I did not take the course very seriously and spent too much time gadding around Boston and, surprisingly, hunting with the Groton foxhounds.

One of the whips, Roger Prouty, rang me up one day and asked if I could ride and would like to go out hunting. Naturally, thinking of those days before the war, I said yes, so Roger lent me a coat in the smart hunt colours, blue and beige copied from the Beaufort, white breeches, leather boots and cap, and off I went to the meet. He had borrowed a 17-hand racehorse, Sharon, who had been sick and was thought to be quiet and reliable. Never having mounted anything larger than our agent's cob, I was filled with apprehension at the sight of this enormous-looking thoroughbred. So I stroked her nose and gave her lumps of sugar and was then given a leg up. Trotting was the first problem — I had forgotten all about rising up and down at the trot, and in any case the movement of a large horse was totally unlike that of the small pony I had been used to.

However, the field got moving and Sharon, being a fine jumper, cleared a series of solid stone walls without my falling off. Then we had to pass through a sawmill; perhaps Sharon took an aversion to the sawdust or, more likely, I was pulling too hard on her mouth. Anyhow, she refused to go forward and started backing right into a large bush. Suddenly she lunged forward, leaving me behind in the bush from where I landed gently on the ground. Sharon was quickly caught by a very impressive-looking lady, Isabella Grandin, who turned out to be one of the backers for the hunt and who helped me to remount.

At the end of the meet, the Master, Bill McGuickin, came up and said to me, 'I hear you're a very fine rider. Would you like to ride in the Myopia Hunt Cup Team?' I readily agreed, not having the slightest idea what he was talking about. The Myopia had, in fact, some of the largest jumps in New England. 'Half the field have broken backs and legs — very tough going.'

So Roger took me out three days a week to practise over the Groton jumps. Sharon was a superb jumper but had a habit every now and then of veering sideways towards the corner of a jump and, as I was expecting her to go straight, we parted company at about every fourth jump and I landed in the dirt on the other side; luckily without breaking anything. Roger and Bill became a bit concerned and suggested after five or six trials that it was a mistake, so that was the end of my riding there.

Towards the end of the summer term a student back at the school who knew that I was planning a gigantic tour of the United States with a friend, John Hale, winner of the Henry Fellowship from Cambridge, offered me the sales agency of Genii Safety-matic gas nozzles. (These nozzles went on the end of a petrol pump and were designed to cut off the flow of petrol automatically once the car's tank was full.) So, armed with route maps prepared by Conoco, we set off in a brand-new car which I had bought because I had plenty of cash – not from the Fellowship but because Hugh Trevor-Roper had made me his publishing agent in the United States for *The Last Days of Hitler* and for arranging publication of articles in the *New York Times* and other papers; in fact, shortly after my arrival, $32,000 was paid into my account.

Unfortunately there was a recession down the East Coast, which had already been covered by other agents, and it was not until we had made hundreds of unsuccessful attempts that we found a ready market – and that was 15,000 miles and eight weeks later in Butte, Montana, where we sold our entire stock. Butte was off the agents' usual round and we had a clear run.

Two other episodes stick in my mind: the fabulous caverns at Carlsbad in New Mexico, which gave me the idea of opening the Caves at West Wycombe; and winning the jackpot twice on a fifty-cent fruit machine in Baltimore and on a dime ten-cent one in Flagstaff, Arizona.

Another incident involved a huge pile of letters of introduction, together with a short note describing each person, which Isabella Grandin had very generously supplied. We were seldom able to make use of them as our itinerary did not correspond with the location of the addresses, but when we reached Seattle on the north-west coast we rummaged about and found a descriptive card for a Mrs Smith; the letter had unfortunately got mislaid and jumbled up in the boot of the car. So I rang up Mrs Smith and introduced myself, explaining about Isabella's letter of introduction. Mrs Smith hadn't the faintest idea who Isabella Grandin was but invited John and me round to her daughter's twenty-first birthday party. So, on arriving, I apologized for losing the letter and tried to explain the situation. But Mrs Smith was most suspicious and, although I told her about the Groton Hunt and Mrs Grandin, she clearly thought we were imposters. So, in desperation, I said: 'Mrs Grandin gave me a card describing you: perhaps if you saw it it might give you a clue as to who she is.' Mrs Smith took the card (which I had not bothered to read) and proceeded to read it aloud to her guests. It went: 'When you get to Seattle you must look up Mrs Smith — she's not nearly as nice and attractive as her sister, Mrs Brown, and unfortunately the family is not well to do.' I could have crawled under the table, and after apologizing profusely we left.

The tour was a great experience; we covered 28,000 miles and visited forty of the forty-nine States, seeing many of the great National Parks and natural and man-made wonders for which the United States is justly famous, as well as some of the vast industrial complexes ranging from the Ford Motor factories at Detroit to the Weyerhauser lumber plants in Washington. There was seldom a dull moment, as there were always filling stations to be canvassed in the smallest community.

There were also the odd exciting moments. We slept in the open on camp beds without a tent. On one occasion we found a spot in a forest on the Smoky Mountains in Virginia. I had got into my sleeping bag and noticed John standing at the foot of my bed. 'What are you doing?' 'I'm in my sleeping bag trying to go to sleep,' came the reply. So I looked again and it was a large black bear. Luckily I always kept an umbrella under my camp bed in case it rained so I used it to drive the bear away. But we did not have a good night's sleep.

In New Orleans we went on a tour of the night clubs in the old French district which had been the original birthplace of modern jazz, the musicians were on strike, however, and few bands were playing. So naturally I took over the drums for a spell in a bar where there was a solitary pianist.

Under the terms of the Henry Fellowship we were required to return after the year and write a report of our experience. So we both missed the second year of the Business School — fortunately for me as I would probably have failed the exams.

MY FIRST JOB

The time had now come to get a job — a most depressing experience at that time. I had interviews with a good many firms. The interviews were usually badly conducted, the salaries were very modest — about £300 a year — and the management seemed negative and unenterprising compared to what I had learnt about American management from all the case studies at the Business School and from visiting factories round the States.

Typical of these interviews was one with the Rover Car Company at their sales office in Piccadilly.

'Between you and me,' said the manager, 'you're an old Etonian and I am an old Harrovian. You'd be wasting your time working here. You should go and look for a better job somewhere else. But I'd be delighted to have you if you want to join us.'

John Hale had gone straight from Harvard to join the huge and well-run Canadian Aluminum Group in Montreal and encouraged me to go out as there was the chance of a job with them.

But in case I failed to get this job, I took the precaution of obtaining agencies for Dennis Trucks and Fire-engines and also for a patent self-locking nut used in aircraft, and then set off for Montreal. In my spare time I tried to sell these, but the trucks and fire-engines were not designed to travel at great speed on ice and snow and the defrosting equipment was not powerful enough. When I wrote explaining the problem a letter came back ignoring my criticism and saying: 'We think you have failed to appreciate that they are powered by Rolls-Royce engines and further comment is therefore superfluous.'

My job with the Aluminum Company of Canada involved working in the smelter and forge plant at Arvida, the cable mill at Shawinigan Falls, the sheet metal factory at Kingston and elsewhere. One day an old friend from the Business School, Fred Wagner, called at the Kingston factory to see me. I came out wearing a boiler suit and with thick asbestos gloves. 'Say, Dagwood, what a come-down! How come?' I didn't know what to say as I couldn't explain that it was all part of my training before entering politics in Britain.

Kingston was interesting for me because my Canadian grandfather, Colonel Vernon Eaton, who commanded the Canadian Royal Horse Artillery at Vimy Ridge, had earlier been the Commandant here.

After this I returned to the sales side in Montreal and at night I became a door-to-door salesman for Avon cosmetics. It was a tough job. There was thick snow everywhere and one had to trudge the streets knocking on doors. Whenever the door was opened the drill was to whip out a small display case full of shotgun shells filled with lipstick and to offer one as a special Christmas present. While the colour was being selected, one opened the case stacked with samples of the main range, matching nail varnish, rouge as well as powders, deodorants and perfumes. Sales were few and far between and it was a soul-destroying job.

The next evening job was much more entertaining. A friend, Sandy Mills, had bought a company called Touringuide which had large framed maps dotted around Montreal, mainly in front of restaurants, boarding houses and car parks. The idea was to sell advertising space round the edge of the map. Another friend, Doug Campbell, quickly bought 200 copies of some wonderful coloured maps of Montreal for 60 cents each from a department store. They didn't fit the old wooden frames so we bought new aluminium ones. Every night we took over Colonel Mills's dining room and, using his mahogany table, fixed the smart new maps with staple guns on to the board in the new frames. When enough were ready, we put them on the roof of Sandy's Ford Anglia, which was smaller than the frames, and took them to their sites.

Then I chased Sandy's salesman, Harry Jones. He had collected in advance his commissions on sales, some of which never materialized, and was making the minimum of effort; so I went off with him to sell the space. As the customers were mainly restaurants and night clubs, this meant sitting in all sorts of dumps waiting for the arrival of the advertising manager — who sometimes only appeared in the early hours of the morning. Sales went well and we also had about 140 of the maps left over, which we put in cheap wooden frames for $2 and sold them off for $14 to the boarding houses.

By the end of the summer the company had transformed a loss into a decent profit.

We also took on an extra salesman, Percy Horner, who reeked of beer. I took Percy's daughter out one night. When I asked her where she would like to go, the answer was Rockheads Paradise Café, a notorious night club which specialized in mulatto dancers. When it got to midnight I suggested leaving as I had a lot of work to do the next day. She suddenly seized a beer bottle and said, 'Sit down or I'll bash you with this.' Rather taken aback I carefully edged my chair away from the table and got up and said, 'I'm leaving now, do stay if you wish, otherwise meet me outside by the car.' It did the trick.

Alcan then seconded me to help a professional American charitable fund-raiser, Joseph Rose, raise $8 million for the Royal Victoria Hospital. Mr Rose had acquired the names of every rich person in Montreal and had divided these according to whether he considered them to be good for $10,000 or $100,000. Then meetings were arranged at which Mr Rose addressed the potential donors. On one occasion, he asked me to take him to the St James's Club where the $10,000 donors were waiting for his talk. Without my knowing, the venue had been changed to the Ritz Carlton Hotel and there was no one at the St James's Club. Mr Rose was furious.

A few days later there was to be a meeting for him to address the $100,000 donors. 'Now Dagwood, take me to the Racquets Club; for Christ's sake don't make another balls of it.' So we hopped into a taxi and I told the driver to go to the Racquets Club. He took us, unfortunately, to Rockheads Paradise Café, much to Mr Rose's displeasure. We did eventually succeed in raising over $8,000,000, however.

All this time I had been worrying about the future of West Wycombe. Then one Sunday I went to church. The sermon was about the return of the Prodigal Son, and it so moved me that I knew it was time to return. Luckily the Ford Motor Company was having a great sales drive in Canada and I managed to part-exchange my second-hand Rover, which Percy Horner had just driven into a lamp post, for a left-handed Ford Prefect, to be delivered in London.

When I got home in 1951, the demolition of the servants' wing was almost finished, the flats were occupied, the squash club was flourishing, the heating was on and my father was back in residence. What a relief! At last West Wycombe seemed secure for the future.

A FOOT IN INDUSTRY . . .

So now I set about finding a job in industry, this time in England.

After interviews with various companies, I eventually went to work at EMI Limited at Hayes in Middlesex in their Organization and Methods Department. EMI was a large conglomerate of about twelve factories which produced HMV and Marconi records, gramophones, radios and TV sets as well as a good deal of equipment for the Ministry of Defence. The O and M Department was required to advise on methods of improving productivity and their implementation, so we were well placed to see what was going on. And it was clear that a great deal was wrong.

Staff for the middle management, of which I was part, were given lunch in a separate canteen from the line workers. That was bad enough, but lunch was usually taken in silence with hardly a word spoken and in a most unfriendly and uncongenial atmosphere, so I took to having a snack in a café with one of my colleagues.

This lack of rapport was equally apparent between management and the men. To my surprise there was not even a personnel department. But the most obvious difference was the lack of that drive and training which had been so evident across the Atlantic. To make matters worse, the managing director had resigned and the management seemed to be floundering in a sea of indecision. It was indeed a depressing place and an unhappy introduction for me to British industry.

The board were by then casting around for a new managing director, and my boss obviously saw this as a heaven-sent chance for promotion and produced a very good report, supported by organizational charts. I took him to see Sir Edward de Stein, the power behind the board in the City. Sir Edward turned to me and asked, 'Is this your idea, Francis?' 'Unfortunately not,' I said. 'I wish it were. It's all Mr X's.' My boss then chipped in, saying, 'You badly need to appoint a new managing director. The trouble is that you always pick someone through the old boy network.' I nearly fell off my chair at such a foolish and provocative remark, and Sir Edward quite rightly decided not to promote my boss.

It was clearly time for me to go, too, as I had learnt enough from my two years' work at Hayes. My worst fears about British industry had been confirmed and I wanted to enter politics to try to alter the situation.

. . . AND POLITICS

Before I could go into politics I had to find a way of making money without having a full-time job. Non-working underwriting at Lloyd's seemed the obvious solution. My father wisely refused to lend the necessary funds, so the only alternative was to go and work at Lloyd's.

Thus I got a job, again with the help of John Hale, with his uncle's underwriting firm at Lloyd's, starting at the bottom on the very small salary of £350 a year – quite a reduction from £650 at EMI two years earlier and £1300 at Alcan four years earlier still, but at least it was a step in the right direction. After a few months working as a broker, I found a way of doing the month's work in less than a week. So the chairman said, 'There's no point in wasting your time in the market. Why not go and try your hand at getting business?' This was not a success and, in any case, so much was beginning to happen at West Wycombe and with my political activities that I no longer had the time or interest to pursue it, and gradually I dropped out of the business. For the first time in my life, I had some capital as well as income from my share of the sale of the Hanover Square house and I was able to become an underwriting member of Lloyd's.

I had already won a seat on the Bucks County Council at a by-election but promptly lost it at the succeeding election. Now I had to find a parliamentary constituency, and West Bromwich, a mining seat with a Labour majority of 16,000, duly adopted me as their Conservative candidate. No one was much interested in my views about British industry and management but in the general election of 1955 the adverse majority was cut to 12,000. The local chairman said, 'Well done – you're the best candidate we've had.' 'Nonsense,' I said. 'If you'd stuck up a sack of old potatoes you would have had the same result.' And it was not far from the truth. Our result was closely in line with the national swing.

The next seat was Gloucester, the aviation centre, for which I was adopted in 1957. A few months later I married Victoria de Rutzen.

Whilst we were on our honeymoon at my father's house in Majorca, the sitting member died. We had to hurry back for the by-election, which was bound to be an important one; the Labour majority at Gloucester was only 800 and the country was engulfed in the Suez crisis with Harold Macmillan as Prime Minister in place of Anthony Eden, so that a good deal of attention was focused on the Gloucester result.

I had spent hours on our honeymoon brushing up on all the main political subjects and imbibing a mass of relevant information and statistics. This was a useful exercise as there were often three public meetings a day and the press expected a variation of speeches to report.

The principal issues were employment and prices, but especially the new Rent Act which was designed to encourage owners to improve houses for sale or letting; and, of course, Britain's actions over Suez. I supported the Government fully on all these issues. But I also took every opportunity to stress the urgent need for better management and productivity and for business schools to train the managers. Lord Eccles told me: 'I agree with what you have been saying but I should forget about it. No one's in the least interested and it would be better to wait until you get into Parliament where you can do something about it.'

Although I worked flat out, the result was a disaster – the Labour majority shot up from 800 to 8000, mainly because the Liberals intervened in a major way for the first time for years. The chairman said to me, 'You're the worst candidate we've ever had.' So, rather facetiously, I replied: 'Nonsense, if you'd stuck up a sack of old potatoes, the result would have been the same.' Actually I didn't really believe this, but when the subsequent general election was held the swing against the Conservatives was not so different from that at Gloucester. Unfortunately I made some more injudicious remarks, and although I tried for some months to get adopted for other seats, it was in vain and I decided to turn to other things.

Until then I had lived at West Wycombe with my father, with whom I had a very close relationship. He was a most amusing character as well as a kind and generous father.

His favourite pastime was to work in his garden, which he had created by pulling down the game larders and outhouses of the old wing and converting this large area into a beautiful walled rose garden. He could usually be found there wearing his blue Tank Corps beret amongst all his roses. Once when he was busy in the garden and there was an excessive number of visitors to the house, a man came up to him and said, 'I pity the poor bugger who lives here.' 'So do I,' was my father's reply.

Apart from the garden and his interest in the beech woods he had mixed feelings about West Wycombe, and was perpetually worried about the cost of living here and the difficulty of finding staff.

By 1957, when I was thirty-two, I had a feeling that my father was slightly concerned that I was still a bachelor and showing no sign of settling down, although I had had quite a few girlfriends. One of my first loves was an attractive blonde called Caroline and as the next, who was tall and very beautiful, was also called Caroline and her name was Thynne, pronounced 'thin', they were nicknamed Thick and Thin. When two more Carolines appeared, they were renamed Mark 1, 2, 3, and 4 after the tanks used by the Rhine Army.

Later, there was a run of girls whose names began with a V.

When I started taking Victoria de Rutzen out, I kept calling her Vanessa. 'If you call me that again I'll fling something at you.' I apologized profusely, but when I repeated the name Victoria rightly threw a cream cake which hit me full in the face.

Some weeks later she invited me to stay with her mother, Sheila, who had married Randal Plunkett (now Lord Dunsany) after the war, her husband John de Rutzen having been killed serving with the Welsh Guards in Italy in 1944.

Some great friends of Victoria's, John (Sir John) and David Nugent, took me out snipe shooting at Ballinlough Castle and as we were crossing a bog covered with ice, I suddenly disappeared up to my neck in freezing mud and water. Luckily David hauled me out by the tip of my gun barrels. But as there was no transport within sight and no telephone for miles, we had to go on across those awful bogs until lunchtime when we had a rendezvous in a pub.

It seemed to me that it was a choice of dying of pneumonia or taking the plunge and proposing to Victoria, and to my everlasting luck she accepted and we were able to announce our engagement at a grand ball given by Aileen Plunket at Luthrellstown Castle two nights later. This marked the beginning of nineteen years of the most blissfully happy of marriages.

Victoria came from an illustrious and colourful Austrian-Polish family who traced their descent from a Roman patrician. In the late seventeenth century Baron Augustus de Rutzen was sent by John Casmin, King of Poland, to negotiate a treaty with Mahommed IV at Constantinople. Unfortunately Augustus, who was a heavy gambler, lost at cards his servants, carriages and horses and his estates near Cracow, but managed to recover most of his land including his estates in the heart of Russia. His son was in the army of 'winged horses' who rode with Sobieski to the relief of Vienna in 1683.

During the eighteenth century the de Rutzens intermarried with the Potemkins, and were thus connected with Field-Marshal Potemkin, the favourite of Catherine the Great. It was this Russian connection which encouraged me to start my collection of porcelain figures made by Gardner at the Czar's porcelain factory at St

Petersburg in the late eighteenth century.

In 1822 Charles Frederick, Baron de Rutzen, who was in the Russian Embassy in Rome, fell in love with an heiress from Wales, Dorothea, the daughter of Nathaniel Phillips. Nathaniel had made a fortune from his sugar plantations in Jamaica and had bought the picturesque Slebech estate overlooking the Milford Haven in south-west Wales. It was here that Charles and Dorothea settled, the former giving up by non-appearance his rights to the estates in Poland to his younger brother but retaining his ancient Polish title by special royal warrant from Queen Victoria.

The year before Victoria and I were married, my father took the brave decision to hand over the whole estate as well as the contents of the house to me.

After the débâcle at Gloucester, we were up to our necks moving into our new home Chipps, which my father had occupied in 1946, and reorganizing the estate. This involved modernizing and repairing more than fifty farmhouses and cottages, expanding the forestry activities and starting from scratch my own farming and shooting enterprises. It also meant enlarging the staff of carpenters, bricklayers, woodmen, keepers and tractor drivers, as well as those for the estate office, Caves and tourist attractions.

Whilst all this was in progress, I became heavily involved with a drive to sell machine tools to Russia. I had started learning Russian at Eton and was, I believe, the first to give a speech in Russian at the annual Speech Day on the fourth of June. I had also studied the language briefly at Oxford after getting my degree in PPE. Now it seemed important to be well informed about Russia and Communism in order to be in a position to repudiate the arguments of the Left in Britain. I also believed that the best way to improve the chances of lasting peace was to develop trade with Russia to help raise her abysmal standard of living; the better off the Russians were, the less likely they would be to resort to war. And I decided that, instead of just going to the Soviet Union as a tourist which I had already done, I would get a far better insight into all sorts of industries by representing a British machine-tool manufacturer.

So I got an assignment as a salesman for Molin's Machine Company which was the leading manufacturer of cigarette making and packaging machines in the world, and later as an interpreter for James Neill of Sheffield, who made permanent magnet chucks, devices for holding metal securely in position by means of powerful magnets so that it could be machined on a lathe or metal-working machine without the need for a normal jig. This meant attending crash courses in their factories at Deptford and Sheffield, and in the evening at Chipps learning by heart tape recordings which I had had translated into Russian and which gave all the relevant information about the machine tools. Eventually I was able to answer almost any technical question put to me in Russian.

All went well, including a spell of six weeks when I acted as an interpreter at the British Machine Tool Exhibition in Moscow in 1961. However, this event coincided with the publication of a report by a British delegation about the Russian machine-tool industry. Its chief findings were that their machine tools were badly designed and made and of no great significance.

I knew this to be incorrect as I had seen a great many of the latest Russian machine tools, including sonic drilling machines, as well as their automated production lines which were well ahead of anything we had in Britain. So I wrote a long article for the *Manchester Guardian* contradicting this report. In due course, I was rung up by a friend in the Foreign Service. 'We read your article in the *Manchester Guardian* and have come to the conclusion that you've hit the nail on the head. Where on earth did you get all this information?'

A few months later Molins asked me to return again to negotiate a huge order which was in the pipeline, but I was advised by the Foreign Office to decline. In any case I had learnt everything I had set out to ascertain, had been utterly exhausted by the experience and didn't relish the prospect of being picked up by the Russians, so I refused.

It was not until 1976 that I ventured there again with a party of friends, as I particularly wanted to see what changes had occurred over the intervening twenty years. Finally, I took my second wife Marcella and all our children with some Italian friends in 1979 for a long weekend in Leningrad. My experiences in Russia were quite extraordinary and utterly different from any I have ever read about and will, I hope, be the subject of my next book.

10

Securing the Future

THE CAVES

DURING the years 1951–52, while I was working at EMI, I had spent all my spare time opening up the Caves at West Wycombe. The idea of making the Caves into a tourist attraction originated from my visit to the Carlsbad Caverns in New Mexico in 1949. I had been amazed at the hordes of visitors there and was convinced that the Caves at West Wycombe could also be made into a profitable venture which would help towards the cost of the vast amount of restoration work needed on all the buildings, monuments and follies.

Since early times there had been an open-cast quarry on the side of the hill for mining chalk for the foundations of houses in the village and for roads; it is shown in one of Hannan's paintings of the 1750s. Sir Francis, the 2nd Baronet, set about extending these works in order to relieve serious local unemployment which had been caused by three successive harvest failures in 1748, 1749 and 1750, and to provide material for a new main road between West Wycombe and High Wycombe. The men were paid one shilling a day, enough in those times to keep body and soul together. The old road ran along the valley bottom and had become so deeply rutted that carriages frequently overturned, especially during wet weather. The new road, which was on a straight line to Wycombe, was also intended to provide a three-mile vista of the church tower capped with its glittering golden ball on top of the hill.

The project was very much in keeping with the proposals which Sir Francis had already introduced into Parliament for stimulating the creation of work to relieve rural unemployment. Why he chose to have a long winding tunnel dug a quarter of a mile into the hill with all sorts of chambers and divided passages instead of just enlarging the quarry is still, however, a mystery. The design is obviously symbolic and is thought to have something to do with the Eleusinian mysteries of ancient Greece.

Another, though much smaller, cave was also dug out close to the small studio house outside Marlow on the road to Medmenham which was occupied by Giuseppe Borgnis, the painter whom Sir Francis had brought over from Italy to decorate West Wycombe. But it is unlikely that either of these caves had any pseudo-religious significance. It is true that there were anti-religious cults in northern Italy at that time as well as Masonic societies in Rome and Florence, but there is no evidence that Borgnis, who was a prolific painter of church interiors in his local area of Craveggia near Milan, was involved in any of these.

I believe that Sir Francis was just having a bit of fun. It was a time when follies and artificial caves were fashionable – Horace Walpole had built a cave at his London house, Strawberry Hill, and had purloined some stalactites from the natural caves at Wookey Hole in Somerset, and there were many other examples such as those at Stourhead and Stowe – but Sir Francis's artificial cave is the largest and most curious of all.

Over the arched entrance to the cave he created a tall flint façade with a vaulted window which was divided by two slender stone columns. On either side of this façade are high walls of flint, with arches and recesses for statues, which encompass a large open courtyard. From the house across the valley this was clearly intended as another feature in the landscape – this time a Gothic church.

When we were children we used to make occasional expeditions to the Caves. The key to the heavy oak door, which was at the end of the brick tunnel at the entrance, was kept by Mr Fryer who lived in the house opposite. Mr Fryer charged a few pennies and in return handed over the key and some candle stubs. My father had stipulated that part of the proceeds was to go towards the upkeep of the church.

These visits were an alarming experience to us children. Water dripped everywhere, the floor was wet and slippery and there were puddles of water as well as several huge boulders which we had to climb over. When we got to the end chamber, it was the custom to blow out all the candles and stand in silence for a minute – all rather eerie and spooky. Several elderly ladies have since told me, however, of the fun and games they used to have being chased round the Caves by their boyfriends.

Although the Caves seem to have been open to visitors ever since they were built, no one besides the locals knew about them and they can only have attracted a small number of visitors.

At this time the Caves were in a terrible state. The entrance was protected by the remains of the original iron railings, with barbed wire filling the gaps. The flint-faced arch and columns over the entrance tunnel had been knocked down at the beginning of the war on the orders of our agent, Captain Hill, to form a barricade to protect the villagers from bomb blast, as the Caves were intended to be used as an air-raid shelter. No maintenance work had been carried out in the Caves themselves since the eighteenth century; the main passage was littered with small lumps of chalk and in one place was half-blocked by huge boulders which had fallen out of the wall. In the Great Hall chalk lumps were scattered all over the floor amongst puddles of water, and the River Styx was full of enormous boulders which had fallen from the ceiling.

First, of course, the Caves had to be surveyed. The preliminary survey concluded that £5000 or more would have to be spent to shore up dangerous areas and build supporting arches. As I only had £50 in the bank I asked my father to help, but he refused to become involved although he agreed to lease the Caves to me for £1 a year. 'Damned silly idea,' was his comment, and in some ways he was right. It was, therefore, a question of going ahead or waiting, perhaps for years, until I had enough capital. So I decided to take the risk and opened the Caves in 1951 at a charge of one shilling and with candles provided free. A wave of publicity ensued and visitors started to roll in, especially when the vicar, Father Allen, told the *Daily Mirror* that 'my tummy wobbles like a jelly every time I pass the entrance.' He followed this with a sermon denouncing the evil influence which emanated from the Caves. I took exactly the opposite view. If there was any evil in the Caves, I was convinced it would soon evaporate when the place was subjected to the eyes of crowds of sceptical visitors; the worst solution was to bottle it all up by keeping the Caves shut and lending credibility to such nonsense.

At weekends, débutantes who had come to stay often helped by selling soft drinks at the entrance, and by the end of that first summer nearly 10,000 visitors had paid their shilling and the Caves had made a tiny profit. It was better than nothing and seemed to offer scope for the future.

So that winter, 1951, I set to work tidying up the passages. Various friends who came to stay helped to split with picks the giant boulders which partially blocked the passage and must have weighed several tons, and to cart out all the lumps of chalk in wheelbarrows.

I arranged for a local blacksmith, Mr Smallwood, to erect steel scaffolding round one side of the Great Hall to protect visitors from any falls of chalk. He had finished putting up all the upright poles, but when he returned the following week he found his scaffolding half-buried under a huge pile of chalk which had fallen from the roof. The fall was partly due to the collapse of the arch on the far side of the chamber, which had given way when he dug holes near it to take the bases of the scaffolding poles.

That was the last I saw of Mr Smallwood. He was too shocked to go near the place again, and so was I.

Not surprisingly, I could not sleep for weeks at the thought of the visitors who had passed through. But after much agonizing, I decided to try again. It seemed absolutely crucial to make the Caves into a successful venture, as they would then act as a magnet and attract visitors to the other sites at West Wycombe, particularly the church and the house.

So I bought a large load of surplus Anderson steel shelters which had been used for protection against bombs in air-raids, and erected these wherever needed in the passages and also across the Great Hall as far as the huge pile of fallen chalk. I did this work myself in case there was any danger, but with some help in carrying the heavy steel sections from a pensioner, Mr Boniface, whom I also employed selling tickets at the entrance.

During the next season the Caves attracted about the same number of visitors, although there was even less to see as I had shut off the half of the Caves past the Great Hall and the latter looked awful with long sections of steel arches leading across it to the pile of fallen chalk.

When the season ended, I decided that it would be better to remove the steel shelters from the Great Hall and seal it off with metal gates. So I unbolted the Anderson shelters in the Great Hall and stacked them, with Boniface's help, against the side walls. It was hard and warm work, so we went up to have a drink. Ten minutes later when we returned there was a pile of chalk ten feet high where we had been working. That, I thought, was the end. We had narrowly escaped being killed and I decided it was too dangerous to go on. I was terribly shocked for months, and went off with my brother to Rome for a break, to reconsider the whole venture. I felt that if there was any supernatural influence in the caves, it was certainly a divine one which had preserved our lives! I was determined to have yet another try, for I could see no other means of rescuing West Wycombe.

So I sold my little car for £300 and arranged for several surveys of the caves to be carried out. Each came up with conflicting advice. One engineer from Yorkshire took me aside and said, 'You will have to carry out major structural repairs to the Caves and if you employ my firm it will certainly cost you at least £10,000. My personal advice to you is to forget about it and have a tunnel dug out by hand, bypassing the Great Hall; it should not cost you more than a few hundred pounds. You'll have to find some miners to do it and you can easily shore up the other defective places in the passages with pit props.'

To my amazement, an advertisement in the local newspaper produced an ex-Sapper, Jim Powney, who had been with the Guards Armoured Division. Jim agreed to come and work at nights and at weekends with another friend, Les Lawrence, and to dig out a tunnel 150 feet long by hand for £350, in order to bypass the Great Hall which was clearly the main danger.

Jim and Les took about four months to dig out the tunnel, depositing all the chalk in the Great Hall and raising the floor level by four or five feet. I used to help too at weekends, although using a pick was hard work and my hands got very sore.

After the tunnel was finished, Jim and Les erected pit props all the way down the caves wherever they were needed.

One night, arriving back from work, I went down the Cave through the new tunnel and just past it saw, to my horror, a huge boulder with a man's coat underneath it. I thought, 'God Almighty, Jim has caught it.' In fact he had nailed a steel spike into the wall to hang his coat on and the whole wall had then fallen off with the coat and steel spike, but luckily missing him.

When it was all finished, Jim let off a whole lot of explosives in the Great Hall and also poked the roof with aluminium poles, thereafter pronouncing that it was as safe as a house.

Shortly after this I came into some money. My father had sold the lease of our London property which ran from the north of Hanover Square right back to Oxford Street, where it included the site of Dolcis Shoes. In a way it was rather sad, as the early eighteenth-century house by Isaac Ware was still standing in the north-west corner of Hanover Square with a separate ballroom in the garden behind. On the other hand, it enabled me to put capital into the Caves and to become an underwriting member of Lloyd's, and it was also a great help to my sister and brother.

So improvements to the Caves sailed ahead. Electric lighting was installed, the wooden pit props were replaced with brick or chalk tunnelling (this actually took years and was done by my estate building staff during the depth of winter) and an elegant café was erected at the entrance by Guy Shepherd who had previously designed Schweppes Grotto for the Festival of Britain Fun Fair at Battersea.

Soon the numbers of visitors started to rise although there was still little to see. So I had a waxwork scene erected under an awning in the Great Hall which was, of course, still shut off to visitors; it showed members of the Hell-Fire Club wining and dining. And I installed a commentary with sound effects, the first underground 'sound and vision' programme in the world.

Unfortunately another large boulder dropped from the ceiling and badly damaged the waxwork scene. So I closed off the Great Hall completely, and visitors could only glimpse through the iron gates this large cavern 50 feet high with piles of chalk on the floor. No one, except in an emergency, was allowed to enter it. That is how it stayed for several years, until 1973, when I decided that it would have to be made secure as we were getting many more visitors and this extra space was needed to ease the flow.

So I turned again to the expert who had previously given me such sensible advice. His solution was to drill holes 130 feet down from the top of the hill into the Great Hall. Wire ropes were to be lowered down these boreholes and attached to a protective steel canopy which was to be hoisted up to the ceiling. Then 300 stainless steel bolts 10 to 15 feet long and with large plates at the end were drilled into the chalk ceiling and walls to make the chamber absolutely safe.

The work got off to a bad start because some hooligans tipped an expensive new air compressor, which the contractors had left overnight, down the hill and smashed it.

The project was eventually finished, however, and the Great Hall made completely secure – so safe that some years later I was even persuaded to give a dance there for my daughter Georgina's birthday.

One of the first visitors to file through the Great Hall after it was reopened in 1974 was a Mr William Brooks of High Wycombe. He discovered a lump of chalk in a crack in the wall and embedded in it were various coins dating from 1748 to 1754. One had initials scratched on it – possibly those of the foremen in charge of the work.

Recently, in some of the smaller caves and recesses, I have installed colourful scenes with artificial stalagmites and stalactites imitating those I had seen in the caves of Campanella and Hams in Majorca. In other caves there are scenes showing Sir Francis in conversation with Benjamin Franklin, who must have toured the

Caves during one of his visits to West Wycombe. He wrote in 1772 to Mr d'Acourt of Philadelphia: 'His Lordship's [Sir Francis's] imagery, puzzling and whimsical as it may seem is as much evident below the earth as it is above it.'

Paul Whitehead, the steward of the Hell-Fire Club, is shown in another cave sitting at a table and writing up the Medmenham Abbey Cellar Book. At his death in 1774, Whitehead left his heart to Sir Francis together with £50 for a marble urn to hold it, so Sir Francis arranged an elaborate ceremony to carry out his friend's wishes. The heart was placed in the urn on a bier in the hall of the house and then carried up the hill by six Grenadiers, 'The Dead March was played by the flutes horns and bassoons, successively with the fifes and the drums of the Bucks Militia and great guns [from the frigate] were discharged every three and a half minutes.' The cortège went three times round the inside of the Mausoleum still playing Saul's Funeral March whilst a special oratorio composed by Dr Arnold was sung in the church. Its theme was 'Whitehead's soul to Heaven fled – Hallelujah!' After depositing the heart, 'the soldiers fired a salute (triple) with great exactness and precision.'

The heart was frequently taken out and shown to visitors until 1829 when it was pinched by an Australian soldier. But the splendid urn with a marble medallion representing Aesculepius, the ancient Greek physician, still stands in its niche. According to tradition, Whitehead's ghost used to be seen flitting about the gardens. Whether it did or not, the Caves remain rather creepy to this day.

Other scenes show Sir George Dashwood, the 5th Baronet, and his sister Mary, Mrs Berkeley, as little children exploring with a candle and dressed as they appear in two delightful paintings in about 1800; miners at work under a foreman digging out the chalk; and, finally, in the end chamber, a group consisting of Sir Francis, John Wilkes, Lord Sandwich and Lord Melcombe Regis with lady friends toasting a statue of Venus de Milo.

All these scenes are enlivened by sound effects and the principal characters can be heard repeating extracts from letters which they wrote to each other.

By the time of writing, 1987, the Caves have attracted about two million visitors, and I have been able to hand over the profits to the National Trust to help pay for restoration and maintenance work.

The struggle has finally paid off, but it was a close shave and Providence has undoubtedly been on my side.

LIFE AT CHIPPS

Victoria took my Russian activities in her stride, and meanwhile made Chipps into the happiest of homes. The house, which was part Elizabethan and part eighteenth-century, had been leased by Christopher Hussey and Lord Gerald Wellesley in the 1930s and restored by the latter.

It was at Chipps that my three daughters, Emily, Georgina and Caroline, were born.

And it was also at Chipps that I started my pig farming.

The Domesday Book of 1086 recorded that a thousand pigs had been kept on pannage at West Wycombe. Pannage meant running the pigs in the beech woods where they lived off the mast or seeds from the beech trees. This seemed the ideal solution. Most of the beech trees were well over a hundred years old and would, before long, have to be felled; and despite my father's efforts there were relatively few young ones growing to take their place. I hoped that by filling the woods with pigs I would ensure that the undergrowth was cleared and the ground manured, and that this would encourage growth of the trees and make replanting a great deal easier. And the pigs would cost less to feed and keep, as they would live in cheap tin arks in the woods without any pigsties to clean out.

So I bought six Britwell Blue sows from Richard Roadnight, a very successful breeder, who kept all his pigs out in the open near Watlington, and let them loose in a paddock with tin arks at Chipps. I also went off to the Harper Adams Agricultural College for a short course on pig breeding. In my absence the pigs were fed by our Italian butler, and before long lots of little piglets appeared. In due course we had three hundred sows living in the the woods.

The pig enterprise lasted for about fifteen years. The pigs tore up all the brambles and undergrowth and turned the ground over, and the growth of young trees was phenomenal. The only drawback was that odd sows took to stripping the bark off some of the mature beech trees which then had to be felled, but on balance the scheme was a success.

My farming activities were also beginning to expand considerably. Several farms had become vacant, including the key one in the centre of the estate, and I took them over, not least because they had been badly farmed and were in a dreadful state – the farmhouses were very dilapidated, the barns and sheds needed reroofing with brick tiles and recladding with timber, and miles of new fencing and piped water were required.

Under the management of my agent, Dick Long, and an energetic farm manager, Harry Dugdale, the ravages caused by the seventy-year depression in agriculture were slowly overcome. Better working conditions for the men, especially in the new milking parlours, different rotations of crops, greater use of fertilizers and much more mechanization all resulted in better returns, and the farms began to prosper.

Since then the farming enterprises have just grown and grown. There have been, of course, some major setbacks, but the results for the past six or seven years have been very impressive under the management of my able and experienced partners. We now have in hand well over 2000 acres at West Wycombe, and my partners have won many of the top awards for farming in the Chilterns.

The shooting at West Wycombe also had to be started from scratch. All our old keepers had died or retired, and there had been no restocking of pheasants or partridges since 1938. We could still hold an occasional wild duck shoot and there were a few coveys of partridges, but it was a rarity to see a pheasant and the estate was crawling with vermin, especially foxes.

I knew next to nothing about running a shoot so I collected a few beaters for some trial days and advertised for guns. One of the beaters, Fred King, took charge and drove the partridges very efficiently over the guns. He was keen to run the shoot so, impressed by his obvious experience and references, I gave him the job.

The first day was very disappointing. We shot one brace of partridge and a hare but there was no sign of a pheasant. However, the prospective guns seemed keen to join. Later I discovered the reason.

King used to chat up each gun in turn. 'I used to work for Lord Dudley at Great Westwood. We had a very good partridge shoot. I expect you know his Lordship?'

'No, I don't.'

'I remember once, when I was loading for the Duke of Marlborough. I expect you know His Grace?'

'No, I only know of him.'

'Anyhow, His Grace said to me, "King, Mr Churchill's in a rotten stand. Tell him to move over closer to me." I expect you know Mr Winston Churchill, sir?' The guns were, of course, suitably impressed, gave King £5 and decided to join the shoot.

It ran quite well for some years until I decided to expand it considerably and went to have a look at some very well-run shoots. Whereupon I wrote a résumé on 'How to run a shoot' which I gave to King. A day or two later he marched into the office, banged the résumé down on the table, saying, 'It says everything except when I'm to go to the toilet,' and promptly gave notice.

The shoot has since grown dramatically. For twenty years I ran my own syndicate, but now most of the shooting on the estate is let off and has become quite a useful asset.

By 1962 Victoria and I with our three little girls were finding Chipps too small, so we began planning to alter the house.

When my father heard this, and prompted by my brother John, he asked, 'Would you like me to move out of West Wycombe and you move in? It's half empty and I spend most of my time in Majorca.'

'I wouldn't dream of asking you to move out. But if you really decide to go, I'd be happy to take over the lease from the National Trust.'

'The only problem, dear boy, is your mother. I can't afford to keep her in the style to which she is accustomed. You'll have to help.'

I asked him to give me the weekend to come up with some proposals.

My father had been incredibly generous and trusting when he had handed the family estate to me. However, it had transpired that his lawyers had made a dreadful mistake and that, although my father had survived the crucial five years following the gift so that no estate duty was liable, certain benefits had been retained by my father and the entire transaction was invalid. So he had little confidence in them.

'My solicitors are no damned good. You'd better get yours to sort it out and do whatever is best for you.'

Now, when it was my turn, I was determined to do my best for him and my mother, and the figure which I proposed turned out to be four times what he had hoped for.

'In that case, I'll pack and go by the end of the week — but you must never tell your mother the details of the deal.'

He had already given his Mannlicher rifle to the head-keeper at Kinveachy, Nina Seafield's principal grouse moor, his gramophone records to his secretary and many of his books to local charities and, true to his word, left a week later.

My mother was persuaded to agree provided a suitable flat in London could be found; it had to have a drawing room large enough to accommodate two grand pianos so that she could continue to play duets.

So it was that Victoria and I took over West Wycombe on 1 January 1963 and immediately embarked on a massive programme of restoration and redecoration. We moved in during March the following year and six months later, in September 1964, Victoria produced my son and heir, Edward.

The restoration programme turned out to cost a great deal, and the shortage of cash which had always bedevilled my father soon developed into a crisis for me. Something drastic had to be done. So I decided that I would have to sell a farm and chose one at Downley which consisted of about 120 acres on the outskirts of High

Wycombe. The moment the borough council got wind of my plans, they slapped a compulsory purchase order on the farm which they wanted for housing and offered me £20,000 for it, about £200 per acre. I refused – the land was worth at least ten times as much, and, luckily for me, the compulsory purchase order had by mistake included the site of a church built in 1938; consequently the order had to be withdrawn so that it could be amended and served again but with a statutory delay of six months.

In the interval I approached several builders who made verbal offers of £2000 to £3000 an acre.

Under legislation passed by the Conservative Government in 1956, public authorities were no longer able to get away with the artificially low price fixed by the local district valuer but had to pay the proper market price for land which was compulsorily acquired. So when the amended order was again presented, I refused the offer and disputed the valuation of £200 an acre submitted by the district valuer. We went on arguing for eighteen months. 'If you can prove it's worth more, we will accept it,' he kept on repeating.

'I have had numerous verbal offers.'

'That's not good enough – they must be in writing. If you can produce offers in writing, that's good enough.'

'I'm sure I haven't got offers in writing.'

'Exactly, that's what I thought. If you produced just one, it would prove your point.'

'Just one. I'll certainly have a look.' So I rushed to the safe where I had the written offer for £2000 per acre from a reputable firm of builders, Comben and Wakeling, and this did the trick. The council had to pay the proper market value of over £200,000.

So I was able to eliminate my terrifying overdraft and decided, at the same time, to help my sister Sarah and my brother John, who had not fared anything like as well as I had, through the law of primogeniture which gives most of the assets to the eldest son – as well as, incidentally, the liabilities. So John too was able to become a member of Lloyd's. I also set up a trust to buy a flat in London and look after my mother.

All this dissipated most of the cash from the land.

Other areas of Downley were, however, also clearly ripe for

development and I was faced with various choices: to sit back with a house and a Rolls-Royce on the Riviera, to expand my holding of land by buying hill land in Breconshire which could be acquired for a song – it lies just over half-way from West Wycombe to our land in Wales – or to do something more constructive.

The designs of small houses seemed to me to be generally very poor, and this was particularly true of the Downley area with which I had been concerned. So I decided to try to build a whole new village of six hundred houses to the most advanced and attractive design and layout in order to encourage a major transformation in the design of such houses. The plan would also have the advantage of providing long-term work for my building staff who would become redundant once the cottages, farms and main houses were finished.

First I invited Lord Esher, who had been closely involved in the development of Stevenage New Town, to submit a plan. But I realized that his proposals, attractive as they were, were essentially neo-Georgian and did not embrace any radical departure from existing designs.

So I then went off on a tour of Holland, Denmark and Germany to look at the best of modern European small houses and was particularly struck with the work of Arne Jacobsen in Copenhagen.

I also interviewed several young architects, winners of the RIBA's small house competitions, and eventually selected Gilbert Marsh to undertake the work. Gilbert introduced me to his senior partner, and the partnership produced some very attractive drawings in the style of Jacobsen's work. Some time later, Gilbert came to see me to announce his break up with his partner and to ask which of them I wished to employ. Sadly, I opted for safety and backed the older and more experienced man instead of my original choice.

Work proceeded rapidly. I asked Lanning Roper to help landscape the garden areas – there were to be no small fenced gardens in front, only open space as in New England – and David Hicks to design the interior of the show houses. I also took Victoria and my architect on a grand tour of the United States to look at the best designed small houses in Boston, Phoenix, Tucson and San Francisco, and especially their marvellous labour-saving kitchens.

The first stage involving thirty houses was a disaster. The foundations had to be altered and relaid; and the ceilings all had to be raised six inches when the houses were half-built because they were too low to pass the building by-laws, which meant that the prefabricated wooden fronts and backs also had to be remade. The final disaster came when the houses were finished and the public relations campaign arranged by J. Walter Thompson was in full swing; we applied for planning approval for the second stage of 128 houses, but this was refused because they had wooden fronts and backs and as the houses were within 15 feet of each other, these features contravened another by-law. So the wooden fronts and backs of Phase I had to be altered; the white wooden weatherboard planks were replaced with unattractive plastic panels which let the rain in round the edges.

For the next few years, all too frequently and at night, my telephone rang and an infuriated husband or wife screamed, 'There's water all over my bedroom floor – leaking through the windows – what are you going to do about it?'

I dared not put my own excellent building staff to work as litigation was pending with both the architect and the builders. So I brought in a consultant architect to try and sort matters out; that process took eight years and cost me a fortune.

In retrospect I realized that it had been a great mistake to embark on an enterprise of such an ambitious nature, especially as I personally was never expecting to do other than lose. The powerful incentive and discipline of the profit motive was essential to ensure that such an enterprise succeeded. The failure of Dashwood Village upset me for years. It had proved nothing except that it was easier and safer to stick to traditional designs, it had destroyed the prospect of maintenance work for my own building staff and had lost a lot of money.

Still, I made several more efforts to continue with alternative schemes and engaged, after a careful search, another prize-winning firm of architects, Andrew Renton and Partners. The designs looked superb on paper, but when it had been costed out it became apparent that I stood to lose another £150,000, so that was the end of that.

My final ploy was to look at a multitude of prefabricated houses. Some very attractive aluminium ones were being made in Warwick but the planners turned the application down which, in retrospect, was just as well. My building company, Breachwoods, is, however, still operating and has had some limited successes.

A few years ago the Residents' Association which controls the open gardens, playing field and tennis court at Dashwood Village arranged to meet me. I was rather nervous at the prospect of such a meeting and started by apologizing for the disastrous train of events and briefly recounting what had gone wrong. 'We have only come for one reason,' said the chairman. 'The residents have decided unanimously that these are the best designed small houses we will ever live in and we wanted to tell you so.' I very nearly burst into tears.

WALES

Whilst all this was under way at West Wycombe, Victoria and I were busy with similar activities in Wales. The tenant farms were all undergoing major modernization programmes; we ourselves had taken over two farms, and the promotion of tourist activities was in full swing.

The first we tackled was Manorbier Castle, in what was then Pembrokeshire (now Dyfed). This enchanting castle had been built in the eleventh century by Gerald de Barri, a Norman baron who was in the vanguard of the Norman army sent later to conquer Ireland.

In this castle Giraldus Cambrensis, the Archdeacon of Wales, wrote his account of his pilgrimages through Wales to recruit for the Crusades, and of the conquest of Ireland. The castle has suffered little over the centuries and is today one of the best examples of a Norman baron's castle in Britain.

When Victoria, who had lived in Wales, first took me there after our wedding in 1957 it was let to a Major Lees for a nominal £150 a year, and a modest income was generated by him from visitors. So when his lease expired I persuaded my mother-in-law, Lady Dunsany, to recover the castle and allow me to transform it into a tourist attraction.

My building staff went down from West Wycombe and camped in the cottage, which Victoria's grandmother had occupied, and proceeded to modernize the interior. We converted the guardroom into a gift shop and stocked it with the same souvenirs as the Caves shop at West Wycombe; then we created realistic scenes with wax and fibreglass statues in the Towers and the Dungeon. One of these was naturally of Giraldus himself. When the wax figure arrived we dressed him up in his Archdeacon's robes and set him down in our drawing room with a copy of *The Times* in his hands. I told our agent, Tom Blois-Brooke, who played a vital role in all the restoration work, to go and sit inside as I was busy. We heard him coughing and grunting as he tried to introduce himself to Giraldus. We left Giraldus there for several days but he began to take on a presence and became rather spooky so we finally removed him to one of the Tower rooms. Manorbier eventually had 50,000 visitors in its best year and is now a thriving attraction.

Then Victoria and I decided to turn our attention to the large, derelict corn mill at Black Pool on her estate at Slebech a few miles away; it stands on the banks of the East Cleddau, the river down which the Blue Stones were floated from the Prescelli Mountains to Stonehenge in 1800 BC. The mill has probably the earliest example of Armfield milling machinery in Britain; it was installed in 1813. So we restored the building and the machinery and, of course, set up a café and a gift shop, and I had to research and produce the inevitable booklet.

It was, however, never a tremendous success, partly because visitors to Pembrokeshire always stay on the coast which has such fantastic beaches and only go visiting historic sites when the weather is poor. But two years ago my daughter Georgina said, 'Daddy, the Caves at West Wycombe are such a success why don't you convert the base of the mill into caves?' So openings were duly cut through the huge masonry foundations at Black Pool Mill and a series of caves constructed of polystyrene. These have been filled with prehistoric animals from Wales, including hyenas, black bear, wolf, reindeer and other smaller mammals and a huge model of the legendary Welsh Dragon. I have also added sound and lighting effects as at West Wycombe, and the programme ends with the Welsh Dragon singing a line from 'Land of my Father's' – the Welsh National anthem! Now Black Pool Mill with its caverns is attracting many thousands of visitors a year.

Through all my research into the history of Manorbier and Black Pool, I discovered there was a very interesting cave just outside Tenby, called Hoyles Mouth. One day I crawled down it with Tom Blois-Brooke. Near the end there is a narrow fissure which leads into the Treasury. I managed to squeeze some way along it and then got stuck, but Tom, with a lot of heaving and pulling, eventually managed to pull me out. In this cave were found the bones of ancient animals which roamed this part of the country, and it is these that I have had copied and placed at Black Pool.

Hoyles Mouth is a natural tourist attraction, so I offered to buy it from the farmer who owned it and had it carefully surveyed. Sadly we could not reach agreement, and nothing has been made of it.

Another venture which caused a lot of headaches was Lawrenny Ferry. This was an old coal bunkering point for ships going to and fro up the Milford Haven. It had served during the war as a base for seaplanes and had a good slipway as well as a large tarmac apron and a dilapidated pub and some cottages.

In 1968 three of us, Lady Dunsany, John Hodson (a steel boiler manufacturer from Cardiff) and I put in £13,000 each and bought the site with the intention of making it into a really fine yachting centre. We erected a large ship repair shed, with a chandlery shop, a floating jetty, provisions shop and café and a number of wooden chalets, and enlarged the caravan site. We modernized the pub and built a motel behind. But Lawrenny made only tiny profits and involved an enormous amount of work and aggravation, so in 1974 we sold it off; it actually made five or six times our investment, which was incredibly lucky as it is difficult to make money out of marinas and other leisure enterprises.

FINANCIAL CRISIS

By 1969 my financial situation had again become precarious and extremely worrying. To safeguard West Wycombe for future generations I had handed over the estate in trust for my son Edward, so all the income from the rents went to the Trustees and I was desperately short of income. Lloyd's had done extremely badly and I had lost about £15,000, which seemed a great deal of money as I had never made much in the previous twelve years; there were structural faults in the Caves where areas were showing signs of collapsing; the diversification of tourist activities into a new restaurant, a gift shop, model museum and a miniature donkey stud was now proving uneconomic and causing headaches. Even my farm was starting to run at a loss, and my farm manager had run off with the manageress of the donkey stud.

Encouraged by Peter Carrington, later Foreign Secretary, who had a gun in my shoot, I went off to Australia with Victoria. We were planning to invest my remaining capital in a farm near Perth in Western Australia, for I had been told that there were great opportunities to improve agricultural productivity there and I thought that my experience in reorganizing the farms in Buckinghamshire and in Wales could be applied to land in another country.

Luckily we went first to Sydney. The next day I went to the ANZ Bank, of which Peter was chairman. The manager introduced me to his chief economist, John McLeod. 'You're another Pommy and I'll bet you're going to buy land in Western Australia on the advice of some English real estate agents.'

'Certainly, what's wrong with that? They told me one would double one's money every two or three years.'

'In my view you'll probably lose a bloody fortune but I expect you're stinking rich and can afford to lose it and if you're lucky you'll be able to sell it in fifteen years' time with a twenty per cent gain.'

I asked him why; after all Perth was growing at 10 per cent and Sydney and Melbourne at 5 per cent so Perth appeared to be growing twice as fast as the latter. John explained that this was not the case, and in fact the reverse was true. The population of Sydney and Melbourne was far larger and they were growing twelve times faster than Perth.

Shaken to bits, I said, 'I'm going to jump on the next plane and fly home again.'

'Don't do that – I've worked out a way of making a fortune but no one will listen to me.'

'Go right ahead and I'll listen.'

'You mustn't try and compete with Australians. They'll have you over a barrel as they're bound to know the local scene and will buy anything worth having. But generally they haven't got real money and can't afford to wait. You should buy land on the outskirts of Sydney and Melbourne and wait five to ten years. You could make a bonanza, especially if you make use of your experience in Britain and go in for the lastest methods such as the application of trace elements to step up productivity.'

So then I went to see the planning officer for Sydney. 'I'm a landowner who has fallen on hard times – I've given everything away and was thinking of buying a farm for one of my three daughters in case one of them marries a young Australian and decides to settle here. But I don't want the farm to be two or three hundred miles away in the outback because my grandchildren won't get a proper education and I don't relish the prospect of trying to run a farm thirteen thousand miles away with a manager in case he upsticks and goes if there's a drought and leaves me holding the baby. And I don't want a farm too close to the city as it will be built over and ruin the farm and we've always lived in the country.'

'Don't worry – I'll show you the provisional confidential town plan of Sydney which will show you where it's going.'

Out came the plan: Sydney was going to expand to the north at Gosford, to the west at Richmond and to the south at Wollongong. So I took a taxi and spent the next week tramping over every farm over a hundred acres at Richmond and Gosford and finally bought 250 acres at Wamberal some way from Gosford. I had also noticed the new Expressway from Sydney under construction – it was going to by-pass Gosford but was similar to the M40 which had had such a fortuitous impact on land prices at High Wycombe. I felt this would make it easier to find someone to run the farm or, at worst, to let it, and that if I was ever forced to sell, there would always be a market for such an attractive, well-situated farm.

Then Victoria and I drove down to Melbourne and started looking at farms there. Sam Goodenough took me to a mountain farm of 1500 acres called Yarraloch and insisted that I climb to the top to see the distant view of Melbourne. But the farm was a scene of devastation. A thousand acres had been bulldozed, leaving vast piles of gum trees and their roots and boulders. So I said to Sam, 'I'll give you a dollar for every farm you take me to see as long as it doesn't look like this.'

'I just thought you should have a look at it — it's the largest acreage within striking distance of Melbourne which has been on the market since the 1930s and offers great scope for improvement. You could make a smashing farm of it.'

We looked at several more farms all costing a great deal more. Someone at a cocktail party said, 'You should get up in the air — that's the best way to see everything.' So up we went and circled Melbourne for two or three hours. Every twenty minutes we passed Yarraloch which was easily recognizable as the bulldozed ground looked white in the heat. Suddenly I realized that it reminded me of West Wycombe, only thirty miles from London — this was twenty-six from Melbourne. They were asking £120 an acre so I made a bid for half that amount and left for England.

On our arrival home we were greeted with the news that I had bought the 1500 acres for £60,000 and that Theo Coles, the nice old chairman of my broking firm, had died.

So now I had spent all my free capital and had to do something about Lloyd's. As I had been with Hinton Hill and Coles for sixteen years I felt bound to stay, especially as there seemed to be the prospect of an exciting future for underwriting agents; in fact before leaving for Australia I had tried hard to persuade Coles to set up a proper underwriting agency but he was totally deaf to such an idea. So now, with the help of Lazards, I made an offer to buy up the broking firm; luckily it was rejected and I felt free to leave and start my own agency.

The idea which had partly originated with a friend of mine, Ronnie

Kershaw, was to pinpoint the best of the four hundred syndicates at Lloyd's and to enroll new members who would have a small share each on a wide range of these carefully selected syndicates.

It was, in fact, a brilliant new departure from the existing system, although it was extremely difficult to get going. Eventually, however, my small agency, Dashwood Underwriting Agencies, was officially accepted with Ronnie as a director. I had found very cheap offices over an Indian restaurant in an old building which was destined for demolition, which cost only £1 per square foot (the going rate was £6 or more).

I worked long hours there – in fact the janitor locked me in one evening and I had to get the fire brigade to let me out through a top window.

Suddenly in 1972, when Victoria and I were having scrambled eggs in the kitchen at West Wycombe, a telegram arrived with an amazing offer for the Sydney farm. I said to her, 'It can't be true. There must be a nought wrong or perhaps I'm overworking and seeing double digits.' Victoria said, 'You must fly out at once and see what's really happening.' So out I went and arranged to meet the original farmer from whom I had bought Wamberal.

'When you offered me $250 an acre I thought you were the biggest fool I'd ever met – another crazy Pommy – I had to go out of the room every five minutes for another can of beer because I couldn't believe my luck. But you did me a very good turn – I've just made ten times the money on a farm further out at Wyong. My advice to you is don't sell. Sydney has to come this way – you'll be as rich as Croesus if you hang on, but prices will go up and down like a yo-yo.'

I took his advice and returned to Sydney to celebrate becoming, at least theoretically, a millionaire. But I decided to hang on to Wamberal, as the idea was to rear calves and then transport them to my farm at Yarraloch in Victoria for fattening. It was not until 1980 that I decided to sell it, and the result was all that I could have wished.

Then I flew down to Melbourne to look round Yarraloch. I had had to borrow a quarter of a million dollars to clear about 800 acres of bulldozed gum trees, repair the badly built water dams, erect 30 miles or so of new fencing and put down several hundred acres to grass. So the outlook seemed far from rosy.

On the walk round, Ken Hayes and I passed a couple of bulldozers working on the farm. 'What are they doing?'

'Oh, nothing much – just some gravel workings of no value.'

At the top we passed a large hole. 'What is that?'

'No idea – haven't walked this way before, probably some old antimony working.'

On the way down, Ken said, 'What about meeting your neighbour, Mr Robertson – he sold Yarraloch to the psychiatrist who went bust and whose partner shot himself just before you bought it.'

This was all news to me. So I asked Mr Robertson, 'What about the gravel?'

'Oh, they're only second-grade deposits – I use them for roads in eastern Melbourne and in return maintain all the roads on your farm – bloody miles of them.'

'And what about the antimony working?'

'Antimony, my foot, that's an old gold mine. Hasn't been worked since 1890 but with the price of gold rising, you'd better open it up.'

Back home I told everyone about my gold mine. Actually it turned out to have virtually no gold in it, but the farm is now considered one of the most beautiful in Victoria. And not unnaturally the State Government decided in 1974 to take it into public ownership. So I wrote to the Premier of Victoria, Mr Hamer, pointing out that I had spent most of my life conserving and preserving West Wycombe and was trying to do the same at Yarraloch, to which I was becoming greatly attached.

A public meeting was duly called on the farm and Ken got a hundred or so of my cows to gallop past the crowd and the cameras. When Mr Hamer read out my letter and asked for a vote, 96 per cent voted against his proposals. So Yarraloch escaped nationalization and now runs a herd of about 250 Hereford cattle.

Hansard covered it with two pages extolling my improvements and congratulating me on being the most far-sighted and constructive landowner in Victoria.

Impressed by this turn of events, I decided to have a go in North America in order to spread my farming enterprises between the three continents. Naturally I turned to Montreal, which I had known so well. (I discovered some years later letters relating to a large area of land at Longueil in Montreal which Sir Francis had considered buying in the 1770s – rather a coincidence.)

With the proceeds of Lawrenny Ferry and an overdraft from the bank, I bought in 1974 a farm of 300 acres at St Joseph about twenty miles west of Montreal, adopting the same technique of aerial reconnaissance and paying little attention to local advice. This farm seemed to offer the prospect of producing substantial farming profits.

On the advice of MacDonald University, I had the farm underlaid with field drains to improve the yield of maize. It certainly did that – the yield trebled, but the manager tried to bill me for draining his farm at the same time and after the harvest most of my maize mysteriously disappeared.

The financial situation was rapidly deteriorating and I was extremely fortunate in 1976 to find a French neighbour who wanted my farm to amalgamate with his so, after paying off a massive overdraft, I came out with a useful gain.

I still wanted to have a farm in North America, however, and had been studying Colorado, having particularly remembered Denver from my visit in 1950. But what a problem! I was taken by real estate dealers all over Colorado to look at picturesque mountain farms with trout, potential skiing resorts, acres of windswept desert in Wyoming and wheat land with possible oil deposits; everything except what I was seeking. Eventually we landed up at Cheyenne. 'This is the ideal place for an investment by you. It's the fastest growing area in Colorado at 12 per cent – and Denver's only 5 per cent.'

I asked about the population. 'Cheyenne's got 6000, Denver 1.25 million.'

I knew this one from John McLeod's comparison of Perth and Sydney. 'You mean Denver's growing at about 60,000 and Cheyenne at 700. You must be joking, this is a total waste of time, I'll take the next plane back to Denver.' The dealers, who had given a dinner party, nearly hit me. I later discovered that they had bought a vast tract of farmland near Cheyenne and were peddling it off to unsuspecting doctors and other professionals as a long-term tax investment.

After such an arduous week I very nearly gave up, but next morning the sun was pouring through the window of my hotel bedroom and there was a fantastic sight – the Rocky Mountains in all their glory and majesty and slowly changing colours.

So I contacted another land dealer who took me south-east of Denver to two little villages, Parker and Elizabeth. I knew instinctively that was the area for me, but as the dealer tried to pull a fast one on the way home over his fees, I dropped him and rang another, Sam Perry. This time I told him precisely the opposite of what I had previously been told and insisted on looking at land to the north, the opposite side of Denver. Sam was amazed. 'Can't think why you're so keen on this dry wheat land. The south and front range is a far better bet.' So I agreed to go south with him, and in no time we were back in Elizabeth and Parker.

To check it better, I hired a Cessna and flew round and round watching the traffic flows. I ended up buying 500 acres of delightful rolling farmland with plenty of Corsican pine trees and rocky outcrop. The owner had sunk two water wells to a depth of a thousand feet and had found plenty of water as well as coal and traces of oil.

So, when I got home, I sent the plan of the farm to Colonel Merrilees, a leading water diviner who had impressed me tremendously in locating underground water flows at West Wycombe, and asked him if he thought there was any oil on my farm. Back came the reply: 'You're sitting on a large basin of top-quality oil similar to the best Arabian – its about 3000 feet down.'

I have not yet discovered if he was right or not, but something just as important has recently come to light. The farm is richly endowed with water which is potentially very valuable. This fortuitous bonus has come about through the growth of Colorado Springs and Denver, causing a huge demand for water.

Sam also found me an excellent share-cropper with whom I run

cattle on the farm. The outlook is so exciting that I have now
bought more farms for my family, and have also expanded the cattle
enterprise which runs with the minimum of management and no
investment in buildings and equipment – the best formula for
running farms at so great a distance.

DANCES

West Wycombe was designed and built for entertainment, and
during the past thirty years it must have witnessed more dances and
balls than at any previous time in its history. I can recall about
twenty, starting with the small dance for my sister Sarah during the
war in 1941 at which my band provided the music.

Many balls were held in the house, which has the magnificent
Music Saloon for dancing, but some of the most amusing have been
in the Temple of Music on the island in the lake. One of the
paintings by Thomas Daniell in 1781 shows this Temple full of
guests and more arriving in an elegant long boat with a prow like a
gondola. The Temple consists of one room which will take about
eighty people squeezed rather tightly together. Underneath are the
cellars. There is a long rectangle in the middle of the wooden floor
which may originally have been a sort of stage for lifting food or
props.

My first party there was in 1953, the year of Queen Elizabeth's
Coronation. The theme was 'the Underworld' and my guests went
to great trouble to dress the part. Roy Harrod, leading protégé of
John Maynard Keynes and my tutor in economics at Oxford, came
as Mephistopheles; Maureen, Marchioness of Dufferin and Ava
as 'The Celebrated Lady Sandwich'; John Julius Cooper (Lord
Norwich) as Orpheus; and my father was dressed as Pluto's Stoker.

The only slight mishap occurred in the cellar which we used as a
bar for refreshments. One of the servants from Christ Church, my

Oxford college, was busy stirring scrambled eggs in a saucepan when a lump of plaster fell from the ceiling straight into the eggs, splattering his stiff white shirt and black tails. The floor had a lot of give when couples were dancing energetically and we had to install a vertical prop before the next party.

That had a 'Tropical' theme: luckily it was a lovely warm night, otherwise the girls would have been cold in their grass skirts. The only mishap then occurred as the last guests were leaving at about 5 a.m. I asked the band, as I always do, to play the National Anthem, whereupon several in the punts stood to attention and one punt slowly sank in the middle of the lake. Actually it might not have been at all amusing as one of the occupants, Antonia Fraser, was not a strong swimmer and had to be helped ashore.

A few months later a fisherman hooked a purse which had been lying on the bottom of the lake. It contained a High Wycombe bus ticket and a ten shilling note, both in reasonable condition; it belonged to a neighbour who had also gone down in the boat.

Easily the most amusing was the 'Harem' party which Victoria and I gave in 1967. We erected a wooden façade representing the entrance to Ali Baba's palace at the end of the Broad Walk on the edge of the lake; it had an arched entrance and walls surmounted with domes and towers and heavily veiled ladies peering over.

The costumes were astonishing – generals in nineteenth-century British and Turkish uniforms, sultans, pashas, sheiks and nabobs. Randal Dunsany was spotted hailing a taxi outside the Cavalry and Guards Club in Piccadilly wearing, appropriately, a long djallabieh with an Arab headdress and old gym shoes (he commanded the Guides Cavalry, the crack Indian regiment, during the war).

The girls were not to be outdone. 'Harem' dress ranged from flowing silk robes to practically nothing except the odd well-placed jewel and jewelled headpiece. Two had just returned from Marrakesh where they had bought the genuine thing. My brother-in-law, Morys Aberdare, afterwards wrote to Victoria: 'You were at your best and would have been my No. 1 choice for my Harem if I could have separated you from that terrible Pasha with the Phallic headdress.' That was me.

I had booked a genuine Turkish belly-dancer to do her act at midnight, but a message was brought over in a punt to say that she had gone to West Wickham in Kent by mistake and would not arrive until 2 a.m. When she finally appeared at 3 a.m. it turned out she could not speak a word of English. Nevertheless, she went through her routine, which took a long time and was rather dull. So Confrey Phillips, the band leader, said: 'I'll take her down to the cellar and get her gassed up; we'll get her to take everything off.' Twenty minutes later she reappeared to great applause, but to everyone's dismay repeated the same tedious routine. I gathered, however, that she was a ball of fire in the bushes when the party was ending.

The balls in the house tend to be more sedate affairs but still highly enjoyable. We did, however, have one most unfortunate incident at 'Pa's Ball' which my brother John and I gave in 1956 to celebrate my father's sixtieth birthday.

I thought it would be an original idea and would also amuse my father to have his birthday cake made as a model of our family Mausoleum which is hexagonal in shape. Marabel Weldon, an old friend of his, offered to have her cook make it – so I sent her photographs of this enormous classical building.

In the meantime my father had become rather ill. I think he overdid himself stalking at Kinveachy in the Scottish Highlands, where he used to stay frequently with his kinswoman, Nina Seafield. He talked incessantly of his impending death, and the outlook looked pretty grim as he had just failed a medical test which was required before insurance could be arranged to cover the potential estate duty.

My father gamely struggled out of bed for the party, and at midnight Marabel appeared with the splendid cake looking like the Mausoleum with its columns and arches and niches for funerary urns. I said to her, 'For God's sake, don't show it to the old man – he'll have a fit as he's not at all well. It will have to stay in the pantry.' Marabel burst into tears. 'My cook has been at it for six weeks – she'll be so upset and will give notice.' So my father never saw the cake. But an *Evening Standard* reporter had sneaked into the pantry, and the story came out the following day and was read by my father on his sick bed.

Two dances I remember especially. One was given by Felix Fenston in 1962 for his daughter's coming out. Unfortunately she ran off with a young man so Felix gave it with my mother instead. It was a fantastic affair; David Hicks carried out all the décor, making the old dining room with its dark red tattered silk walls and maroon curtains sensational with his scarlet table cloths and brilliant flower and lighting effects. A huge marquee was erected on the lawn, and the wonderful old band from the 400 Night Club under Tim Clayton played. The garden was full of little Chinese pagodas serving Chinese delicatessen, and for breakfast there was everything from caviar, lobsters, quails' eggs and salmon to kedgeree and eggs and bacon.

That was the last dance before my parents moved out, although they did have a final dinner party that winter for Bill and Bronwen Astor. My mother rang me at Chipps. 'Do come down early and look after the guests.' As I arrived all the lights went out, and our Austrian butler, Fritz, was rushing round to find out why. Luckily it turned out to be due to an electric fire which had been plugged into a light socket. The house was bitterly cold so my mother had asked the handyman, James Elton, to stoke up the boilers, but he had firm instructions from my father to take no notice. My mother then had the grates in the drawing room piled high with huge logs which she had ordered the woods staff to cut specially for the occasion. She had been staying at Boughton with the Duchess of Buccleuch and had been impressed by their lovely large fires. The grates at West Wycombe, however, have small cast-iron baskets for coal burning, and as these enormous logs would not fit they had to go on top. It looked as if there would be a chimney fire at any moment so Fritz and I yanked them off and stood them to one side.

Then there was only one bottle of gin and one of sherry for thirty guests. 'Those were Sir John's orders,' said Fritz with a superior smile. So I made a Los Angeles dry Martini with three parts of gin to one of sherry, and by using tiny liqueur glasses we managed to make the drink go round.

After dinner my mother braved the cold in the Music Saloon where she played the piano to a small group of frozen guests; others huddled in front of the fire in the Blue Drawing Room or played bridge in their fur wraps. But they all seemed to enjoy it even though everything was falling to bits, the carpets were full of holes, the curtains in shreds and the leather of the chair seats in loose patches scattered over the horsehair stuffing.

The most ambitious party, however, was the one which Marcella and I gave in 1979 for Emily and Georgina's coming out. It was really far too large a party – there were 900 guests – but luckily we had a fine warm night. There was a disco in the Music Temple with punts from Oxford and punters dressed in red and white. A Jamaican steel band strolled along the Colonnade, and in the Hall an Italian string trio played those lovely tunes one hears in St Mark's Square in Venice. And we had Confrey Phillips's orchestra in the Music Saloon. But it was exhausting organizing it and I was too tired to enjoy it; I had to go to bed for a week afterwards to recover.

In 1985 we decided to have the ball of our lives to celebrate my sixtieth birthday. To begin with everything went wrong.

Lester Lanin's band from New York had not got the necessary work permits and were stopped at Heathrow; all the silver candelabra had been sent to another do at Hampton Court by mistake; and a calor gas cylinder which we tried out the night before, to heat the Colonnade, went off with a loud bang and caught fire. And the guest list kept changing, which was a nightmare for Marcella who was sorting out the placement for three hundred people – thirty tables of ten each inside the house or on the Colonnade. Funnily enough I was not in the least perturbed. 'Everything's going wrong – it's bound to be a great success,' I told everyone.

And so it proved. I can only quote from some of the letters. 'I think Heaven must be very like last night,' wrote Lady de Zulueta. 'What a fantasmorgorical party – I have seldom seen or been in such a perfect in every way gala night. The setting, the lights, the guests all in their best dresses, the flowers, the lit-up gardens, the superlative dinner, the great excitement when the remarkable fireworks started, the American orchestra, Lester Lanin, and last, but not least you and Marcella giving an atmosphere of happiness, gaiety and love,' enthused Lady Russell.

'You know I have enough imagination to realise how ecstatically happy you must be this morning after having, between you, produced such a magical evening,' wrote Fleur Cowles (Mrs Tom Meyer). She continued: 'The house looked a dream; the garden lighting was extraordinarily beautiful; the food was *delicious;* the music delightful – and that is about the end of the adjectives (I am running out of them!). It would be an evening hard for anyone else ever to reproduce.'

The fireworks were sensational. They were made and fired by the Rev. Ron Lancaster to a version of Handel's *Firework and Water Music,* with the grand finale from Tchaikovsky's *1812 Overture.* The music took me weeks to cut and rearrange. Over the years I had floodlit the Temples of Venus, of Daphne and of Music and the four elegant flint bridges round the lake, as well as the Mausoleum and church tower with the golden ball on the hill beyond. 'The fireworks were so beautiful that I saw some people with tears in their eyes,' said the Duchess of Buccleuch. And Alistair Horne wrote:

I recall (though not personally!) the adjective used to describe Louis-Napoleon's great Paris ball of 1867 – 'fierique' – and can't think of a better word (but I hope you will continue to live more happily than did poor L-Nap!). I think the two greatest fireworks displays I remember were at de Gaulle's visit here in 1961 and at the Inauguration in Washington in 1980 – but yours eclipsed them both by the setting, the marvellous reflection on the lake, etc.'

I can see no point in having all the work and problems of running a stately home with thousands of visitors tramping round unless Marcella and I can entertain our friends in style too.

MY FAMILY NOW

Living at West Wycombe has been the greatest fun and I have had the most wonderful help and support, first from Victoria and then from Marcella.

Marcella first came to stay at West Wycombe with her husband in 1954 and I remember my father chasing her round the dining-room table trying to pinch her behind. She was then a stunning model and was regarded by the famous photographer, Baron, as one of the ten most beautiful women in the world. She was also a favourite subject of such eminent photographers as John French, Norman Parkinson, David Bailey and Richard Dormer. Her modelling career took her all over the world, and she was the leading model for magazines such as *Harper's Bazaar, Vogue* and *Elle,* as well as the major Italian and French collections.

Marcella also starred in a number of films, with Roger Moore and Tony Hancock, with Rod Steiger in *Across the Bridge* and with Peter Cushing and Christopher Lee in *The Hound of the Baskervilles.* With her fluent knowledge of English, she also did the whole BBC television series of 'Parliamo Italiano'.

Besides all this, she started and developed her own wig-making business, Marla Wigs, which became internationally successful.

Over the years I had more or less lost touch with her, but following Victoria's death in 1976, my sister Sarah gave a dinner party as she felt that Marcella, whose husband had also recently died, and I were well suited for each other. Shortly after this I went off on a cruise in the Carribean in a French ship. It was full of elderly couples, and by the time it reached Barbados I was feeling absolutely miserable. So I rang my sister, who was staying with Jackie Ward (Colonel E. J. S. Ward) and his wife, Susan. She and Susan persuaded me to abandon the cruise and installed me in an hotel near Sandy Lane, where I started to write this book.

Two days later Marcella arrived to stay with the Wards and that was the beginning of a new and happy era for me.

I have also been blessed with a large and happy family. Emily is married to an Irish farmer and has two dear little boys, Nicholas and

West Wycombe as it is today, showing the East Portico and Cockpit Arch to the left.

This capriccio painting of the Colonnade, the Temple of Venus and Edward's bridge is by Felix Kelly and was given to me by friends on my sixtieth birthday.

*The marbled entrance lobby and
Colonnade with Roman and
eighteenth-century busts.*

Above: The main Hall with its ceiling copied from the Sun Temple at Palmyra, 1770, and marble floor replaced by me in 1964.
Below: The Blue Drawing Room, originally the Breakfast Room, with the figure beloved by Sir Francis, the Venus de Medici.

The Cascade, flanked by reclining nymphs, frames the Temple of Music,
designed by Nicholas Revett and completed in 1770.

Marcella and me relaxing in the Music Saloon, photographed by Lord Snowdon. The ceiling by Giuseppe Borgnis is based on Raphael's Banquet of the Gods *in the Palazzo Farnesina. The elaborate mantelpiece (above) is by Sir Henry Cheere. I have since replaced the Louis XVI sofa and chairs with the Chippendale pieces seen in the large photograph.*

Me in the Library upstairs,
where we live, amongst my
architectural books, busts and
statues.

Right: The seventeenth-century
brass-bound 'Yale' chest from
Portuguese Goa, and the 1705
mirror with the family crest in
verre eglomisé which I bought
back in 1964.

Edward. She and Charlie, her husband, have converted a derelict orangery into a delightful house where she is building up her business restoring and gilding furniture and pictures.

Georgina leads a hectic social life with her large circle of friends, with one of whom she started her own Montessori School in London. It goes from strength to strength and is bursting at the seams. She also manages somehow to find the time to help run an interior decorating business. Caroline worked for a spell in my firm at Lloyd's and is now at a London hospital where she has almost finished qualifying as a doctor.

Edward took a degree in Land Management at Reading University and is now a land agent with one of the leading firms in Wales. He has a passion for fishing, shooting and the countryside, which he must have inherited from his grandfather, Baron de Rutzen. My stepson, Marco, read Politics, History and English at Buckingham University. He is a fluent linguist, which should be greatly to his advantage if he goes, as he hopes to do, into the world of art.

Life at West Wycombe is now very different, not least because of the problem of finding suitable staff. When our family butler 'Bung-Ho' Bryndley left in 1971 (he was so nicknamed by the *Daily Mirror* for plugging a leaking tap in a bathroom – which was being used by one of our guests, Sir Philip de Zulueta* – with his thumb until the stop-cock was turned off) we despaired of finding a replacement. But we were soon proved wrong, for the new butler, Edwards, who had arrived with impeccable references, was a gem. He looked extremely smart in his black and red striped waistcoat and some of his suits had even come from Huntsman's, the most expensive tailor in Savile Row. Within hours of his arrival he had all the silver out of the silver safe and was busy checking and polishing. Then he went down to inspect the cellars and took a very dim view, especially of my champagne. 'No proper air-conditioning – you'll need to put that right.'

For serving at the table he wore white gloves, which I thought was odd. 'What's wrong with that?' said Marcella. 'All butlers in

---

* Private Secretary to Harold Macmillan.

Europe wear them.' 'Well, English butlers don't.'

My sister Sarah was also surprised when he served the wrong way round the table. The only explanation I could think of was that: 'He's been working for a retired industrialist in Birmingham. After his wife died it probably didn't matter which way round he went, and he must have forgotten the form.'

The dailies didn't take to him, and when we asked why the answer was, 'Oh! he's always shuffling backwards and forwards.'

At the time Marcella and I were busy organizing a huge coming-out ball for my daughters, Emily and Georgina. We had to have extra police security, as several members of the Government were coming. Early one morning Edwards stuck his head round the door of the library where I was talking to two uniformed policemen and promptly disappeared. That was the last we saw of him. So I asked the police to check, and that evening they rang back. 'Edwards is one of the most dangerous criminals around. He's known as "the shuffling butler" and has been involved in any number of armed robberies; he's even suspected of being involved in a case of murder; he's had twenty-eight years inside. But he's always unlucky and usually gets caught.'

When the police found him, Edwards asked, 'How did you get on to me?'

'We didn't – we had no idea you were at West Wycombe. We only came to discuss security.'

'Sod me,' said Edwards, 'I could have bluffed it out.'

We had one more try, this time with a young trainee who was very willing but not too reliable. In the early hours of the morning, after the ball, I found him in his tails being chased across the kitchen tables in the catering marquee by two or three burly chefs waving saucepans and making war cries like a pack of Apache Indians in a Western film.

So Marcella gamely trained our dailies to do the work instead. 'If I can lift a table or climb a ladder to dust a bust, so can you.' And they all set to and have, like my secretary Mrs Bird, proved themselves wonderfully adaptable and willing.

The gardens were another problem. We had 47 acres consisting of 15 acres of lawn and about the same of shrubberies and wooded areas, 9 acres of lake with three islands as well as streams and a river, three walled gardens and a large modern greenhouse.

They could easily have swallowed four or five gardeners, so when we took over in 1963 Victoria and I decided to do some replanning and asked Lanning Roper and, later, Russell Page to come and help. Gravel paths were grassed over, grass paths were replaced with stone or brick paving, banks and difficult areas were covered with periwinkle, hypericum, cotoneaster and lamium. In the greenhouse we subsequently concentrated on large pot plants for the house, azaleas, bilbergias, Birds of Paradise, camellias, clivias, hippeastrums, orange trees, orchids, sparmannia stephanotis and urn plants, as well as some rare exotics, many of which came from Marcella's greenhouse at her previous home in Sussex. We also invested in the latest labour-saving equipment, including a weed-cutting boat, a motorized sprayer, a leaf sweeper and semi-automatic watering in the greenhouse.

Marcella is a remarkably fast worker with a considerable knowledge of gardening, so I leave the wall gardens and shrubberies to her and concern myself mainly with the landscape garden, the lake and the greenhouse. We employ only one young gardener, who is highly adaptable and skilled in a remarkable variety of activities. At peak periods, when the weed has to be cleared from the lake or the grass is at maximum growth, he has some extra help. Now the whole place looks immaculate and delightful, especially when the snowdrops and daffodils, of which we have planted 100,000 are in flower; at such times we open the gardens to raise funds for various charities.

Farming is, of course, the main activity on the estate, but there are a great many others. Besides the Caves, which is the most successful financially, there are squash racquets courts, football and cricket grounds, an elaborate network of footpaths and riding trails to provide better access to the country, and a riding school. There is also drag hunting, when bloodhounds chase a man pulling a foul-smelling stocking over a ten-mile course with 30 or 40 jumps for the horses and riders to negotiate, trout fishing in the lake and river, and shooting of pheasant, partridge and duck. The shooting is mainly organized through syndicates, although I do have a small private shoot for which I use horse-drawn carriages instead of motor vehicles for moving the guns around.

These days I am as concerned as any landowner or farmer must be at the decline in agriculture being brought about by over-production in the Western world. This situation seems likely to continue to deteriorate, and farmers could suffer disastrously if massive increases of output occur as a result of recent developments in the United States, where the cloning of wheat can triple the output of grain and injecting dairy cows can dramatically increase milk yields. This must mean much more land going out of production in Britain, and we are therefore contemplating diversifying into other activities, such as a shooting school, dry skiing and a toboggan run. Being so close to London and the City, as well as to Heathrow airport, West Wycombe is ideally placed, so whatever the problems here I am not unduly pessimistic about the future.

The great joy is living in a house with such a happy atmosphere, and I hope it will continue to be the family home of the Dashwoods for many years to come.

WEST WYCOMBE

11

The House

WEST WYCOMBE is not a vast country house like Blenheim Palace, Woburn Abbey or Chatsworth. With its separate wing it never had more than about seventy rooms, and I had half of that wing demolished in 1950 and the other half converted into a squash racquets club and estate offices, so the house is now reduced to about forty rooms. But what it so fortuitously lacks in size is more than made up for by the elegance of the architecture and the beauty of the interior.

The ground floor has a large hall with marbled columns and walls which leads into a series of magnificent reception rooms; their ceilings were copied from those in Roman palaces such as the Farnese, widely considered the quintessence of sixteenth-century décor, and from fragments from the third-century ruins at Palmyra near Damascus.

Upstairs is the beautiful Library, with breathtaking views over the lake and garden; we use this as our principal living room. At the top of the house is a vast room, known as the Masonic Room, which was designed for secret meetings in the eighteenth century. In the centre of the ceiling is a circle filled with a variety of different instruments in plaster used for surveying, cartography and architecture; they include compasses, protractors, rulers, a quadrant, a telescope and a circumferentor (an instrument used mainly by mine surveyors for taking or measuring horizontal angles) with a fleur-de-lis.

The first view of the house as one comes up the drive is the massive entrance portico which was erected in 1771; it was copied from the ancient temple of Bacchus at Teos near Smyrna and is one of the most important buildings of the Greek revival in England. Inside the portico stands, appropriately, a massive statue of Bacchus next to the front door of the house.

The original entrance, however, which is on the south side of the house, is even more impressive for it is in the centre of a double colonnade which stretches almost the length of the house. The Colonnade is the most distinctive and original feature of West Wycombe. The top columns are Corinthian and those beneath are Doric, and at each end, as well as in some of the ceiling panels, there are colourful frescoes by the Italian artists who were employed here in the eighteenth century.

The frescoes in the ceiling show scenes of amorous and cavorting cherubs; they are particularly well preserved and have undergone little restoration, whereas those on the end walls, especially that at the east end which represents the Fountain of Diana, have suffered much damage – partly, I regret to say, because I used to bounce balls against them when I was a boy.

Sir Francis, the 2nd Baronet, toyed in 1739 with the idea of pulling down the red brick Georgian house built by his father in about 1700, but decided instead to remodel it. He was greatly influenced by the designs of the famous sixteenth-century Italian architect, Andrea Palladio, and was also encouraged by his uncle, John Earl of Westmorland, who in 1719 had employed Colen Campbell to build Mereworth Castle in Kent – a replica of the most splendid of Palladio's villas, the Villa Rotonda, which stands on a hill just outside Vicenza.

This, together with the brilliant achievements of Lord Burlington at Burlington House and Chiswick, virtually launched the Palladian movement which had been introduced earlier by Inigo Jones into England and is, therefore, one of the most important landmarks in the history of architecture in this country.

Sir Francis did not entrust the alterations to his father's Georgian house to any one architect, as he wanted to put into practice his own ideas which he no doubt discussed with equally discerning and

Plan of the entrance portico by Nicholas Revett, 1770.

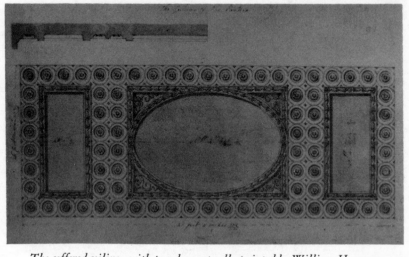

The coffered ceiling, with panels eventually painted by William Hannan.

knowledgeable friends in the Dilettanti Society; this accounts for the multitude of plans submitted by various hands. Three men can be singled out, however. The first was the French architect of whom Sir Francis wrote to the Dilettanti Society in 1752, 'my rascally French architect who has left nothing but debts.' He has recently been identified as Niccolo Servandoni. Another Frenchman was also involved, Morise Lewes Jolivet; he signed a survey of the house and gardens in 1752 but I have been unable to discover anything about him, although there was a Jolivet working for Le Nôtre at Versailles earlier in the century. Servandoni was followed by John Donowell who was working here in 1755 and had been one of Lord Burlington's draughtsmen at Chiswick. Donowell claimed responsibility for the north and south fronts. He was fired in 1764 and went to work for the Marquis of Salisbury at Hatfield House. Finally there was Nicholas Revett, who was responsible for the West Portico and most of the temples and bridges, especially during the last twenty years or so up to Sir Francis's death in 1781.

The north front and the East Portico were completed by 1753, but the south front posed a problem and took longer, for it consisted of a long façade with a small central entrance loggia between two wings which jutted out at each end. Numerous alternative schemes were submitted until finally Sir Francis hit on the brilliant idea of connecting the two ends with the 112-feet long two-tiered Colonnade. This was inspired partly by the façade of the Church of St Sulpice in Paris, built by Servandoni in 1732 (which in turn, owed much to Sir Christopher Wren's façade for St Paul's Cathedral in London), and partly by other Palladian buildings with tiers of colonnades in Venice and in Vicenza.

The original front door, which had an impressive stone surround surmounted by a griffon, my family's crest, was removed and re-erected at the Temple of the Winds east of the house in 1759, and both top and bottom colonnades were furnished with a mixture of Roman and eighteenth-century heads on brackets fixed to the walls and on wooden pedestals painted to look like genuine porphyry.

The beautiful marble statue lying on a couch always intrigues visitors as on close inspection it can be seen to be half-man,

Early designs for the Colonnade front, c. 1750. The top one may have been by Sir Francis himself; the others were by John Donowell.

half-woman and is, in fact, a copy of the famous Hermaphrodite in the Palatine Museum in Rome, described by Lady Townsend as 'the only happy couple I ever saw.' It is now thought that this may be the original marble copy which was made for Versailles in 1679–80 but which disappeared soon afterwards.

THE GREAT HALL

The entrance for visitors to the house is through a door in the centre of the lower Colonnade. This leads directly into the Great Hall.

The Hall was created in 1770 by knocking down the walls on either side of the original small entrance hall; with its scagliola columns and walls it was intended to simulate the atrium or courtyard of a grand Roman villa. The ceiling was copied from fragments of the ruined Temple of Bel at Palmyra near Damascus which had been built in the second or third century AD and had been carefully measured and drawn by Robert Wood and published in his *Ruins of Palmyra* in 1752.

When Victoria and I took over the house from my father in 1963, the hall had dark brown walls hung with huge paintings and a dark oak floor. However, we knew that my grandfather had covered the original floor with oak boards from trees which he had had cut from our woods at Downley near High Wycombe, so we had the centre boards lifted and underneath we found intact a beautiful centrepiece in black and white marble as well as several sections of the original Portland and red stone floor which had a Greek key pattern surround. Beneath the Portland slabs were two ducts, one for conducting hot smoke up from the furnaces in the cellars and the other, which ran alongside it, for conveying clean warm air up through small grilles in the floor into the Hall. This was the remains of a remarkable eighteenth-century underfloor warm-air heating system which was based on the Roman hypocaust found by the antiquary Dr William Stukely at Lincoln in 1740.

Whilst this restoration was going on, Victoria urged me to try cleaning off the dirty marks left by the picture frames on the walls. So, with wire wool, cotton wool, methylated spirits and turpentine, I started, rather grudgingly, to clean a small area. After an hour or so, the brown colour started to move and underneath I found, to my astonishment, colours of the most delicate shades. So with the help of our Austrian butler, Fritz Doppler, and estate painter, Charles Syred, we spent the following six months cleaning the whole of this vast Hall to reveal the most exquisite fresco marbling beneath.

We had also discovered ten brass studs in the walls in line with the tops of the doorways and found, in the furniture list of 1781, that there had been ten busts on brackets against the walls and five more over the doorways. The brackets had all gone but the busts, mainly of Roman emperors, still stood on top of the door achitraves, three to a door. So new brackets to a William Kent design, produced by John Fowler, were made by Jacksons and the busts of Caesar and other Roman emperors replaced in their original positions.

My father told me that he used to play rounders in the Hall using an old Chinese vase as a base. In 1921 he sent the vase, together with much priceless furniture, to Sotheby's to sell. It turned out to be a K'Hangsi one and fetched the then enormous sum of £4600. My father was so amazed that he pushed off to the Ritz to down champagne with my step-grandfather, Captain Alec Fraser, whilst suites of Chippendale chairs and other wonderful furniture went for a song.

The Hall is full of busts of the men who figured most prominently in the rebuilding of West Wycombe: Lord Cobham, the builder of Stowe, Lord Westmorland, Sir Francis and, appropriately, Palladio himself. The two marble sphinxes represent Sir Francis and his wife, Sarah, and must have been carved in about 1740 after Sir Francis's tour of the Ottoman Empire. The marble bust of Lord Sandwich was until recently outside on the Colonnade. It had been painted black.

The bust of Giuseppe Borgnis was originally in the Mausoleum but I removed it to stop it disintegrating. Borgnis came from Italy, at Sir Francis's instigation, with his son Giovanni and carried out much of the decorative work in the house and church. He died at West Wycombe in 1761, reputedly from a fall from scaffolding which had been engineered by jealous English rivals, and was buried in the Mausoleum; his son continued working here and lived in a small house with a studio outside Marlow built by his father in 1753.

The finest bust of all is a marble one by Roubiliac which is thought to represent the great William Pitt, Earl of Chatham.

Another noteworthy feature of the Hall is the very beautiful staircase of Spanish mahogany inlaid with satinwood and with walnut bannisters, the work of a highly skilled joiner or cabinet maker. It is similar to other marquetry work in the house, the dado in the Music Saloon and the bookcases in the Study, and I am inclined to think it was by the painter William Hannan who was employed here from 1749 and died at West Wycombe in about 1775. Hannan was described as a 'Scottish cabinet maker who showed such aptitude for painting that he was encouraged to take up painting by his patron.'

On the walls of the staircase are frescoes copied from those by Raphael in the loggie at the Vatican and by Carracci and Domenichino in the Palazzo Farnese; they show, amongst others, Angerona, the goddess of silence, beckoning with a hand to her lips, the temptation of Eve, and Abimelech finding his wife Rebecca being embraced by Isaac – a curious mixture of motifs for anyone going upstairs to bed!

THE KING'S ROOM

The State Bedchamber, which we now call the King's Room, was intended as a bedroom for members of the Royal Family; it was probably used by Frederick, Prince of Wales, and by King George III. The furniture included a very fine leather chest, brass-studded with Royal crowns, and the magnificent Chippendale state bed which had gilded pineapples on the top corners and was covered in pale blue silk. In those days the state bed was frequently the most valuable piece of furniture in a house. During the nineteenth century the room was used as a small dining room and the state bed was stored upstairs in the Masonic Room. The bed was sold at Sotheby's in 1921 for £58 and the chest for £85.

My grandfather had thought of closing down the servants' wing, which must have been most inconvenient as the kitchen was 70 yards from the main dining room and food had to be carried along a stone-floored passage known as 'The Tube', through several doors and across three halls. He also had a plan to improve the maids' bedrooms at the top of the house by inserting dormer windows, and to add a small service wing next to the King's Room, matching the bathroom wing which he had already added to the opposite end of the house. But nothing further came of this rather sensible idea, for he died suddenly in 1908.

When it came to my father's turn to tackle the problem in 1926, he opted for a relatively simple and inexpensive solution. The servants' wing or 'old wing' was closed down, the kitchen was converted into a squash racquets court and the King's Room became the new kitchen; the green silk was stripped from the walls, the ceiling was covered in white paint and the eighteenth-century fireplace was removed and replaced with a cooking range. A hatch was punched through into the Palmyra Room which was divided up to form a servants' hall and a telephone room with a long dark passage connecting the pantry with the Great Hall, and the marbled walls were given liberal coatings of cream oil paint.

This arrangement was obviously a great improvement but food still had to be carried a fair distance from the hatch along the passage and across the Great Hall to the dining room.

So in 1950, on my return from America, where I had seen many well-designed modern kitchens, I suggested converting the scullery into a small kitchen and restoring the King's Room into a dining room. Although my father did not really like the idea, he eventually gave his approval and instructed the clerk of works to see if the paint could be removed from the ceiling to reveal the original décor. The clerk of works reported that it could not be done. So, one evening, when my father had gone out to dinner with his friend Dr Hugh Jones, I carried in the long ladder used for reaching the lights in the squash court, and started cleaning a circular panel in one corner with wire wool and methylated spirits whilst my mother held the ladder. After about an hour of hard rubbing, followed by cleaning with turpentine and cotton wool, a beautifully painted basket of flowers began to show and proved to be completely undamaged. My father must have suspected that something was brewing because he suddenly popped his head round the door, although it was only 9 p.m. and his dinners usually lasted until much later. He was, of course, very annoyed, but my mother eventually persuaded him to allow the work to proceed. So scaffolding was erected, and she spent the rest of the year with the help of a picture restorer, Miss Mavis McKnight, uncovering the rest of this beautiful ceiling with its panels depicting cherubs floating among the clouds and swags of flowers all surrounded by gilded enrichments.

My mother even studied how to gild and regilded much of the original stucco, as it was almost impossible to remove the white paint. She then had the walls covered in an elegant green paper, not unlike the original silk; with Dutch still-life paintings on the walls and a light yellow carpet, the effect was very pretty.

When Victoria and I took over the house in 1963, we recovered the painted chimney piece which my father had transferred to Chipps, the Queen Anne house to which he had moved in 1946, and I asked John Fowler* to help us.

* In England and America between 1930 and 1970, John Fowler was unequalled in his knowledge of English country house interiors with their supremely elegant and relaxed look and in the use of old wallpapers, silks and chintzes which he had discovered through the most painstaking research and documentation.

For the King's Room, we had already determined to hang six glorious paintings of West Wycombe in 1781 by Thomas Daniell which were seldom seen as they were hanging in a spare bedroom. These were Daniell's most important commission before 1785 when he left for India, where he and his nephew William were to make their names through their paintings of Indian scenes. They are my favourite pictures in the house and we frequently study them to check features in the park. Russell Page, who helped us so much in the landscape garden, paid particular attention to them as they showed the original siting and species of shrubs and trees, and he encouraged Victoria and me to visit Kew Gardens to try to find similar species for replanting.

We had also found a piece of very beautiful and finely carved architrave in a cupboard upstairs and thought that it belonged to the room. John Fowler said, 'Of course, it must be part of the door surround. You'll have to have it properly copied and put back.' As this was obviously going to be very expensive, I asked the foreman of the firm restoring the roof if he could have the satinwood and mahogany key pattern copied in plaster and then painted. Luckily, when he was walking round the house with the piece of architrave he bumped into the gardener-handyman who said, 'What on earth are you doing with that – there's feet of it in the roof of my workshop. It's been there ever since I have.' Round we rushed and found all the magnificent surrounds, not only for the door but also for the windows, as well as the strips of gilded wood used for battening the silk to the walls.

Finally the room was redecorated in a wonderful shade of dragged tangerine, skilfully mixed by Cyril Wopshott under John Fowler's directions.

We use the King's Room now as a dining room, except in the summer when we have lunch on the Colonnade or when we have large lunch or dinner parties and use the Palmyra Room instead.

THE TAPESTRY ROOM

This was originally the dressing room for the State Bedchamber or King's Room and seems to have been redecorated in about 1766. John Fowler considered it the best example of a room of that date in England.

The richly decorated doorways, frieze, dado and chimney piece in shades of salmon pink picked out with gold are almost unequalled, as so much ornamentation in other houses was overpainted in the nineteenth and twentieth centuries.

The ceiling, which is derived from panels in the loggie of the Vatican, is by William Hannan after drawings by Francesco Bartoli which are now in the Library at Eton College.

The walls are covered in Flemish tapestry which was made by Josse de Voss c.1710 and cut to fit the room. The tapestries depict scenes of a 'Game of Bowls', the 'Return from Harvest' and the 'Fish Market', and are identical to other sets belonging to Lord Digby at Minterne and Lord Stair at Stranraer. It is possible that all these sets were presented to his generals by the Duke of Marlborough after his victorious campaign in the Netherlands and that the West Wycombe ones belonged to the Earl of Westmorland, who was Paymaster-General of the Army.

When I had the tapestries removed for cleaning and repair, we found signs of extensive fire damage in the timbers of the east wall, so this and the Yellow Room were possibly the two rooms which caught fire in 1765.

Sir Francis was deeply concerned over the danger of fire, especially as two houses in the village had been destroyed by fire in 1756. As a precaution he had sheets of copper laid beneath the entire first floor of the house and covered the top Colonnade with it too. For sound-proofing, the space between the copper sheeting and the ceiling below was packed with sawdust.

Benjamin Franklin was so impressed by Sir Francis's use of copper sheeting that, in 1770, he encouraged its use in Philadelphia since the wooden colonial houses were very prone to catch fire, quoting the covering of the floor of the top Colonnade at West Wycombe with copper sheeting as 'one of the few instances only' in England of such a practice.

A few years later, on 9 July 1774, Sir Francis decided to test the system. Two rooms were set alight 'in the old part of the house' (this part) and the experiment, possibly the first public test of the system, proved a great success. Thomas Hartley, an MP, who was closely involved with the project, attended the West Wycombe experiment and subsequently patented the system.

Unfortunately all this sheeting had to be cut away in 1964 to permit inspection of the timber joists and removal of the sawdust which was used for sound-proofing since it tended to encourage dry rot, especially where there was any damp. So I am no longer so sanguine about the fire hazard.

The Tapestry Room was my mother's writing room, and it was the only drawing room left for our use during the war as the others were all occupied for wartime purposes.

THE PALMYRA ROOM

In the nineteenth century this room was used as a billiard room and the original marble floor was probably ripped out by my grandfather.

Victoria and I had the partition walls, which my father had built to enclose the servants' hall and telephone room, knocked down in 1963. The estate painter, Charlie Syred, managed to remove all the whitewash covering the painted ceiling to reveal the original décor in grey, brown and maroon, and the circular centre piece in shades of grey and black derived from Woods's drawings of a sepulchre at Palmyra. We tried to remove the thick layers of oil paint from the walls but it proved too difficult, so we gave up and had the walls freshly marbled by a specialist firm, Roffés.

The room continued to irritate me, however, so after Victoria died in 1976, and as a sort of therapy, I decided to have another go at the walls and floor. Fortunately a local painter, Ken Small, found a paint stripper with which he removed most of the thick oil paint. On the frieze he uncovered the honeysuckle theme from Palmyra and on the walls the most colourful frescoed marbling; but the paint removal process had inevitably done much damage. So John Fowler arranged for Jean Hornak to carry out the restoration work and Jean, her son Mark and Marya Farr stayed for nearly six months that winter. What a relief it was to return home from the City and have dinner with them rather than alone in a sad and empty house! They did a brilliant job and restored this unique and richly coloured fresco which has an orange-red base overlaid with veining in green, brown and blue. The recesses in the window frames were in pseudo lapis lazuli, the door frames in white marbling with black veins and the skirting in black and gold marbling.

Having gone so far I decided to restore the marble floor, but when the wooden boards were lifted we found no trace of the original floor — only a mass of sheep bones which had been laid down apparently to keep the floor dry. Beneath were the arched tops of three cellars which we didn't know existed. I had a hole punched through the top of one but all we could see was a large empty cellar. We could not take more time to explore the others as the next day I had to leave for Australia and the ready-mix concrete was due to arrive. So a new floor was laid, of red Wilderness and Portland stone with a centrepiece of black, white and yellow Sienna marble, copied from the marble one in the church and with a Greek key pattern as in the Hall, designed by Ross Britain.

All this work was, of course, expensive, so to finance it I decided to sell a very fine second-century Greek bronze head which Sir Francis had bought and which had never been much noticed.

The pictures in this room, by Adrien Carpentiers and George Knapton, are particularly interesting. On the north wall are the portraits of members of the Divan Club in frames surmounted with turbans. (Qualification for membership of the Divan Club was to have visited the Ottoman Empire.) On the east wall are two more portraits of Sir Francis, as Pope Pontius VIII toasting a statue of Venus, also by Carpentiers, and as Postmaster-General painted in

1776 by Nathaniel Dance; in the latter he holds a book which looks like the Book of Common Prayer which he and Benjamin Franklin produced for use in the Church of England.

Apart from the pictures, mirrors and chairs, the rest of the furniture was bought by me — the chandelier from Mrs Ionides at Buxted Park, the Chippendale pedestals from Lulworth Castle, the mahogany side tables by Giles Gendrey from Chandos House, the gilded consoles with yew tops from Mrs FitzGerald at Heathfield Park, and the George III screen from Lord Burnham at Hall Barn. The two candelabra by Thomire I found standing on the floor of an antique shop behind the Sacher Hotel in Vienna in 1969.

I have not, however, replaced the statue of the two wrestlers which stood at the west end of this room behind the porphyry columns. It was stored up 'The Tube' until 1951 when, unfortunately, I took it down to the Caves where it disintegrated.

THE YELLOW ROOM

This was the dining room until 1952 when my mother finished restoring the King's Room from a kitchen back to a small dining room as it had been for most of the nineteenth century.

My earliest memory of it is when my sister Sarah and I, after lunch in the nursery, were made to dress in our smartest clothes to salute the guests. We were ushered in by one of the footmen in maroon tailcoats and black and gold striped waistcoats, and after a curtsey from Sarah and a bow from me, we had to say 'Bonjour Messieurs' and 'Bonjour Mesdames' and then go round the table shaking hands or getting a pat on the head — quite an ordeal.

As we grew older we had our meals at a separate table for 'la jeunesse' in a corner by the window. One of our ploys was to stare at my grandmother when the strawberries, freshly picked from the garden, were being handed round to embarrass her from taking too many as then there would be none left for us.

During the war the dining room became a sort of restaurant for all the people staying in the house. Wartime rations were very small, and we resorted to eating coots and moorhens which were cooked in aspic and served cold. On one occasion we even decided to shoot a swan. My brother John and I thought it rather unsporting to shoot one on the water so our old keeper, Low, chased them round in a punt until they took off over the waterfall, below which John and I were stationed. Luckily we got one, but we then had to pluck it which took most of the day and filled two large bags with feather and down. The following week I invited a party of friends from Eton and we sat down in the dining room and ate the whole swan.

Soon after this, in 1942, the dining room was taken over to house Sir Robert Witt's collection and we resorted to having our meals in the servants' hall, the only room left on the ground floor besides the small Tapestry Room.

When the war ended, the whole house became empty and had a very rundown appearance. The red silk brocade on the walls of the dining room was in tatters, so my mother, in her indomitable way, set about restoring it. She persuaded her wartime working party of village ladies, Mrs Harris, Mrs Woodward, Mrs Herman and other volunteers who had been sewing and knitting socks and pyjamas for the troops, to tackle this mammoth task. First of all, the torn and rotten material had to be gently washed in a soapy liquid made from a common garden weed called saponaria (from the Latin for soap). Lady Meade-Featherstonehaugh had discovered the recipe and had been using it for her monumental restoration work at Uppark in Sussex, but she refused to divulge the secret without receiving a royalty. So my mother advertized in *The Times* and got it from another source. Then the washed silk was laboriously tacked on to a canvas backing, set up on rollers in the Library. Eventually one half of the long wall opposite the windows was completed and rehung.

When our turn came in 1965 to deal with this room, all the silk had been removed as the whole of the plaster cornice of the north wall had to be taken down so that steel beams could be inserted to support the floor of the Library above. The bare walls showed clearly not only the marks where the pictures had been before the silk brocade was hung in 1854 but also the earlier colour of the walls – a light grey with undercoats of olive green followed by pale blue.

It was the usual practice in the eighteenth century only to plaster walls which were going to be painted. When silk or chintz was to be used, wooden battens were fixed straight to the bare brickwork. At West Wycombe this treatment was used in the King's Room and Red Drawing Room, which were intended to be hung with silk, and upstairs in the principal bedroom where chintz was used; the rest of the rooms were all painted.

So we decided to forget about the red silk which was in shreds and too rotten to restore, and I had the few better pieces made into cushions for the Red Drawing Room, partly to record my mother's valiant efforts. The problem was to choose the right colour for the walls. I wanted to copy a brilliant yellow from the dress of one of the goddesses on the ceiling, the National Trust committee wanted a Sienna yellow to match the marble surround of the fireplace and doorway, and John Fowler a pale yellow silk. We tried the Sienna but it looked dreadful against the chestnut and satinwood dado so Hal Baxby (who had begun his career in decorative painting with John Fowler) painted the walls a startling yellow. It certainly gave the room life and colour, which it needed, but it was not until Nancy Lancaster suggested glazing the walls, as she had done in her fabulous drawing room over her shop, Colefax and Fowler, in London, that the result for which I was aiming was achieved.

Nancy gave me invaluable advice, too, over the dado, window frames and shutters, which had been painted to look like satinwood and chestnut. 'Leave them as they are – everyone's having their dados and woodwork done in different shades of white – so boring – and this is exceptional and so beautifully done.' So I left it alone.

Today the room is more or less as it was in the eighteenth century, apart from the painted woodwork and the window glass with its coloured roundels designed by Lady Dashwood from drawings in a book which she dedicated to the Queen in 1797; it still has the ceiling by Borgnis representing the 'Council of the Gods and the admission of Psyche to the celebrated hierachy', after Raphael's in the Villa Farnesina in Rome; the magnificent marble chimney piece with Androcles and the Lion by Henry Cheere; the matching door frame by Thomas Carter surmounted by the marble bust of the Earl of Westmorland in 1739 by Thomas Ady, sculptor to the Dilettanti Society; and the four marble Seasons by Laurent Delvaux, 1731, which came from Sir Richard Ellys's collection at Nocton via his widow, Sarah.

The pictures look very grand but are not of the same quality as the furniture and statuary, apart from a fine Genoese nobleman by Andrea Sacchi and two views of Rome by Orizonte.

There is, however, one interesting picture in this room, of the poet John Milton. It was noted in Langley's *History of Bucks* in 1797 as 'Milton – fine, said to be an original', and must have come from Sarah Moore whom Sir John Dashwood-King married in 1761. She was the granddaughter of Milton's sister, Ann Agar, and inherited most of the Moore family's property in Chertsey as well as all their chattels, and these would certainly have included any paintings belonging to Ann Agar of her famous brother.

THE RED DRAWING ROOM

We used this room as our main living room before and after the war. It was then called the Brown Drawing Room as my mother had had it decorated with beige walls and orange-brown curtains edged with silver embroidery.

John Fowler was determined to have it painted in dragged pink with yellow curtains, a theme which he had used very successfully in other houses. Victoria was against the idea. 'We've already got enough pink; the Music Saloon has pink with gold curtains, the Blue Drawing Room has yellow curtains, the Study is to be pink and so is my bedroom – I don't want any more.' John insisted, however, so pink it became. But it did not look right even with all the pictures hung. So the pink was shaded, then it was glazed and this process was repeated two or three times, with the pictures going up and down like yoyos until Victoria finally burst into tears and refused to have anything more to do with it.

One of the earlier inventories indicated that the room had been covered in red, and a small tuft of deep red silk which I found in one of the door hinges confirmed this. Shortly afterwards I was sauntering along South Molton Street and happened to see some red silk draped over a chair in Mann and Fleming's shop near the Connaught Hotel. I went in and had a closer look: the colour and pattern seemed just right and later proved to be identical to the silk from the walls of the dining room. So I said, 'If you've got enough of that silk and can do the job in time for my wife's birthday in six weeks, I'll order it.' It turned out that they had 80 metres in stock and the room needed 76. Bumping of course had first to be fixed to the original battens, then the silk was hung and edged with gold battens. With the pictures all hung the room looked superb, and Victoria was delighted with the result.

Soon after this, John Fowler returned to advise on other rooms. 'I must look at my pink drawing room; it must be splendid with the yellow curtains.' As I didn't want to upset him and have a scene, it was imperative to stop him seeing the red silk. I told him, 'The floor is full of death-watch beetle and is very unsafe; no one is allowed in.' Of course he didn't believe me and tried the handles of both doors, which I had taken care to lock, so he eventually gave up and we continued round the rest of the house.

In fact the floorboards were rather loose and furniture used to wobble when anyone entered the room, causing lights to flicker, so I asked one of my carpenters to take up the boards and find out what was wrong. He soon came back: 'The floor joists are riddled with death-watch beetle; luckily it does not seem to be active but the boards all need taking up and the joists replacing.' Such an idea filled me with horror – it meant removing all the pictures and furniture and making a fearful mess. So I told him to treat the beetle and to screw the boards down again and forget about it.

The National Trust recently decided that the floor could not be left in this state, so in 1986 it was decided to renew all the joists and replace the original floorboards. This turned out to be a much more difficult job than one might have supposed, as beneath the joists was a thick layer of pugging, a material composed of clay and mortar which was a very effective insulating medium used in the eighteenth century. The worst problem was the dust caused in removing it, which spread throughout the house and with which my poor wife Marcella had to cope.

The ceiling of this room, which shows nymphs bathing, was painted by William Hannan and consists of a series of colourful panels with classical figures and with two insets: the *Sleeping Cupid* from the Palazzo Barberini and a fragment from Caesar Augustus's house in Rome found in 1737 by the antiquary Dr Mead who lived nearby in Aylesbury.

Besides decorating much of the interior of the house, Hannan was commissioned to paint four views of the house and gardens which were engraved by William Woollett and printed in 1754 by John Tinney. They must have sold readily because Hannan's pupils were put to copying the four originals, most of which are now scattered round the country. These paintings are very colourful, and of particular interest as they were painted over a period of three or four years and show the changes which took place in the house and the landscape at that time.

The best pieces of furniture in this room are the commodes and the brass-studded jewel chest. The commodes were considered to be of no great interest and little value until research by Anthony Coleridge of Christie's revealed that they had been made in the 1760s by Pierre Langlois, a leading cabinet maker who had come from France to England and was commissioned to make similar commodes for George III, the Duke of Bedford, the Marquess of Zetland and others.

The jewel chest always fascinated me as a boy. It has a secret catch and a false bottom, as well as lots of hidden compartments. At the top of each side there is a tiny piece of sliding inlay beneath which is a long screw used for clamping the chest firmly down to stop it being stolen.

This chest is identical to one in America which belonged to Elihu Yale, the British agent for the East India Company in Madras in the 1680s. Yale University was named after him in gratitude for his gift of goods which fetched £800 and was the largest donation at that critical moment. The key of my chest actually fits the Yale one. So perhaps this chest was in the consignment of furniture from Madras over which the first Sir Francis had a dispute with Elihu Yale in 1704.

One of my treasured possessions is a little porcelain cream jug which was made at Meissen and has a painting of Hannan's finest view of the house and lake with the frigate riding at anchor. It was found by Major Arthur Ladenberg, an old friend and antique dealer who lived in the Apple Orchard in the village and was always on the lookout on my behalf for china and furniture which had originally been here.

The most interesting of the other pictures in this room is the one over the fireplace by Bartolomeo Nazari; it shows figures in a ship's cabin off the coast of Genoa and is thought to commemorate the founding of the Dilettanti Society in 1732.

THE STUDY

My father made this room his den after the war and created a cosy atmosphere here, in spite of the unattractive oak shelves which he had erected for his books. He also installed a gramophone behind the door into the Blue Drawing Room, underneath which he stored his supply of drink which was severely limited by rationing. A drinks cabinet was also kept in the Hall; on Fridays, before the weekend guests arrived, the butler used to remove all the whisky, gin and sherry from the cabinet so that only the guest privileged to be invited into the Study got a drink. Another economy measure was the installation of a pay telephone in the telephone room for the use of guests and children, the only direct lines being to my mother's bedroom and also one from the Study which went through the Estate Office's switchboard.

The Study was the only room in which I gave John Fowler a free hand, and the stippled red walls with the matching curtains are very elegant and effective.

Recently, when the ceiling was being restored, the National Trust agreed to decorate the frieze which was plain but may originally have had a decorated motif in paper. Marcella and I chose a design from amongst a set of six in the Library which had been produced by James Gandon in 1767, and this has been brilliantly reproduced by John Dives.

The early eighteenth-century mirror in *verre eglomisé*, with the Dashwood coat of arms and the initials MJD, for Mary Jennings Dashwood, came to us by a stroke of luck. Barbara Hutton, the Woolworth heiress, had lent it to the American Ambassador, John Wynant, for the Embassy at Winfield House in London. She decided to sell it back to Mallett's, the antique dealers, in 1965 and they immediately offered it to me. It must originally have been hung in the Study, as the furniture list of 1781 describes 'a Chimney Glass 3 plates ornamented with a Coat of Arms' over the mantelpiece. I didn't feel I could afford it but my solicitor, Lord Nathan, said, 'Why don't you sell some of those dreary Dutch still-lifes which I seem to remember in the dining room. You really should get the mirror back.' Which is precisely what I did, and how right he was.

Another find was a mass of architectural drawings wrapped up in brown paper in the Library. The best of these I had framed and hung in my bedroom, and John Fowler had the remainder framed for the Study. The collection is of great significance for West Wycombe; it shows a wide range of the architectural proposals for the house and temples by various architects and also includes a number of the actual working drawings which the builder himself used – a rare feature.

Initially Sir Francis seems to have tried his own hand and drew one or two elevations in 1739. Several are by a French hand and the others are by various architects, including Robert Adam for the West Portico and kitchens and Roger Morris for the north and south elevations. The majority, however, are by John Donowell and Nicholas Revett.

Amongst this collection of drawings are ones for a small fort, a 'Turkish Chiosk' and a Turkish mosque and two gondola-like boats; some of these were actually built, although no traces of them survive.

The two bookcases in this room were sold in 1921 but I managed to buy them back in 1983 from the Metropolitan Museum in New York. The marquetry doors beneath them have similar inlay to those in the Music Saloon and on the staircase, and must be by the same hand.

I had another stroke of luck when I found a leather trunk covered in brass studs with the Royal crown in Christopher Hodsal's shop in Pimlico. It was made for George II and is similar to the one which used to be in the King's Room and which was sold in 1921.

So this is now my Study where most of this book has been written.

THE BLUE DRAWING ROOM

This is Marcella's and my favourite drawing room. The blue flock walls and the yellow-gold curtains date from the 1850s. The traditional method of applying flock was by blowing minute pieces of velvet on to an adhesive with bellows. This flock was very badly worn and had to be replaced, but it was really out of the question to adopt the original method and I had to have rolls of identical flock paper made instead.

My mother had tried to save the brocade curtains by tacking them to a backing but they were too rotten to last, so I had the best pieces removed and made into cushions for the sofa and armchairs. For the curtains I managed to find a wonderful matching silk in Bangkok which cost a fraction of the price quoted by other suppliers.

The theme of this room is the Power of Love, in which the wedding of Bacchus and Ariadne, shown on the ceiling, is given pride of place. It was painted in the early 1750s by Giuseppe Borgnis and is a copy of Annibale Carracci's masterpiece the *Triumph of Bacchus and Ariadne* which he painted in about 1600 in the Palazzo Farnese (now the French Embassy) in Rome. It is easily the most colourful and lively of all the ceilings at West Wycombe, with so many naked nymphs and satyrs revelling in the wedding procession.

The sumptuous effect is enhanced by the dazzle of gilded pier glasses and the finest of Georgian furniture, Langlois commodes, Chinese lacquer cabinets and Chippendale tables. And presiding over all this, the statue of Venus de Medici in a niche − evidence of the 2nd Baronet's 'devotion to this paragon of classical beauty'.

It was in this room, known as the Breakfast or Dining Room, that Benjamin Franklin perpetrated one of his famous hoaxes known as the 'King of Prussia Edict'. This is the way Benjamin Franklin described the reaction to the hoax in a letter to his son William in 1773:

I was down at Lord le Despencer's when the post brought the day's papers. Paul Whitehead was there too who runs early through all the papers and tells the company what he finds remarkable. He had them in another room and we were chatting in the breakfast parlor, when he came running into us, out of breath, with the paper in his hand. 'Here,' he says, 'Here's news for ye. Here's the King of Prussia claiming a right to this Kingdom.' All stared, and I as much as any body: And he went on to read it. When he had read two or three paragraphs a gentleman present said 'Damn his impudence; I dare say, we shall hear by next post that he is upon his march with one hundred thousand men to back this. Whitehead, who is very shrewd, soon after began to smoke it, and looking in my face said, 'I'll be hanged if this is not some of your American jokes upon us.' The reading went on, and ended with abundance of laughing, and a general verdict that it was a fair hit: And the piece was cut out of the paper and preserved in my Lord's collection.

The edict purported to be an announcement emanating from Frederick the Great. In solemn, burlesque style it cited the fact that Britain was first settled by Saxon colonies, that it had been decided to raise a revenue from these colonies to defray expenses, and that certain measures had been ordered to be put into execution. These measures were the same as Britain had ordained from America. One such command was: 'That all the thieves, highway and street robbers, housebreakers, forgerers, sodomites, and villaines of every denomination, who have forfeited their lives in Prussia, but whom we in our great clemency do not think fit here to hang, shall be emptied out of our gaols into the said island of Great Britain, for the better peopling of that country.'

At the beginning of the war, my mother used this room for her sewing parties of volunteers from the village. Later it was used for storing part of the Wallace Collection. At weekends the guardians were sometimes persuaded to take out and show us such masterpieces as *The Laughing Cavalier* by Franz Hals, *The Rainbow Landscape* by Rubens or *A Dance to the Music of Time* by Poussin.

In the 1960s the ceiling of the Blue Drawing Room was showing cracks, and it was found that the joists and beams had all rotted at the ends. My grandfather had inserted a vertical steel rod which supported the central beam from the roof trusses above, but complete restoration was now required. So the ceiling was propped up, and the beams and joists were completely removed and replaced with new ones. The lath and plaster of the ceiling was then fixed back to the new joists using hessian soaked in glue and small nails; the cracks were filled and finally the whole ceiling was carefully cleaned. All this was meticulously done by those master craftsmen, Michael and Benjamin Gibbon.

Marcella unearthed a lovely photograph which showed her in a corner of this room in front of the Adam mirrors when she was on a modelling assignment for the *Tatler* in the 1960s. I thought she was absolutely stunning then just as I do now, but never dreamt that we were destined to be married one day.

Now we use the Red and Blue Drawing Rooms for drinks before lunch and dinner parties, as we like to keep all the rooms alive.

THE MUSIC SALOON

This is the grandest room in the house with its coved and painted ceiling and the richly ornamented plasterwork of the frieze and cornice. The centre ceiling panel is a copy of Raphael's *Banquet of the Gods*, and the cove panels are after various frescoes by Carracci. The frieze has bold plasterwork mouldings with stags' heads and bows and arrows mixed with garlands of flowers.

This scene and the one in the Blue Drawing Room are of the greatest significance. Raphael's *Banquet of the Gods*, which he painted in 1518 in the Villa Farnesina, was one of the earliest 'Humanist' painted ceilings using classical mythology as subject matter. Annibale Carracci's ceiling in the Palazzo Farnese, the great palace on the opposite side of the Tiber to the Farnesina, was painted deliberately to challenge comparison with Raphael's, and these two ceilings were the starting point of the baroque ceilings which multiplied all over Italy and southern Europe and finally reached England at the end of the seventeenth century.

By the 1750s, when Sir Francis had the scenes reproduced here, this kind of décor was out of date and about to disappear. It says much of his lively character and independent taste that he chose what he liked and not what was then fashionable, and made Borgnis reproduce the work of masters of the High Renaissance.

Luckily the ceiling is in near-mint condition and no restoration work was required here. I merely stripped off the nineteenth-century pink wallpaper with its gold and black design and was lucky to find ample traces of the original eighteenth-century red ochre. After rubbing down and undercoating with white, it took Hal Baxby precisely three days to paint the walls of this large room, using the spongeing technique which he and John Fowler had learnt as apprentices together.

Originally the window wall of this room was covered in mirrors, two vertical in the piers and three horizontal ones across the tops of the windows to create a glittering appearance like the Great Hall of Mirrors at Versailles. Two tall Chippendale mirrors still stand between the windows, but the three narrow horizontal ones over the windows must have been removed in 1854, when a new frieze was added below the cornice. The mirrors were replaced by the gold brocade curtains which were restored by the Royal School of Needlework in 1966.

The other outstanding features of this room are the marble mantelpiece by Sir Henry Cheere with the four matching columns surmounted with busts of Milton, Locke, Newton and Addison, and the Sienna marble doorcases with plaques showing nymphs riding a dolphin and playing with a ram by a temple. Also notable is the dado inlaid with cherry and satinwood stars and Greek key surrounds.

The furniture is of the same standard. The set of large armchairs and settees are similar to those which the Earl of Shaftesbury sold from St Giles's in 1982, and are now so rare that one hardly dare sit on them.

The pictures, on the other hand, are disappointing. Sir Francis is said to have paid £1500, a vast amount in the eighteenth century, for Rubens's *Poultry Market* which turns out to be by Jan Rombouts and Adriaen van Utrecht; an identical right half is in the Hermitage in Leningrad. Few of the pictures at West Wycombe are outstanding but they do show Sir Francis's intense love of Italian art, and in those days few patrons minded whether what they bought was original; in fact they often spent as much, or even more, on copies since the quality of appreciation was not considered to be diminished thereby. What a sensible attitude! Unfortunately Sir Francis left the selection mainly to Mr Charron of Leghorn; unlike his partner, Mr Lefroy, who concentrated on supplying statuary, Mr Charron was rather a rogue and took advantage of his clients.

Pictures as well as busts, figures and marble slabs were shipped from Genoa regularly in the *Fortune,* which was part-owned by Sir Francis, together with lemons and oranges, Arteminia wine and 'an olive tree for your garden' and, for the return journey, the *Fortune* was loaded with crates of red herrings.

After the war the Music Saloon reverted to being used as a ballroom and it has been the scene of some marvellous dances.

EAST PORTICO

The Music Saloon gives on to the East Portico which was built by 1753. It is an exact reproduction of the porticoes of the two pavilions thought to have been built by Roger Morris for Lord Westmorland at Mereworth Castle in about 1740, and is the most colourful and ornate of the façades of the house.

In the ceiling there is a fresco of Aurora the sun goddess with her chariot, a copy of the Guido Reni in the Palazzo Rospigliosi in Rome. The back wall is decorated in *trompe l'oeil* with two medallions enclosing the heads of Carracci and Correggio. But far the most popular features of this portico are the two lead lions which were probably by John Cheere in about 1770. With children sitting on them, they make a perfect setting for a family photograph.

WEST PORTICO

Originally service buildings were grouped at this end, but they were all swept away in 1770 and this became the main entrance. The original proposals were by Robert Adam, but these were discarded by Sir Francis in favour of a similar scheme which Nicholas Revett produced following his expedition to Asia Minor in 1764–66.

The aim was to build an exact reproduction of the façade of the ruined Temple of Bacchus at Teos near Smyrna. With its giant Ionic columns, massive statue of Bacchus and paintings – the *Chariot of the Night* and, inevitably, *Bacchus and Ariadne* – let into the coffered ceiling, the result was a complete success and is one of the most important examples of neo-classical architecture in England.

Naturally the completion of this portico was too good an

opportunity for a celebration for Sir Francis to miss, and its dedication in September 1771 was fully in keeping with his love of providing amusement and entertainment for his friends, whether at West Wycombe, Medmenham Abbey, Dunston or Hanover Square. Paul Whitehead, poet and member of the Hell-Fire Club, described it thus: a procession of 'Bacchanals, Priests, Priestesses, Pan, Fauns, Satyrs, Silenus, &c. all in proper habits & skins wreathed with vine leaves' made a sacrifice to the statue and then repaired to the lake for more 'Paeans and libations' and 'discharges of cannon' from several boats. The tradition continues, happily, to this day.

THE NORTH FRONT

The elegance of this typical Palladian façade, which was completed in 1753, is eclipsed by the breath-taking view which unfurls to the north. It gives me a thrill every time I look at it, and one of my favourite weekend relaxations is to lie upstairs on the Chippendale day bed in the Library and gaze out of the windows, with classical music playing in the background.

12

The Gardens

As one walks from the house down towards the lake one sees on the hill to the left the glistening golden ball on top of the church tower. The original Norman tower was much lower and had a flagstaff for flying the national ensign on special occasions. In 1740 another storey was added to this tower with a flagstaff to fly the Union Jack. A sailor climbed the flagstaff and lodged his chin on top of it. He then issued a challenge to anyone who would repeat the act and William Rolfe, who lived in the parish, managed to do just that, 'to the great surprise and alarm of the astonished crowd'.

The tower was finally surmounted in 1751 by a golden ball similar to the Ball of Fortune which stands on top of the tower on the island where the Grand Canal and the Giudecca Canal meet in Venice, just across from the quay of San Marco. The ball is 8 feet in diameter and made of wood covered with gold leaf; inside are bench seats which, with a squeeze, can take about six people. Sir Francis used to signal through the portholes by heliograph (a mirror device for reflecting the rays of the sun) to his friend John Norris in an identical tower with a golden ball which the latter had erected at Camberley, 34 miles away – one of the earliest examples of overland signalling by this means. All but the lower half of the Camberley tower, which is in the grounds of a convent, has since disappeared. Norris lived at nearby Hughenden, which was to become Disraeli's home. It was Disraeli who bought the Abbot's chair from Medmenham Abbey, which can still be seen at Hughenden.

Wilkes wrote of the golden ball: 'it is the best globe tavern I was ever in — I admire likewise the silence and secrecy which reigns in that great globe, undisturbed but by his jolly songs very unfit for the profane ears of the world below,' and went on to refer to a meeting which took place there between himself, Sir Francis and Charles Churchill in 1762. The purpose of this particular meeting seems to have been to try to persuade Wilkes and Churchill to drop their campaign against the Ministry in return for any further action against them being suspended. But 'if from perverseness neither of these gentlemen then yielded to his wise reason, nor to his dazzling offers, they were both delighted with his divine milk punch.'

The wooden steps to the hatch in the golden ball have had to be removed because vandals started tearing out the wooden seats, so the ball is now empty.

Sir Francis went on to rebuild the church in imitation of the Temple of Bel at Palmyra. Visitors accustomed to the austere and simple beauty of English Norman interiors are often astounded by the magnificence of this interior with its vast red porphyry columns against yellow ochre walls, its richly ornamented frieze and splendid ceiling in a geometric pattern of circles and hexagons painted to look like plaster; but the atmosphere, especially during evening services when it is lit by candles, is both holy and inspiring.

When the black and white marble floor with a centrepiece in the shape of a twelve-pointed star in yellow Sienna and black marble was laid, the parishioners entered into a covenant not to bury anyone beneath it, and if the floor was ever moved, to return it to Sir Francis.

When we were children my brother and sister and I used to climb the hill to attend Sunday services and would try to put our feet in the sunken footprints which led up the hillside. These were known as the Devil's footprints; when the church was originally being built at the top of the hill, the Devil was reputed to have come at night to take the stones down the hill to the bottom. Modern psychologists assert that this was merely an explanation of a long dispute between those who lived at the top of the hill and those at the bottom. Wilkes cynically remarked of Sir Francis's rebuilding effort: 'the church he has just built on the top of a hill for the convenience and devotion of the town at the bottom of it . . . this is the first church which has ever been built for a prospect. . . . The words "Memento" in immense letters on the Steeple surprised and perplexed me. I could not find the MORI or perhaps MERI from the Practice as well as the Precept of the Noble Lord.' (*Memento mori* means 'Remember you must die' and *Memento meri* 'Do not forget the wine'.)

In the round face of a sundial fixed to the exterior of the south wall of the church were the words 'Keep thy tongue from evil speaking, lying and slandering' – possibly an admonition by Sir Francis to those like Wilkes who sought to blacken his reputation.

To the right of the church lies the vast roofless hexagonal Mausoleum. Its six walls are of dark grey flint with great open arches and massive stone columns. They are, in fact, repetitions of the single archway known as the Temple of Apollo, near the house, which was derived from various antique arches in Rome, such as Constantine's Arch.

The Mausoleum was built with a legacy of £500 left by Bubb Dodington, Lord Melcombe Regis, to 'build an arch or temple at

A view of the lake and gardens in an eighteenth-century etching by William Hannan.

whichever of His Lordship's seats was likely to remain the longest.' It was completed in 1765 at a cost of £495. Besides memorials to members of my family, it also had in the niches the urn with Whitehead's heart and busts of Lord Melcombe Regis, Dr Thompson (George III's doctor) and Giuseppe Borgnis.

The Mausoleum was the first building apart from estate cottages which I restored; that was in 1956 and the frieze alone cost £6000. I tackled the interior of the church in 1962, and the work has gone on continuously ever since, although now, at last, the end is in sight.

Further down the hillside can be seen the entrance to the Caves, with its high flint side walls and tall flint piers forming an archway in which are set stone columns. It looks at a distance like the façade of a Gothic church, which was no doubt the intention.

The lake which adds so greatly to the beauty of the park was created before 1739, probably by Sir Francis, the 2nd Baronet, or by his father. It is in the shape of a swan, the legs being represented by the two small streams which are crossed by charming little bridges of rough and knapped flints designed by Revett; on the

opposite side the neck is represented by the river which leaves the lake at the Cascade and bends round to its head, a large pond, further down the park to the east, just above Sawmill House.

The first little flint bridge leads to the Broad Walk in the middle of which I erected a tall pillar with a magnificent statue of Britannia on the top in honour of the Queen's birthday. The inscription, which reads 'BRITANNIAM BRITANNIARVM REGINAE ELIZABETHAE II ANNIS SEXAGINTA DEI GRATIA PERACTIS IN HONOREM EXAEDIFICAVIT ANNO MCMXXXVI FRANCISCVS DASHWOOD BARONETTVS' was devised by the orator of Cambridge University. We are eagerly awaiting the visit by Her Majesty for the unveiling ceremony later this year.

Further on stands the Temple of Venus on a large mound where the original house stood. The Temple was built in 1748. Beneath it is Venus's Parlour which Wilkes described as follows:

> For the entrance to it is the same entrance by which we all come into the world, and the door is what some idle wits have called the Door of Life. It is reported that, on a late visit to his Chancellor, Lord Bute particularly admired this building and advised the noble owner to lay out the £500 bequeathed him by Lord Melcomb's will, for an erection in a Paphian column to stand at the entrance, and it is said he advised it to be made of Scottish pebbles. . . . And, at the entrance to the temple . . . are two urns sacred to the Ephesian matron [heroine of a mildly obscene ancient novel] and to Potiphar's wife, with the inscriptions MATRONAE EPHEFIAE CINERES, DOMINAE POTIPHAR CINERES [The ashes of the Ephesian matron, the ashes of Potiphar's mistress]. You ascend to the top of the building, which is crowned with a particular column, designed, I suppose, to represent our former very upright state, when we could say FUIMES TORIES, FUIT INGENS GLORIA [We were Tories, there was great glory], and is skirted with very pretty underwood . . .

The paintings by William Hannan of this temple show on top of it Leda embraced by a swan and inside the statue of Venus. Over Venus's Parlour was a statue of Mercury, and there were a great many more statues on the mound itself and on the flat ground in front of Venus's Parlour. The inventory of 1781 lists 4 boys with shields, 2 flower pots, 2 vases in the two niches, 5 large lead figures in Venus's Parlour, 25 small figures in different attitudes. All of these were subsequently removed, perhaps at the instigation of Lady Dashwood-King, the descendant of the poet John Milton, leaving only Venus, and even she was taken away in 1796 and sold.

The temple itself was removed in 1819 by Sir John Dashwood-King and the mount partially levelled; eventually it became covered with ash trees, elder bushes and stinging nettles, whilst the brick and flint façade of Venus's Parlour had crumbled away, leaving only the oval entrance into the brick chamber with the remains of one oval niche; this cave was used in my father's time for storing gunpowder for blowing out tree-stumps.

The temple had been such a prominent and delightful feature of this part of the garden near the lake that I decided it would have to be rebuilt. So after the ash trees had been felled, Marcella and I, helped by our children and their friends, went at weekends and dug at the top of the mound. About eighteen inches down we found the remains of the base of the temple consisting of chalk blocks with a few broken red floor tiles still in place. Along one side was buried a large tree branch and it looked as if this might have fallen on the temple; there were also signs of a slip at one end where the chalk base had given way, so these may have been the reasons for the removal of the temple during the nineteenth century. Right in the middle was found a large rectangular brick base which had supported the plinth and statue of Venus.

We also found that the base of the temple was oval in shape, and on closer inspection the brick cave beneath with its oval entrance turned out to be oval too – all clearly an erotic design representing the female anatomy.

Although the temple is shown in various paintings and the original design for Venus's Parlour is here, there are few if any similar oval temples anywhere. The final scheme, designed by Quinlan Terry and completed in 1982, is a triumph and must, I think, be close to the original one. In 1986 I installed an exact copy of the Venus de Milo inside it as well as a figure of Mercury over the cave entrance beneath, but I do not plan to add any more statues as I think they were overdone and must have looked rather like the decoration on a birthday cake.

According to Langley, in 1797, 'Temples, statues and vases by turns attracted and wearied the attention – nevertheless the character of the place is beauty; there is nothing grand or sublime, but the whole scene is cheerful and animated.' He goes on to refer to his Lordship's 'fondness for trifling decoration which formerly appeared in every direction.'

To mark all the help and encouragement given by Marcella, I have just had a white bridge erected across the little canal; it was copied by David Hicks from one designed for Lord Burlington at Chiswick, but this one has the initial M let into each side. At the far end of the canal there is now a 20-foot fountain gushing out of the huge vase which originally stood on the Colonnade.

The flint bridge near Venus's Mound was built in about 1770 to replace the original wooden one, which was a copy of the bridge built in 1748–50 by William Etheridge over the Thames at Walton and was recorded in a famous painting by Canaletto. The bridge at Walton was claimed to be the longest single-span wooden bridge in the world.

Beyond this bridge is the Temple of Daphne, the first of the follies to be built at West Wycombe in the 1730s.

Hannan chose a spot near here on the edge of the lake to paint the most delightful of his four views of the house and gardens. One shows a frigate at anchor and there is a similar one of the same frigate with smoke belching from its guns. We have a full description of the scene in 1754 from Thomas Phillibrown's diary:

In ye Grand Canal are various vessels, one of which is a Snow, Burthen about 60 Tun; it is completely rigg'd and carries several brass carriage guns which were taken out of a French Privateer and a sailor constantly is kept who lives abord this snow to keep it in proper order; we all went on board it and there is a neat pretty cabin, forecastle or cork room and both under decks and outside is neatly painted and everything in missalure and quite pretty order and well worth seeing. There is also another 2 mast vessel, a little in the Venetian manner, also a 1 mast vessel like a sloop and also a barge which little Fleet makes a beautiful appearance. There are also swans on ye canal to add to ye beauty. We were told by ye sailor at one time a battery of guns in form of a fort was erected on ye side of ye canal in order to make a sham-fight between it and ye little fleet but in ye engagement a Capt. who commanded ye Snow comeing to near ye battery, received damage from ye wadding of a gun which occasion'd him to spit blood and so put an end to ye battle.

No one knows what happened to the 60-ton frigate. I was told by my old cowman that timber from the *Mayflower* had been used for the roof of Park Farm so perhaps that is where the frigate timbers went. As for the cannons, there was, at the turn of the century, a row of cannons on the Oxford side of the village, standing upright along the main road as a traffic barrier against the stream. One large cannon was, until recently, embedded as a bollard outside the cottage opposite the main gates and another smaller one in the stable yard. So I had them removed and mounted on carriages; one now stands by the Cascade and the other on Boat-house Island. Both are early eighteenth-century and probably came off the frigate.

On the far side of the lake one can see down the river to the left a replica of the original wooden bridge which we rebuilt in 1985 to Quinlan Terry's design; it was my son Edward's idea to erect it there and it has been named after him to mark his twenty-first birthday. Beyond it is Flora's Temple, which originally consisted of an open portico on the first floor with pilasters at each side and metal railings along the front. The front has, unfortunately, been bricked up and filled with two extra pilasters, presumably to make it more habitable, but it calls for restoration. In front of this temple there was a small island known as the Citadel on which Sir Francis erected a wooden fort.

Continuing round the lake one comes to Revett's Cascade. The original cascade consisted of a mass of stone boulders with a reclining statue of Father Neptune in the centre and grottoes on either side through which the water poured. Another very elaborate scheme, by a French architect, was prepared with a fountain set inside an ornamental arch at the centre of an enormous stone and flint wall punctuated by stone recesses and niches which was to run along the entire side of the lake. It would have been a very expensive and formal affair and fortunately the idea was dropped.

Revett's Cascade consists of flint arches with pedestals above and the sloping waterfall between. On the pedestals are two splendid reclining statues of nymphs, one a copy of a Roman statue in the Capitoline Museum. My father removed the original lead statues to the house, mainly because the plinths were disintegrating, and I have replaced them with fibreglass copies on the Cascade.

Inside one of the arches is a small waterwheel, 4 feet 6 inches in diameter, which Sir Francis installed in 1767; it was used to pump water up to the house into a tank behind the Dovecot Temple to supplement the supply of well water. During dry summers the level of the lake gets very low – in fact it has dried up completely three times during my lifetime – and I remember our bath water being brown and dirty until mains water arrived in about 1935. The waterwheel also supplied a tank in the roof of the Temple of the Winds which was later used for watering the tennis court.

Looking eastwards one can see in the distance Sawmill House, which marks the head of the swan. This was one of the first industrial buildings to be designed in a classical manner and was used until the late nineteenth century to turn out timber for the estate and also hop poles for making beer for the house. According to my father, the beer was quite revolting. The Dashwoods, who were brewers in the City in the early seventeenth century, especially William who was Master of the Brewers' Company in 1667, would have turned in their graves!

On the roof stood a statue of William Penn of Pennsylvania, flanked by statues of the haymaker and haymistress on the pepper pots on either side. The statue was erected in 1774 and Benjamin Franklin's advice was sought over the words on the plaque held in William Penn's hand. Franklin felt that too many words were to be inscribed on the plaque, and wrote: 'My dear Lord, I apprehend there will hardly be room for *so much*, in Characters large enough to be read from below. If the Sculptor should be of that Opinion, perhaps it may be well enough still, if we begin with the Words,

My dear Lord

I apprehend there will hardly room for so much, in Characters large enough to be read from below. If the Sculptor should be of that Opinion, perhaps it may be well enough still if we begin with the Words, Almighty God being, etc. and end with, Persuasion, omitting what is before & after.

I happen to be engag'd at Dinner, but propose waiting on your Lordship between 1 & 2. With unalterable Attachment, I am ever

Your most obed. humble servant

B. Franklin

Craven Street
Apr. 12. 74.

Letter from Benjamin Franklin to Sir Francis, 1774.

Almighty God being, etc. and end with, *Persuasion,* omitting what is before and after.' The inscription finally read:

CHARTER OF PRIVILEGES TO PENNSYLVANIA MDCC. ALMIGHTY GOD, BEING THE ONLY LORD OF CONSCIENCE, I DO GRANT AND DECLARE, THAT NO PERSON, WHO SHALL ACKNOWLEDGE ONE ALMIGHTY GOD, AND PROFESS HIMSELF OBLIGED TO LIVE QUIETLY UNDER THE CIVIL GOVERNMENT, SHALL BE IN ANY CASE MOLESTED OR PREJUDICED.

All those statues were removed at the instigation of Humphry Repton in 1798 or 1799. The one of William Penn went to Stoke Park and was later sent to Philadelphia and erected in the garden of the Pennsylvania Hospital, where it still stands.

In the far distance, to the left of Sawmill House, one may just espy the spireless top of the tower of St Crispin's, a charming folly which was designed by Captain Moody to look from the distance like a church. Unfortunately, Repton had the spire removed on the grounds that 'a cathedral in miniature must in itself be absurd; and when we know that it was only the residence of a shoemaker, and actually dedicated to St Crispin, it becomes truly ridiculous.' St Crispin was the patron saint of shoemakers.

Repton's ony worthwhile contribution to West Wycombe was to remove a number of very large trees which obscured the view of the lake; in other respects he was not at all a match for Sir Francis's skill in landscape gardening.

In the centre of the lake stands Revett's Temple of Music, built in about 1770, which owes something to the Temple of Vesta in Rome. There are earlier but similar plans for this in the same French hand as the Cascade drawings. The temple consists of a single room in the shape of a horseshoe. For dances forty couples can be squeezed into it. On the outside there is a colonnade which runs right round the back, and beneath it a series of cellars. In the middle of the floor there is a large rectangular panel which perhaps formed part of a stage which could be lowered or raised. The inventory of 1781 mentions such a stage. The temple was used, and is still used, for summer parties; one of Daniell's paintings of 1781 shows it full of guests, with others arriving in gondola-shaped boats.

Up beyond the Cascade to the south is the Temple of the Winds, which is octagonal to correspond with the eight classical winds and derived from the Roman version in Athens. Above the flint façade can be seen the front door surmounted by a griffon, from the original early eighteenth-century house. This temple was not a mere folly. At the back of the flint archway there is a narrow passage leading to a large sunken brick chamber which was packed with ice and used as a deep freeze for storing meat.

I once used this temple for a cricket match lunch. On the platform over the flint archway a small band played, and the cricketers were given sandwiches and an ample supply of vin rosé — too much, because two of the village's star performers had to lie down after lunch and this naturally affected the result of the match. Next day the wicket-keeper's wife stormed in to complain that her husband had had to stay away from work because of a hangover.

Along the south side of the temple runs a ha-ha – a ditch with a retaining wall which enabled cattle, deer and sheep to graze right up to the edge of the lawn without the view being spoilt by a fence. I think the idea originated in China or Japan. The word 'ha' in Japanese means, among other things, an edge.

At the far end of the ha-ha is another delightful little temple, or perhaps one should call it a 'conceit' since it hides the circular tower which housed the tanks filled with water from the lake.

Up above the ha-ha one can see the new ride which I opened up recently – to furious objections from members of the local Council who felt they should have been consulted. It follows the line of the original ride shown in the 1752 survey and crosses an ancient sunken track which was filled in at that time. At the top is a splendid statue of a Roman soldier on horseback in fibreglass which I bought from Pinewood Studios.

Finally, just to the left of the colonnade front, stands the Temple of Apollo or Cockpit Arch, with a fine statue of the Apollo Belvedere in a flint recess at the back.

Beneath the archway there used to be a sandpit where cock fights were held, and above is a room which used to house cages for the cocks. In a panel over the arch is the inscription 'Libertati Amicatiaeque Sac' (Sacred to liberty and friendship), the motto of the Hell-Fire Club.

The restoration of the landscape has taken a long time. All round can be seen a great many trees and shrubs which have been planted in recent years. Where the trees have had to be protected against cattle and sheep, I have erected elegant tree guards which owe their Chinese Chippendale design to ones which the late Earl Spencer had made for Althorp.

Invaluable help has been given to me, first by Lanning Roper, then by Russell Page and finally by John Sales, the National Trust gardens adviser. And both my dear wives, Victoria and Marcella, have taken a very keen interest in it all too, especially the walled gardens and the shrubberies.

Now little else remains to be done in the landscape garden, apart from rebuilding the brick and flint façade to the boathouse and replacing the spire on the tower of St Crispin's. But the church tower has become infested with deathwatch beetle, the fibreglass cornice on the north front of the house has become defective, and the frescoes on the end walls of the Colonnade need to be restored. So I suppose the work will never really end and West Wycombe will always require constant love and attention.

CHRONOLOGY

1658   Francis Dashwood made Alderman of the City of London
1698   His son Francis buys West Wycombe
1707   Francis created Baronet
1708   Son Francis born
1724   Sir Francis, 1st Baronet, dies
1726   Sir Francis, 2nd Baronet, begins Grand Tour in Italy
1733   Travels to Russia
1739   Begins alterations to West Wycombe
1748   Founder of the Hell-Fire Club
1750   Medmenham Abbey acquired
1762   Made Chancellor of the Exchequer
1771   Alterations to West Wycombe completed
1773   Revised Prayer Book published
1781   Sir Francis dies; his half-brother, John Dashwood-King, becomes 3rd Baronet
1793   Sir John Dashwood-King dies; succeeded by his son John
1796   Sir John, 4th Baronet, becomes MP (for 35 years)
1832   His son George becomes MP (for 31 years)
1849   Sir John dies; George becomes 5th Baronet
1863   Sir George, 5th Baronet, dies; his nephew Edwin (from New Zealand) becomes 7th Baronet
1874   Sir Edwin's son Edwin goes back to New Zealand
1882   Sir Edwin dies; his son Edwin becomes 8th Baronet and returns from New Zealand
1893   Sir Edwin, 8th Baronet, dies; succeeded by his brother Robert
1908   Sir Robert, 9th Baronet, dies; his son John inherits as a minor
1925   Sir John's son Francis born
1944   Sir John gives West Wycombe to the National Trust
1951   Francis reopens Caves at West Wycombe
1957   Francis marries Victoria de Rutzen (d. 1976)
1964   Francis's son Edward born
1966   Sir John dies; Francis becomes 11th Baronet
1969   Sir Francis starts his own underwriting agency
1976   Buys farming land in Colorado
1977   Marries Marcella Scarafia
1987   HRH The Prince of Wales and HM The Queen visit West Wycombe

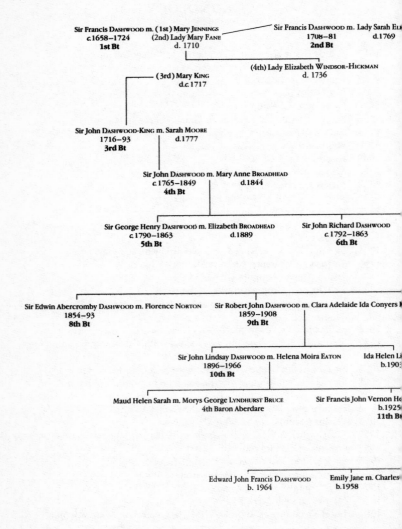

Sir Francis Dashwood m. (1st) Mary **Jennings**
*c.*1658–1724
1st Bt
(2nd) Lady Mary **Fane**
d. 1710

Sir Francis Dashwood m. Lady Sarah **Ell⋯**
1708–81   d.1769
2nd Bt

(3rd) Mary **King**
d.*c.*1717

(4th) Lady Elizabeth **Windsor-Hickman**
d. 1736

Sir John Dashwood-King m. Sarah **Moore**
1716–93   d.1777
3rd Bt

Sir John Dashwood m. Mary Anne **Broadhead**
*c.*1765–1849   d.1844
4th Bt

Sir George Henry Dashwood m. Elizabeth **Broadhead**
*c.*1790–1863   d.1889
5th Bt

Sir John Richard Dashwood
*c.*1792–1863
6th Bt

Sir Edwin Abercromby Dashwood m. Florence **Norton**
1854–93
8th Bt

Sir Robert John Dashwood m. Clara Adelaide Ida Conyers **⋯**
1859–1908
9th Bt

Sir John Lindsay Dashwood m. Helena Moira **Eaton**
1896–1966
10th Bt

Ida Helen Li⋯
b.190⋯

Maud Helen Sarah m. Morys George Lyndhurst **Bruce**
4th Baron Aberdare

Sir Francis John Vernon He⋯
b.1925⋯
11th Bt

Edward John Francis **Dashwood**
b. 1964

Emily Jane m. Charles⋯
b.1958

PRO MAGNÀ CHARTA

THE DASHWOODS OF WEST WYCOMBE

Edwin Sandys DASHWOOD m. Emily HARE
d.1846

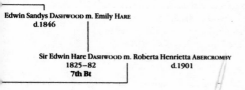

Sir Edwin Hare DASHWOOD m. Roberta Henrietta ABERCROMBY
1825–82   d.1901
7th Bt

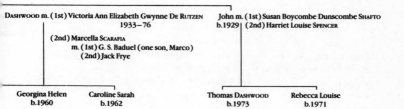

DASHWOOD m. (1st) Victoria Ann Elizabeth Gwynne DE RUTZEN   John m. (1st) Susan Boycombe Dunscombe SHAFTO
1933–76   b.1929 | (2nd) Harriet Louise SPENCER

(2nd) Marcella SCARAFIA
m. (1st) G. S. Baduel (one son, Marco)
(2nd) Jack Frye

Georgina Helen   Caroline Sarah   Thomas DASHWOOD   Rebecca Louise
b.1960   b.1962   b.1973   b.1971

BIBLIOGRAPHY

Almon J., *Letters of J. Wilkes*, 1805.

Almon J. and Wilkes, J., *New Foundling Hospital for Wit*, 6 vols, 1768–84.

Ashford, L. J., *The History of the Borough of High Wycombe*, Routledge and Kegan Paul, 1960.

Annual Register, 1762/5, 1797.

Blake, Robert, *Disraeli*, Eyre and Spottiswoode, 1966.

Briggs, Asa, *How They Lived*, Vol. 3, Basil Blackwell, 1962.

Brown, Wallace C., *Charles Churchill, 1731–64*, University of Kansas Press, 1953.

Bulletin of John Rylands Library, Vol. 37, no. 1, 1954.

Chancellor, Edwin C., *Lives of the Rakes*, Vol. 4, Philip Allan, 1925.

Churchill, Charles, *Genuine Memoirs*, 1765.

Churchill, Charles, *Poems*, 1761, 1764.

Croft, Herbert, *The Abbey of Kilkhampton*, 1780.

Croft-Murray, E., *Decorative Painting in England*, Country Life, 1962, 1970.

Cust, Lionel, *The History of the Dilettanti*, Macmillan, 1914.

Dashwood, Sir Francis, Egerton Manuscripts in the British Museum.

Davis, W., *Olio of Biographical and Literary Anecdotes*, 1814.

Dodington, George Bubb, *Diary of Geo. Dubb Dodington*, 1784.

Dillon, Constantine, Letters, 1849–51.

Doren, Carl van, *Benjamin Franklin*, Putnam, London; Viking Press, New York, 1939.

East India Company, Court Minutes, 1660–1705.

Fforde, Major C. del W., *The Lucknow Siege Diary of Mrs C. N. Brydon*, privately published, 1978.

Fuller, Ronald, *Hell Fire Francis*, Chatto and Windus, 1939.

Gibbs, R., *Worthies of Buckinghamshire and Men of Note in that County*, R. Gibbs, 1886.

Goadby, M., *Nocturnal Revels*, 1779.

Hall-Stevenson, John, *Crazy Tales*, 1772.

Hall-Stevenson, John, *The Works of*, 1795.

Harcourt Smith, C., *The Society of Dilettanti*, printed for the Society, 1932.

Harmon, H., *Notes on West Wycombe*, Blandford, 1934.

Hutchins, John, *The History and Antiquities of the County of Dorset*, J. B. Nichols and Sons, 1861–73.

Johnston, Charles, *Chrysal, or The Adventures of a Guinea*, 2 vols, 1760–5.

Jones, Louis C., *The Clubs of the Georgian Rakes*, Columbia University, Studies in English and Comparative Literature, 1942.

Journal of the Ex Libris Society, 'Medmenham Friars', 1901.

Kemp, Betty, *Sir Francis Dashwood: An Eighteenth Century Independent*, Macmillan, London; St Martin's Press, New York, 1967.

Kidgell, J., *The Priest in Rhyme*, 1763.

Langley, Thomas, *The Hundred of Desborough*, 1797.

Lee, Albert, *The History of the Tenth Foot (The Royal Lincolnshire Regiment)*, 2 vols, Gale and Polden, 1911.

The Letters of Horace Walpole to Sir Horace Mann, R. Bentley, 1843.

Lee, Rachel F. A., *Remarks on a Will*, 1828.

Lindsay, Sir Martin, *The Baronetage*, Unwin Brothers, 1977.

Lipscombe, George, *History of Bucks*, 1847.

London Chronicle, May 1763.

London Magazine, December 1763.

McCormick, Donald, *The Hell-Fire Club*, Jarrolds, 1958.

Marceau, Henri, 'William Penn's Other Statue', *Pennsylvania Magazine of History and Biography,* vol. XCV, no. 4, October 1971.

Mayo, C. H., *Municipal Records of the Borough of Dorchester*, William Pollard, 1908.

Morning Post, August 1776.

Pixley, F. W., *A History of the Baronetage*, Duckworth, 1900.

Plaisted, Rev. Arthur H., *The Manor and Parish Records of Medmenham, Buckinghamshire*, Longmans, Green, 1932.

Plumb, J. H., *England in the Eighteenth Century*, Penguin Books, 1950.

Plumb, J. H., *The First Four Georges*, Batsford, 1956.

The Political Journal of George Bubb Dodington, edited by John Carswell and Lewis Arnold Dralle, Clarendon Press, 1965.

Postgate, Raymond, *'That Devil Wilkes'*, Constable, 1930.

Public Advertiser, 1763, 1772.

Repton, Humphry, *Theory and Practice of Landscape Gardening*, 1803.

Thompson, Edward, *Temple of Venus*, 1763.

Thompson, Edward, *Life of Paul Whitehead*, 1777.

Walpole, Horace, *Horace Walpole's Journals of Visits to Country Seats*, edited by Paget J. Toynbee, the 16th volume of the Walpole Society, 1927/8.

Walpole, Horace, *Memoirs of the Reign of King George III*, 4 vols, R. Bentley, 1845.

Weatherly, E. H., *The Correspondence of John Wilkes and Charles Churchill*, edited and with an introduction, Columbia University Press, 1954.

Wilkes, John, *North Briton*, 1762–3.

Wilkes, John, *Essay on Woman*, 1763; facsimile edition published by André Deutsch, 1972.

Wilkes, John, *History of the Late Minority*, 1766.

Willcox, William B. (ed.), *The Papers of Benjamin Franklin*, Yale University Press, 1972–86.

Wooler, W. U., *A Short History with a Description of the Parish of West Wycombe*, Bucks Free Press, 1934.

Wraxall, N. William, *Historical Memoirs of My Own Time*, 1815.

INDEX

Figures in bold refer to main sections
Abercromby, Sir Robert, 101
Abercromby, Roberta Henrietta *see*
    Dashwood, Lady Roberta Henrietta
Aberdare, Lord, 179
Abingdon, Lord, 82
Adair, Major-General Sir Allan, 112
Adam, Robert, 212, 218
Addison, Joseph, 217
Ady, Thomas, 208
Aga Khan, Begum, 111–12
' Agar, Ann (Milton's sister), 5, 72, 208
Alan Rufus, 108
Albert, Prince Consort, 90
Allen, Father, 156
Aluminum Group of Canada (Alcan),
    143–4, 145, 147
Andrews, Henry, 135
Anglesey, Marquess of, 21
Anne, Czarina, 52, 56
Anne, Queen, 14
Annesley, George (Viscount Valentia),
    74, 75
Anson, Admiral, 24
Anson, Mr, 24
Antiquities of Athens, 20–1
ANZ Bank, 171
Apperley, J. H., 76, 82
Apraksin, Admiral, 53
Arbuthnot, Andrew, 122
Armstrong, John, 37
Armstrong, Sir Thomas, 133
Arnold, Thomas, 96–7, 160
Astor, Viscount, 181
Astor, Hon. Mrs Bronwen, 181
Aubrey, Sir John, 38
Augustine of Hippo, St, 29
Austen, Lady, 72
Australia, author's farms in, 171–3,
    174–5

Bacon, Sir Nicholas, 5
Baden-Powell, General, 108
Bailey, David, 184
Ballachey, Miss, 114
Banks, Sir Joseph, 47
Baron (photographer), 184
Barri, Gerald de, 168
Barry, Frances, 35, 71
Bartoli, Francesco, 202
Bassetsbury, Buckinghamshire, 78, 81, 90
Bateman, Anne, 16
Bates, Dr Benjamin, 38, 50
Baxby, Hal, 207, 216
Bedford, Duke of, 210
Beer, Sydney, 111
Beit, Sir Alfred, 115
Beit, Lady Clementine, 115, 126
Benckendorf, Alex, 127
Berkeley, Hon. Augustus, 82
Berkeley, Mary (née Dashwood), 85, 160
Bird, Frances, 186
Bismarck, Princess Ann-Marie, 111
Bismarck, Prince Otto, 111
Black (butler), 115, 116, 121, 128, 133,
    135, 137
Black Pool Mill, 169–70
Blackburne, Archdeacon, 66–7
Blackford, John, 12
Blackwood, Mr, 24
Blois-Brooke, Captain Tom, 169, 170
Blue Drawing Room, 114, 181, 208,
    211, 213–15, 216
Bluff Run, 100
Blunt, Sir Edward, 82
Bonfoy, Captain, 24
Boniface, Mr, 157
Book of Common Prayer, 65, 66–70
Borgnis, Giovanni, 198
Borgnis, Giuseppe, 22, 28, 103, 154,
    197–8, 207, 213, 216, 223

Boswell, James, 27
Bowles, William, 124–5
Boyle, Sir Edward (later Lord Boyle of Handsworth), 14
Boyne, Lord, 19
Brand, Mrs Simon, 110
Brewers' Company, 12, 15, 228
Britain, Ross F., 204
Broadhead, Augustus, 81–2
Broadhead, Brinckley, 82
Broadhead, Elizabeth see Dashwood, Lady Elizabeth
Broadhead, Sir Theodore, 73
Brooks, William, 159
Brooks's Club, 20, 21
Brown Drawing Room, 114, 208; see also Red Drawing Room
Bryndley, 'Bung-Ho' (butler), 185
Bubb, Brigadier Jingles, 125
Buccleuch, Duchess of, 181, 183
Buckingham, Duke of, 85
Buckinghamshire Militia, 38, 58
Burdett, Sir Francis, 83
Burlington, Lord, 192, 194, 226
Burnett, Ben, 86
Burnham, Lord, 205
Bute, Lord, 39, 40, 44, 59, 61, 63
Butler, R. A. (later Baron Butler of Saffron Walden), 113
Byng, Admiral, 58–9
Byng, J., 75

Calthorpe, Sir Henry, 24
Cameron, Charles, 56
Campbell, Colen, 192
Campbell, Doug, 144
Canada, 106, 113, 122, 143–4
Canaletto, 226
Carracci, Annibale, 198, 213, 216, 218
Carlisle, Lord, 19
Carlsbad Caverns, New Mexico, 141, 153
Carnarvon, 2nd Earl, 16
Carnarvon, Lord, 72
Carpentiers, Adrien, 22, 27, 204
Carrington, 1st Baron, 89
Carrington, Peter, 6th Baron, 171
Carter, Thomas, 208
Cascade, West Wycombe, 227–8

Castlerosse, Lady, 110
Catherine the Great, 53, 56, 150
Catholic Church, 18, 27, 66, 88
Cavendish-Bentinck, Bill (Duke of Portland), 111
Caves, West Wycombe, 3–4, 28, 45–6, 141, 153–61, 171, 187, 223–4
Chandler, Richard, 21
Chandos, Lords, 20, 83, 87
Channon, Sir Henry 'Chips', 111
Chaplin, Sir Robert, 16
Charles, Prince of Wales, 3, 21
Charles II, King of England, 13
Charles XII, King of Sweden, 56
Charron, Mr, 217
Cheere, Sir Henry, 103, 207, 217
Cheere, John, 218
Chippendale, Thomas, 216, 218, 231
Chipps, Buckinghamshire, 135, 138, 151, 161, 163, 200
Christ Church, Oxford, 133
Christie, Agatha, 4
Christie's, 71, 103, 210
Chrysal or the Adventures of a Guinea, 42
Churchill, Charles, 35, 38, 39, 40, 221
Churchill, Randolph, 111
Churchill, Sir Winston, 7
Cicero (spy), 129–30
Clarke, Mr, 38
Clarke, Thomas, 81
Clayton, Tim, 181
Clement XII, Pope, 19
Clerke, John, 30
Cobden, Richard, 89
Cobham, Lord, 197
Cockerell, Sir Charles, 74, 82, 83
Cockpit Arch, West Wycombe, 231
Colefax, Sybil, 111
Colefax and Fowler, 207
Coleridge, Anthony, 210
Coles, Theo, 173
Colonnade, West Wycombe, 79, 81, 90, 104, 114, 192, 194, 201
Colville, Captain Norman, 105
Comben and Wakeling, 165
Congreve, William, 29
Congreve, Sir William, 97
Corn Laws, 85, 89
Cornwallis, Archbishop, 67

Correggio, 218
Cosby, Lady, 83
Courtauld, Sir Sam, 113
Coutts, Mrs, 83
Cowles, Fleur (Mrs Tom Meyer), 183
Cripps, Lt-Col. Hon. Freddie, 113
Crispin, St, 229
Curtois, Rev. John, 26
Curtois, Mary, 26
Cushing, Peter, 184

d'Acourt, Mr, 160
Dance, Nathaniel, 27, 205
Daniell, Thomas, 178, 201, 230
Daniell, William, 201
Dashwood, Captain A. J., 96
Dashwood, Amelia, 93
Dashwood, Caroline (author's daughter), 161, 185
Dashwood, Ensign Charles, 96
Dashwood, Dowager Lady (author's grandmother), 22
Dashwood, Edmund, 12
Dashwood, Edward (mayor of Dorchester), 12
Dashwood, Edward (author's son), 164, 171, 185, 227
Dashwood, Captain Edwin, 84, 93
Dashwood, Sir Edwin, 7th Bt, 93–103
Dashwood, Sir Edwin, 8th Bt, 101, 102
Dashwood, Lady Elizabeth (née Broadhead), 86, 88–90, 91–2, 102–3
Dashwood, Emily (author's daughter), 161, 182, 184–5, 186
Dashwood, Francis (son of Edmund), 12
Dashwood, Alderman Francis, 12–13
Dashwood, Sir Francis (son of Alderman Francis), 13–14, 15–17
Dashwood, Sir Francis, 1st Bt, 72, 82, 211
Dashwood, Sir Francis, 2nd Bt, 5, 17, 176, 197, 214; Grand Tour, 18–19; Dilettanti Society, 19–22; Divan Club, 22–4; Lincoln Club, 25–6; Hell-Fire Club, 26–51; portraits, 27, 204–5; visit to Russia, 52–6; in Parliament, 57–63; as Postmaster-General, 63–5; revision of the Prayer

Book, 65, 66–70; Plan of Reconciliation, 65–6; death, 71; and the Caves, 153–4; and Whitehead's heart, 160; at West Wycombe, 192–4, 216, 217; fire precautions, 202–3; West Portico, 218; church tower, 220–3; gardens, 224, 228, 230
Dashwood, Lieutenant Francis, 35
Dashwood, Francis (Postmaster), 35
Dashwood, Francis (illegitimate son of 2nd Bt), 21, 35, 71–2
Dashwood, Sir Francis, 11th Bt, childhood, 118–21; at Eton, 122–4, 126–7, 151; rabbit farm, 126; in Second World War, 128–32; at Oxford, 133, 151; in America, 139–42, 143; first jobs, 143–7; political life, 147–9; first marriage, 148, 150; takes over West Wycombe, 151; in Russia, 151–2; opens Caves, 153–61; farming enterprises, 161–3, 187–8; at West Wycombe, 163–6, 185–8; Dashwood Village, 166–8; Welsh enterprises, 168–70; Australian farms, 171–3, 174–5; broking agency, 173; Colorado farms, 176–8; dances and parties, 178–83
Dashwood, Alderman George, 15, 16
Dashwood, George (son of 3rd Bt), 76
Dashwood, Sir George, 5th Bt, 73, 80, 160; inherits West Wycombe, 86–7; Parliamentary career, 87–9; financial problems, 90; alterations to West Wycombe, 90–1; death, 91, 101–2
Dashwood, Georgina (author's daughter), 159, 161, 169, 182, 185, 186
Dashwood, Harriet, 120
Dashwood, Helen (Aunty Babs), 105, 120–1
Dashwood, Lady Helen (author's mother), 2, 120–1, 164, 165; background, 106–8, 109–10; at West Wycombe, 110, 113–16, 124–5, 134–5, 200, 206, 213; dances, 181
Dashwood, Rev. Henry, 81, 84, 95
Dashwood, Sir James, 16
Dashwood, Sir John, 4th Bt, 7, 73–85, 86, 87, 95

Dashwood, John (son of 4th Bt), 81, 95
Dashwood, John (son of Captain Edwin), 93
Dashwood, John (author's brother), 112, 114, 118–20, 122, 124–5, 135, 138, 165, 180, 206
Dashwood, Sir John Lindsay, 10th Bt (author's father), 121, 125, 197; at West Wycombe, 104, 106, 110–17, 134–5, 149; in First World War, 105–6; marriage, 106; Assistant Marshal of the Diplomatic Corps, 110, 135–6; in Second World War, 129–30; leases Caves to author, 155; sixtieth birthday, 180; at West Wycombe, 199–200, 211
Dashwood, Lady Marcella (author's second wife), 2, 152, 182, 184, 185–6, 187, 215, 226, 231
Dashwood, Lady Mary (née Broadhead), 73, 76–7, 78, 79, 83, 84
Dashwood, Mary Jennings, 212
Dashwood, Rachel Frances Antonina, 35, 49, 71
Dashwood, Rebecca, 120
Dashwood, Richard, 11
Dashwood, Robert (16th century), 12
Dashwood, Captain Robert (Robin), 105, 106
Dashwood, Sir Robert (17th century), 15–16
Dashwood, Sir Robert, 9th Bt, 101, 102–4, 199
Dashwood, Lady Roberta Henrietta, 100–1
Dashwood, Sir Samuel, 12, 13–16
Dashwood, Samuel (son of Sir Samuel), 16
Dashwood, Sarah (Lady Aberdare, author's sister), 119–20, 127, 132, 137, 165, 178, 184, 186, 205
Dashwood, Sarah (wife of 2nd Bt), 197
Dashwood, Thomas, 120
Dashwood, Lady Victoria (author's first wife), 14, 148, 150–1, 161, 163, 168–9, 184, 187, 197, 203–4, 208–9, 231
Dashwood, William, 15, 228
Dashwood Finance Company, 13

Dashwood House, London, 13
Dashwood-King, Sir John, 3rd Bt, 5, 30, 36, 38, 71, 72–3, 77–8, 208, 225
Dashwood-King, Lady Sarah, 5, 72, 73, 208, 225
Dashwood Underwriting Agencies, 174
Dashwood v. Magniac, 103
Dashwood Village, 166–8
Davis (butler), 79
Dawkins, Henry, 76
Dayshwode, John, 11
De l'Isle, Lord, 21
De La Warr, Lord, 126
Delvaux, Laurent, 208
Digby, Lord, 202
Dilettanti Society, 20–2, 27, 35, 194, 208, 211
Dillon, Constantine, 100
Dillon, Fanny, 100
Dining Room, 91, 116, 128
Diplomatic Corps, 110, 136
Disraeli, Benjamin, 7, 83, 88–9, 92, 220
Disraeli, Mrs J. W., 89
Divan Club, 22–4, 27, 204
Dives, John, 212
Dodington, George Bubb see Melcombe Regis, Lord
Dolci, Carlo, 72
Dolphin, Thomas, 74
Domenichino, 198
Donald, Miss, 135
Donegall, Lord, 113
Donowell, John, 194, 212
Doppler, Fritz (butler), 181, 197
Dormer, Charles see Carnarvon, Earl of
Dormer, Richard, 184
Dormer family, 16
Down, Lesley-Anne, 4
Downley, 92, 164–6, 196
Drake, John, 80
Dudman (groom), 118, 120
Dufferin and Ava, Maureen, Marchioness of, 178
Duffield, Francis, 36, 38, 46, 51
Duffield family, 28, 30, 51
Dugdale, Harry, 162
Duncannon, Lord, 23–4
Dunsany, Lady, 150, 169, 170

Dunsany, Lord, 150, 179
Dunston, Lincolnshire, 73, 80
Dunston Pillar, 25, 26
Dutens, Colonel, 75
Dymoke, Rev. John, 75
Dymoke, Lewis, 75
Dymoke family, 75, 82

Eaker, General Ira C., 125–6
East Portico, 218
Eaton, Evie, 109
Eaton, Helen Moyra *see* Dashwood, Lady
    Helen
Eaton, Myra FitzRandolph (author's
    grandmother), 108, 109, 138–9
Eaton, Nell, 108, 109, 114, 138–9
Eaton, Colonel Vernon, 106–8, 109,
    118, 144
Eccles, Lord, 148–9
Eden, Sir Anthony (later Earl of Avon),
    137, 148
Edenborough, S. B., 101
Edgcumbe, Captain, 24
Edgcumbe, Mr, 23–4
Edward II, King of England, 5
Edward VII, King of England, 105
Edward VIII, King of England, 111
Edwards (butler), 185–6
Egmont, Lord, 62
Egremont, Lord, 21
Elgin, Lord, 21
Elizabeth II, Queen of England, 121,
    133, 225
Ellys, Sir Richard, 25, 29, 208
Ellys, Lady Sarah, 23, 25, 29, 208
Elton, James, 136, 137, 181
Elton, Mrs, 137
EMI, 146–7, 153
Erskine, Agnes, 85
Esher, Viscount, 1, 111, 166
Essay on Woman, 35, 42–3
Etheridge, William, 226
Eton College, 114, 122–4, 126–7, 128,
    133, 151

Falmouth, Earl of, 72
Fane, Jack, 113
Fane, Lady Mary, 17
Fanshaw, Mr, 24

Faringdon, Lord, 21
Farr, Marya, 204
Fawkener, Sir Everard, 24
Featherstonehaugh, Buddy, 127–8
Fellowes, Mrs Reginald, 110
Fenston, Felix, 181
Ferguson (mathematician), 54, 55
Fiennes, N. T. A., 122
FitzGerald, Mrs, 205
FitzRandolph, Edward, 'The Pilgrim',
    108
FitzRandolph, Nathaniel, 108
FitzRandolph, Robert, 109
FitzRandolph family, 108–9
Flora's Temple, 227
Forbes, George, Lord, 52
Forbes-Sempill, Lady Margaret, 114
Ford, Sir Brinsley, 21
Foreign Office, 110, 116, 152
Forester, Lord, 82
Fortescue, Lionel S., 123–4
Fowler, John, 197, 200, 201, 202, 204,
    207, 208–9, 211, 212, 216
Fox, Henry, 59
Franklin, Benjamin, 1–2, 47–9, 64,
    65–6, 67, 69, 159–60, 202–3, 205,
    214, 228–9
Franks, Lt-Col. Thomas Harte, 95
Fraser, Captain Alexander, 121, 197
Fraser, Lady Antonia, 179
Frederick, Prince of Wales, 28, 59, 199
Frederick the Great, 214–15
French, John, 184
Frölick, Mr, 23–4
Fryer, Mr, 154–5

Gage, John, 75, 80, 82
Gandon, James, 212
Gardner (porcelain maker), 150–1
Gendrey, Giles, 205
George II, King of England, 213
George III, King of England, 25, 26, 40,
    59–63, 76, 83, 199, 210, 223
George IV, King of England, 76–7, 83
George V, King of England, 111
George VI, King of England (Duke of
    York), 111, 133
Gerrard, Charlie, 127
Gibbon, Benjamin, 215

Gibbon, Edward, 69
Gibbon, Michael, 215
Gibson, Lord, 21
Gillows, 80, 90
Giraldus Cambrensis, 168, 169
Gloucester, 148–9, 151
Goodenough, Sam, 173
Gore, Charles, 76
Gough, Lt-General Sir Hugh, 93–4
Grafton, Duke of, 80
Granby, Marquis of, 24, 47
Grandin, Isabella, 140, 141–2
Gray, Bill, 130
Gray, Sir James, 19
Great Hall, 196–8
Green, Mrs, 133, 137
Grenville, George, 60, 61, 62
Gresley family, 82
Grey, Sir George, 100
Griffin, Freddie, 126–7
Groton foxhounds, 139–40, 142
Gwyn (mathematician), 55

Hale, John, 141–2, 143, 147
Hals, Franz, 215
Halton, Buckinghamshire, 80–1, 84, 85, 87, 90
Hamer, Mr, 175
Hancock, Tony, 184
Hannan, William, 29, 56, 153, 198, 202, 210, 211, 224, 226
Hardinge of Penshurst, Lord, 111
Hardy, Captain, 7
Harman, 88
Harriman, Harriet, 110
Harris, Sir Arthur 'Bomber', 7, 117
Harris, Mrs, 206
Harris (whaler), 98
Harrod, Sir Roy, 178
Harry (groom), 79
Hartley, Thomas, 203
Harvard Business School, 139, 142, 143
Hayes, Ken, 175
Heathcote, Sir G., 77
Heavy (cook), 131–2
Hell-Fire Club, 5, 26–51, 72, 159, 231
Hemings, Mr, 39
Henry (footman), 119
Henry VIII, King of England, 29

Henry Fellowship, 133–4, 139, 141, 142
Hereward the Wake, 118
Herman, Mrs, 206
Hewett, William, 24
Hicks, David, 166, 181, 226
Hill, Captain J. B., 155
Hinton Hill and Coles, 173
Hitler, Adolf, 113, 114
Hobhouse, John Cam, 90
Hodder-Williams, Christopher, 127
Hodsal, Christopher, 213
Hodson, John, 170
Hogarth, William, 27, 29, 33, 38, 39–40
Holmes, Errol, 113
Hopkins, Richard, 38
Hornak, Jean, 204
Hornak, Mark, 204
Horne, Alistair, 183
Horner, Percy, 145
Hounsum, Edward, 79
Hudson, Robert, 51
Hughenden, 89, 220
Hughes Onslow, Adam, 129
Humblet, Captain Pierre, 131
Hussey, Christopher, 135, 161
Hutton, Barbara, 212

Indian Mutiny, 95–6
Ionides, Mrs, 205

Jacksons, 197
Jacobsen, Arne, 166
James I, King of England, 6
James II, King of England, 13
James, John, 90
Jebb, Gladwyn (Lord Gladwyn), 111
Jennings, Alderman John, 17
Jennings, Mary, 17
Jersey, Earl of, 111
John Casmin, King of Poland, 150
Jolivet, Morise Lewes, 194
Jones, Harry, 144
Jones, Dr Hugh, 200
Jones, Inigo, 192
Jones, Timothy, 127
Jones, Sir Tyrwhitt, 82
Jowitt, Lord, 111

Kemble, Adelaide (Totti), 84
Kemble, Charles, 83–4
Kemble, Fanny, 84
Kemble, Mrs, 84
Kent, William, 197
Kershaw, Ronnie, 173–4
Keynes, John Maynard, 178
Killearn, Lord, 129, 130
King, Major Charles, 72
King, Fred, 163
King, John, 25–6
King, Dr John, 17, 71
King, Mary, 5, 17, 72
King, Colonel Thomas, 71
King's African Rifles, 130, 131
King's Room, 199–201, 202, 205, 207,
    213
Kingham, Bill, 127
Kingston, Duke of, 47
Kirtlington, Oxfordshire, 16, 104
Knapton, George, 20, 22, 27, 204
Knatchbull-Hugessen, Sir Hughe, 130
Knights of St Francis of Wycombe see
    Hell-Fire Club
Krenikov, Madame, 134–5
Krenikov, Nina, 134–5
Kruppa, Gene, 127

Ladenberg, Major Arthur, 127, 135, 211
Lancaster, Nancy, 207
Lancaster, Rev. Ron, 3, 183
Langley, Thomas, 208, 226
Langlois, Pierre, 210, 214
Lanin, Lester, 182
Lansdowne, Marquess of, 78, 89
Lascelles, Hon. Gerald, 127
Lauderdale, Earl of, 72
Lawrence, Les, 158
Lawrenny Ferry, 170, 176
Lazards, 173
Le Nôtre, André, 194
Lechmere family, 82
Lee, Albert, 94
Lee, Christopher, 184
Lees, Major, 169
Lees-Milne, Jim, 114, 115–16
Lefroy, Mr, 217
Leigh, G., 76
Leigh family, 74

Lennox-Boyd, Alan (Viscount Boyd of
    Merton), 111
Leslie, Reggie, 112
Levett, Rev. Richard, 77–8
Lewis, Elizabeth (née Dashwood), 16
Lewis, Alderman Thomas, 16
Library, West Wycombe, 119, 191,
    206, 212
Lincoln Club, 25–6
Lincolnshire, Marquess of, 117
Lincolnshire Regiment, 93–5
Lindsey, Theophilus, 67
Little, John S., 109
Lloyd, Robert, 38, 40, 44
Lloyd, Rupert, 35
Lloyd's, 4, 147–8, 158, 165, 171,
    173–4, 185, 188
Locke, John, 217
Long, Major R. S., 162
Lovibond, Edward, 38
Low (gamekeeper), 124, 126, 206
Low, A. P., 108
Lowe, Lt-Col. Johnny Drury, 112
Lyttelton, Humphrey, 127

Maccartney, Mr, 24
McCartney, Paul, 4
McGuickin, Bill, 140
Mackeurtan, J. G., 122, 123
McKnight, Mavis, 200
McKye, Mr, 24
Maclean, Brigadier Sir Fitzroy, 129
McLeod, John, 171–2
Macmillan, Harold (later Lord Stockton),
    148
Mahommed IV, Sultan, 150
Maitland, Lady Anne, 72
Malcolm, Sir Dougal, 113
Mallett's, 212
'Mammo' (governess), 118
Mann, Kathleen (Marchioness of
    Queensberry), 111
Mann and Fleming, 209
Manorbier Castle, 168–9, 170
Margaret, Princess, 121
Marina, Princess, Duchess of Kent, 111
Marla Wigs, 184
Marlborough, 1st Duke of, 7, 202
Marlborough, 6th Duke of, 90

Marlborough, 10th Duke of, 128
Marriot, Nanny, 137
Marsden, H. K., 'Bloody Bill', 122, 123
Marsh, Gilbert, 166
Martin, St, 14
Mary, Queen, 110–11
Masonic Room, 116, 118, 128, 136–7, 191, 199
Maud, Queen of Norway, 118
Mauritius, 129, 130–1
Mausoleum, West Wycombe, 2, 91, 160, 180, 183, 222
Mead, Dr Richard, 210
Mead, Harold, 127
Meade-Featherstonehaugh, Lady, 206
Mecklenburgh, Duchess of, 55
Medmenham Abbey, 28–37, 39, 42, 45–51, 58, 66, 72, 154, 220
Melbourne, 171–2, 173, 174–5
Melbourne, Lord, 90
Melcombe Regis, Lord, 27–8, 38, 59, 160, 223
Menshikov, Prince, 53
Mereworth Castle, Kent, 72, 80, 192, 218
Merrilees, Colonel Kenneth, 177
Merryfield, Mrs, 134
Metropolitan Museum, New York, 104, 213
Meynell, Hugo, 74–5
Meynell, Mrs, 103
Middlesex, Lord, 19, 20
Miles, Freddie, 112
Mills, Sandy, 144
Milton, John, 5, 32, 72, 73, 208, 217, 225
Minchin, E. C., 100
Mitchell, Captain E. M., 97–100
Mitchelson, Sir Edwin, 102
Mitford, Nancy, 114–16, 126
Molin's Machine Company, 151–2
Monade, Monsieur, 93
Montagu, Lady Mary Wortley, 19, 23
Montreal, 143, 144, 145, 176
Moody, Captain J., 230
Moore, Roger, 184
Moore, Sarah see Dashwood-King, Lady Sarah
Morris, Roger, 212, 218

Morse, Nathaniel G., 96
Morton, Dr John, 36, 38, 46, 51
Motueka, 96, 101, 102
Moyne, Lord, 129
Muir, Robert, 130
Murray, Fanny, 23, 24
Music Saloon, 91, 114, 118, 121, 127, 178, 181, 182, 198, 199, 208, 213, 216–17

Nathan, Lord, 212
National Trust, 1, 2, 3–4, 21, 114, 116, 133, 161, 163, 207, 209, 212, 231
Nazari, Bartolomeo, 19, 211
Neill, James, 152
Nelthorpe, James, 24
New Zealand, 96–102
Newcastle, Lord, 39, 59, 61
Newcome, Major R. K., 97
Newport, Colonel, 82
Newton, Sir Isaac, 54, 217
Neyelov (architect), 56
Nicholson, Peter, 112
Normanby, Marquis of, 21
Norris, John, 36, 38, 220
Norris family, 89
North, Lord, 47, 60, 64
North Briton, 39–40, 42, 43
North Front, 219
Northwich, Lord, 82
Norton, Florence, 102
Norton, Dr Frederick, 102
Norwich, John Julius, Viscount, 178
Nugent, David, 150
Nugent, Sir John, 150
Nye, Henry, 55

Ofner, Bill, 134
O'Neill, Heremon, 6
Oppenheimer, Sir Ernest, 113
Orizonte (Jan Frans van Bloemen), 208
Oss, Oliver van, 123
Ottoboni, Cardinal, 19
Oxford University, 133, 151

Page, Russell, 187, 201, 231
Palladio, Andrea, 192, 197
Palmyra Room, 2, 199, 201, **203–5**

Parkinson, Norman, 184
Pars, William, 21
Parton, Colonel Jimmy, 125
Pasta, Giuditta, 83
Paterson, Miss Florence, 114
Peel, Sir Robert, 83, 89
Penn, William, 79, 228–9
Perry, Sam, 177–8
Peter the Great, 52, 53–6
Petre, Mr, 24
Phillibrown, Thomas, 226–7
Phillimore, Claud, 111
Phillips, Confrey, 180, 182
Phillips, Nathaniel, 151
Pickles, Canon Harold, 128
Pigot, Belle, 77
Pigott family, 90
Pilkington, Robert, 127
Pitt, Sir William, 39, 40, 42, 58, 59, 61–3, 65, 198
Plan of Reconciliation, 65–6
Plunket, Hon. Mrs Aileen, 150
Plymouth, Earl of, 17
Pococke, Dr, 24
Pope, Alexander, 29, 42
Portal, Air-Marshal Sir Charles (later Viscount), 117
Potemkin, Field-Marshal, 150
Potter, Thomas, 35, 38, 43
Poussin, Nicolas, 215
Powys, Caroline Lybbe, 45
Powney, Jim, 157–8
Pratt, Lord Chief Justice, 40–1
Prayer Book, revision of, 65, 66–70
Princeton University, 108
Prouty, Roger, 140

Rabelais, François, 29
RAF Bomber Command, 117, 127–8
Randolph, Sarah, 109
Raper family, 80
Raphael, 72, 198, 207, 216
Rastrelli, Bartolomeo, 53
Red Drawing Room, 207, 208–11, 215
Redesdale, Lord, 82
Reni, Guido, 22, 72, 218
Renton, Andrew and Partners, 167
Repton, Humphry, 79, 229–30
Revett, Nicholas, 21, 28, 194, 212, 218, 224, 230
Reynolds, Burt, 4
Rhodes, J., 80
Ricci, Marco, 72
Richmond, Andrew, 97
Roadnight, Richard, 161
Robert I, King of Scotland, 5
Roberts, General Lord, 108
Robertson, Mr, 175
Rock, Mr, 82
Rockingham, Lord, 62–3
Roffés, 203
Rolfe, William, 220
Rombouts, Jan, 217
Ronaldshay, Earl of, 113
Roper, Lanning, 166, 187, 231
Rose, Joseph, 145
Rothschild, Nathaniel, 90
Rotton, Samuel, 81
Roubiliac, Louis François, 198
Rowe and Pitman, 110
Rowlatt, C. J., 122
Royal School of Needlework, 217
Royal Horse Guards, 84, 93
Roydon, Captain Marmaduke, 15
Rubens, Peter Paul, 215, 217
Rubinstein, Artur, 111
Rumbold, Sir Horace, 114
Rumbold, Lady, 114
Rushout, Lady, 83
Rushout family, 82
Russell, Lady, 182
Russia, 52–6, 151–2
Rutzen, Augustus, Baron de, 150
Rutzen, Charles Frederick, Baron de, 151, 185
Rutzen, Dorothea, Baroness de, 151
Rutzen, John, Baron de, 150
Rutzen, Victoria de see Dashwood, Lady Victoria

Sacchi, Andrea, 208
Sackville-West, Hon. Edward, 111, 114, 115–16
Saddlers' Company, 12
St Albans, Duchess of, 83
St Albans, Duke of, 83, 90
St Crispin's, 79, 81, 229, 231
St Leger, Anthony, 82

St Leger, Elizabeth, 83, 85
St Petersburg, 52–5
Sales, John, 231
Salisbury, Marquis of, 194
Sandwich, Earl of, 22, 23–4, 27, 38, 39, 41–3, 46, 47, 160, 197
Sargent, Sir Malcolm, 111
Saumarez, Lady de, 83
Sawmill House, 224, 228, 229
Scarsdale, Viscount, 111
Schwarzkopf, Elisabeth, 2
Scott, Captain, 116
Seafield, Countess of, 111, 164, 180
Selwyn, George, 38
Servandoni, Niccolo, 194
Shaftesbury, Earl of, 217
Shakespeare, William, 43
Sharp, Granville, 70
Shepherd, Guy, 158
Shields, Brooke, 4
Shilling, Bob, 131
Shrimpton, Joe, 81
Siddons, Sarah, 83
Simond, Sister, 116
Sitwell, Sir Sacheverell, 111
Small, Ken, 204
Smallwood, Mr, 156
Smiley, Sir Hugh, 112
Smith, Mrs, 141–2
Solander, Dr, 47
Somerset, Duke of, 80
Sotheby's, 197, 199
South Africa, 72, 113, 132
Spencer, Earl, 231
Spenser, Edmund, 29
Sportoletti-Baduel, Marco, 185
Squire, Sir Jack, 111–12, 113
Stacey, Brigadier, 94
Stair, Lord, 202
Stanhope, Sir Walter, 28
Stanhope, Sir William, 36, 38
Staniforth family, 90
Stanley (footman), 119
Stapleton, Sir Thomas, 28, 33, 36, 38, 72
Stapleton, Sir William, 30
Starkey, Mrs, 21
Steiger, Rod, 184
Stein, Sir Edward de, 147
Stevenson, John Hall, 35, 38, 39, 44

Stokes, Captain J. L., 98
Stone, Steve, 127
Story, Amelia, 85, 100
Story, Captain Henry, 100
Strahan, William, 65
Stuart, Prince Charles, 18
Stuart, James, 'Athenian', 21, 22
Study, 199, 208, 211–13
Stukely, Dr William, 197
Sublime Society of Beefsteaks, 27, 35
Swift, Jonathan, 29
Syred, Charles, 197, 203

Talbot, Lord, 67
Tapestry Room, 116, 202–3
Temple, Lord, 39, 40
Temple of Apollo, 223, 231
Temple of Daphne, 183, 226
Temple of Music, 119, 178–9, 182, 183, 230
Temple of Venus, 81, 183, 224–6
Temple of the Winds, 194, 228, 230
Terry, Quinlan, 225, 227
Thomire, Pierre, 205
Thompson, Dr, 36, 223
Thompson, J. Walter, 167
Thompson, Julie, 110
Thompson, Dr Thomas, 38
Thomson, James, 29
Thynne, Lady Caroline, 149
Tinney, John, 210
Townsend, Lady, 196
Trefusis, Violet, 115
Tregus (gamekeeper), 86
Trevor-Roper, Hugh (Lord Dacre), 141
Tucker, John, 36, 38, 45

United States of America, 65–6, 108–9, 133–4, 139–42, 143, 166–7
US 8th Air Force, 117, 125
Ustinov, Peter, 4
Utrecht, Adriaen van, 217

Vansittart, Arthur, 33, 38
Vansittart, George, 42
Vansittart, Sir Henry, 33, 38, 42
Vansittart, Robert, 33, 38
Venus's Mount, 79, 81
Venus's Parlour, 224–5

Vernon, Edward, 24
Vernon, Lord, 87
Veronese, 72
Victoria, Queen, 90, 151
Vintners' Company, 12, 14
Voss, Josse de, 202
Vyner, Mr, 82

Wagner, Fred, 143
Walcot, John, 72
Walcot, Mary, 23
Walcot family, 82
Wales, 73, 82, 168–70
Walker, Mr, 77
Walker and Holtzapfel, 119
Wall, Dr, 82
Wallace Collection, 114, 133, 215
Walpole, Horace, 18, 19–20, 29, 33, 36, 56, 154
Walpole, Sir Robert, 61
Walton, Sir William, 111
Warburton, Dr, Bishop of Gloucester, 43
Ward, Colonel Jackie (E. J. S.), 184
Ward, John, 21, 74–5
Ward, Susan, 184
Ware, Isaac, 158
Warrender, Sir George, 90
Waterford, Lord, 87
Weldon, Marabel (Lady Cathcart), 180
Welles, Samuel, 81
Wellesley, Lord Gerald (later 7th Duke of Wellington), 111, 135, 161
Wellington, 1st Duke of, 5, 7
Wesley, John, 49–50, 92
Wesley, Samuel, 49
West (gamekeeper), 124
West, Dame Rebecca, 135
West Portico, 218–19
West Wycombe, Dashwoods acquire, 16; Repton's suggestions, 79; under Sir Francis Dashwood, 79–80; under Sir John Dashwood, 79, 80, 81; under Sir George Dashwood, 90–1; under Sir John Lindsay Dashwood, 106, 110–17, 124–6, 134–5, 149; under Sir Robert, 103–4; ghosts, 128; furnished flats, 136–7, 138; the author lives at, 151, 163–6, 185–8; dances and parties, 178–83;

description, 191–231; gardens, 220–31; see also Caves, Mausoleum and individual rooms
Westmorland, 4th Earl of, 17, 18, 72, 192, 197, 202, 208, 218
Wharton, Duke of, 78
Whatmore (chauffeur), 119
Wheeler, Robert, 81
White, Mrs, 137
Whitehead, Paul, 27, 33, 35, 38, 46, 160, 214, 219, 223
Whites' Club, 27
Why, Jack, 127
Wilkes, John, 29, 30, 31, 32, 35–45, 51, 160, 221, 222, 224
Wilkie (publisher), 69
Wilkinson, Arthur, 130
Willcox, William B., 69
William the Conqueror, 108
William of Orange, 13, 15–16
Willis, Dr, 26, 35
Wilson, Corporal, 106
Windsor, Lady Elizabeth, 17
Winterton, Lord, 111
Witt Collection, 116, 133, 206
Wood, Mr, 24
Wood, Robert, 196, 203
Woodward, Mrs, 206
Woollett, William, 210
Wopshott, Cyril, 201
Wortley, Edward, 24
Wren, Sir Christopher, 194
Wroughton, Rev. W., 25
Wycombe, Lord, 78
Wycombe Abbey, 117, 125
Wynant, John, 212

Yale, Elihu, 15, 210–11
Yarraloch, 173, 174–5
Yellow Room, 202, 205–8
York, Duchess of, 111
Young, Henry, 100
Young, Thomas, 79
Young, Sir W., 87
Younger, George, 127

Zetland, Marquess of, 210
Zulueta, Hon. Lady de, 182
Zulueta, Sir Philip de, 185